Growing Up in the Culture Wars

Growing Up in the Culture Wars

Identity and Generational Conflict

JENNIE BRISTOW
AND ELLIE LEE

polity

First published in 2026 by Polity Press Ltd.

Polity Press Ltd.
65 Bridge Street
Cambridge CB2 1UR, UK

Polity Press Ltd.
111 River Street
Hoboken, NJ 07030, USA

ISBN-13: 978-1-5095-6705-8 (hardback)
ISBN-13: 978-1-5095-6706-5 (paperback)

A catalogue record for this book is available from the British Library.

Library of Congress Control Number: 2026937733

Typeset in 11 on 14pt Warnock Pro
by Cheshire Typesetting Ltd, Cuddington, Cheshire
Printed and bound in Great Britain by Ashford Colour Ltd

For further information on Polity, visit our website:
politybooks.com

For our growing-up children – Emma and Annia, Paul and Lauren. With love.

In memory of Gwen, who would have loved debating the questions raised in this book. *Tu nous manques.*

Contents

Acknowledgements

We have many people to thank for their inspiration, encouragement, and help with this project: Elise Heslinga and the team at Polity, for their enthusiasm and professionalism; Charlotte Faircloth, Frank Furedi, Jan Macvarish, and the many other academics who have contributed to the Centre for Parenting Culture Studies since its birth in 2011; colleagues in the interdisciplinary Generations Network; old friends around the Parents' Forum, who did so much to bring fun, rage, and perspective to our experience of 'parenting'; newer friends in Faversham, for going through their growing-up years with us; Ann Furedi, Emma Gilland, and Joanna Williams, for contributing their thoughts and comments.

Jennie's colleagues at Canterbury Christ Church University gave the book space to grow. Special thanks go to Peter Watts, for mulling over the issues and providing invaluable feedback on the chapters; Jesse Potter, for putting up with the F-bombs; and Bob Bowie, Jim Butcher, John McGowan, and Claire Street, for their persistence in making the case for academic freedom. Our thanks also go to the organisers and editors of the various forums and publications through which we have developed our ideas. These include the Battle of Ideas, Living Freedom,

Compact, spiked, UnHerd, and the *Next Generation* podcast – alongside the many journalists, commentators, and campaigners grappling with the problem of what it means to grow up in the culture wars.

It has been a great privilege to have spent our careers teaching and interacting with students and other inquisitive young people, who have taught us a lot about the nuance and balance needed when dealing with claims about 'the younger generation'. Above all, thank you to our families for their love, support, and exasperation. Without them, we would neither have wanted to write this book nor been able to do it.

1

Introduction

In writing this book, we, as authors, expose ourselves to a range of unflattering stereotypes about stroppy middle-aged mothers who don't go with the progressive *cause du jour* – hags, TERFs, Karens, *women*. From the other side of the culture wars, sociologists working in universities can be pigeonholed as the kind of people responsible for the corruption of young minds through 'woke' ideas. We hope that, as you are reading this, you have taken the old-fashioned view that it's better to read the actual book and critique it later.

One problem with writing about the culture wars is that you never know where the next battle will be fought. Remember the global lockdowns of 2020–1, the biggest social experiment of the twenty-first century to date, an unprecedented event that would change the way we did things forever? They seem like a bad dream now. Remember the Black Lives Matter protests of 2020, imagined by some as a revolutionary overthrow of systemically racist societies? It all became more difficult when the corruption scandals surfaced, along with the lawless devastation of once great American cities.

The mantra 'trans women are women' got trickier once it became clear that this 'be kind' slogan amounted to a full-scale onslaught on women's rights, and the problems with 'gender affirming care' for young people were officially acknowledged (Cass 2024). In any case, by 2024 the lives that mattered most to progressive causes were Palestinian lives. The terrorist slaughter of hundreds of young Israeli festivalgoers and *kibbutzim* and on 7 October 2023 was immediately eclipsed by concerns that Israel would fight back. Greta Thunberg, famous for fronting the all-encompassing 'climate emergency' ('our house is on fire', remember that?), was mainly seen sporting a keffiyeh, shouting 'fuck Israel!', and sailing a performative flotilla into the war zone before being detained and 'forced to hold flags' (Deconinck 2024, Tondo & Carrington 2025).

Flags, of all sorts, have become a flashpoint. From universities to corporations to city high streets, the Pride flag has become institutionalised to signal progressive credentials; to complain about public organisations' attachment to this activist cause would be regarded as transphobic. Partly by way of backlash, summer 2025 brought 'Operation Raise the Colours' (Lawson & Jefford 2025), where small groups of determined blokes across England scaled lampposts to fly the Union Jack and St George's flags, in an inchoate expression of patriotism, cultural rebellion, and objections over illegal immigration, somehow bound up with a peculiar form of muscular Christian nationalism. The UK government tied itself in knots working out what to say about the national flag, while the liberal commentariat muttered darkly and predictably about the return of fascism. By the time this book is published, we'll doubtless be embroiled in another breathless battle for 'the right side of history', on a different cause with a new set of victims and villains.

As the culture wars have escalated, a growing number of brave individuals have spoken out about the excesses and implications of some of the radical positions masquerading as mainstream. We owe a debt of gratitude to those academics, commentators, and campaigners who have doggedly sought to clarify the questions at stake around such emotive issues as gender ideology, the Covid lockdowns, the disciplining of children, the importance of academic freedom, and the rise of populist politics, among others. Aside from informing our own thinking, they have opened up a crucial space for critical enquiry and discussion. Evidently, this growing number of heterodox voices cannot simply be dismissed as 'fascist', 'phobic', 'disinformation', or by some other fashionable cancellation epithet. At stake are some profound questions and disagreements about what we understand our society to be, and what we want it to become. Unless we are prepared to have those arguments out, there is no future for society: only a trap of hostile, defensive, ever-decreasing echo chambers. Is this the world we want for ourselves – let alone our children?

The capacity for dissent is a core feature of open, democratic societies – and now is a moment that demands more discussion, not less. That doesn't mean that all dissenting voices should be flattered by agreement. Reasoned criticisms of the excesses of contemporary progressivism sometimes find themselves drowned out by a performance of competitive victimisation from the identitarian right, shouting about having been let down, ignored, and taken over by a messy conspiracy of governments, migrants, banks, and a host of other baddies – including, of course, Jews (antisemitism being one sentiment that seems to hold appeal for culture warriors of all persuasions).

Women, having been derided by transactivists for their attachment to equal rights and single-sex spaces, also occupy a malign position among sections of the identitarian right, for whom sexual frustration, declining birth rates, unstable employment, and a smorgasbord of other modern problems are all somehow the fault of women, for stealing their trousers.

On any 'side' of any issue, it's hard to find purity. Like many of our fellow citizens, we spend much of our time being bemused and disturbed by the frenetic churn of the culture wars, and we struggle to predict what may come next or where it might end. The difficulty is compounded by the language, which fails to capture adequately the perspectives at stake. Throughout this book, we have tended to refer to the battles between 'progressive' and 'conservative' positions, in preference to more loaded and misleading terms such as 'woke', 'liberal', 'populist', or 'hard right'. But we acknowledge that the term 'progressive' is also loaded – including with positive connotations that bear little relation to the ideas put forward by self-styled progressives today.

The reaction against some aspects of progressive ideology often comes from people who would never consider themselves conservatives – feminists, for example, or supporters of radical populist movements. We ourselves became friends many years ago, through our involvement in what was then termed 'hard left' politics and our commitment to the progressive cause of advancing women's freedom and autonomy. While much of this book is an argument with contemporary progressivism and makes the case for placing more value on traditions and relationships rooted in the past, we wouldn't describe ourselves as 'conservative' – not least because those who do often seem rather confused about what exactly they are trying to conserve.

The battles raging today do not take place between clearly defined camps situated on one or the other side of the culture wars, but are often fought out around specific issues. Staunch allies on the question of gender identity might disagree bitterly about the Israel–Gaza conflict, for example. On the other hand, connections are made between a whole number of disparate and often contradictory causes, as can be seen in the widely ridiculed slogan Queers for Palestine (Navabi 2023). In this confused and hypersensitive situation, rigid positions are drawn up that must be adhered to in order for people to be on the 'right side of history'; and to question, let alone debate, those positions is regarded as an act of violence, a marker of 'literal fascism' – until the discussion moves on and the positions change.

This book can't capture everything about our current moment or resolve the battles that have come to define it. What it can do, however, is draw on some of the knowledge and experience developed in our years of research, teaching, and writing about the predicament of young people and the problem of raising children in a society that seems to be increasingly at odds with itself. We are not seeking to position ourselves on any 'side of history'; rather we aim to bring some historical and sociological perspective on the question of what it means to grow up in today's febrile culture wars.

At the heart of our argument is the understanding that society's survival and progress depend on its ability to reproduce itself through the socialisation of the young. This relies on there being strong or 'thick' ties between children and the adults close to them, to provide them with both stability and space, which they need to work out who they will become. In recent times there has been a pervasive cultural devaluation of the thick ties that bind people together into intimate partnerships, families, and communities. While people continue to live within, and gain meaning from, the concrete relationships that frame their lives, they are under pressure to downplay these relationships and obligations, in deference to politicised, performative forms of thought and behaviour. The result is a further weakening of the ties between children and those who give meaning to their lives. This increases both the estrangement between generations and young people's sense of isolation and insecurity.

Understanding the fragmentary dynamics of this process and seeking ways to counter them do not constitute a merely intellectual project. As university teachers, we interact with young adults on a weekly basis and have learned a lot about how they make sense of their world: what they know and don't know, what they care about and why. From the Covid pandemic onwards, we have struggled to manage the dissonance between the university as an institution dedicated to the education and socialisation of young people and the fragmented, often cynical experience it now breeds as a norm. And as parents of young adults, we have to work out how to guide them in a world that seems very different to the one in which we came of age ourselves.

It would have been nice if we could have produced a self-help book that ended with some top tips. No such luck. Writing this book has made us even more aware of the enormity of the challenge posed by integrating young people into a society that sometimes seems to have given up. But it has also revealed the opportunities offered by the current, confused moment for young people to shape a more open and exciting future than the dreary technocratic conformity that, when we were young, was hailed as 'the end of history' (Fukuyama 1992). History is moving on in a messy and unpredictable way: and if we can help our young to embrace its possibilities rather than shrinking away in fear, we'll have done a pretty good job.

In the following chapters we explore how the dynamics of the culture wars, with their focus on personal identity, interfere with young people's ability to develop a stable, social, adult identity – and what we can do about that.

Chapter 2 explores why historical perspective is so notably absent from contemporary discussions about young people. Across the board, the kids of today are regarded as damaged goods – victimised by historical injustices as much as by current and emerging threats, for example social media and climate change. Such self-indulgent catastrophising evades discussion of the deeper problem: that western societies are now in the grip of a reactive response to the uncertainties of the present day. History is rewritten as a disaster in the making, with the implication that any lessons to be gleaned from our ancestors should be ditched as outdated and irrelevant. The future, meanwhile, is confronted with fear, as though what we can do tomorrow were limited to containing a resurgence of the prejudices of the past.

Attempts to understand the crisis of young people are ultimately expressions of a bigger crisis, of shared norms and social time. The response to the Covid pandemic of 2020 was the most visible and visceral expression of this bigger crisis. When confronted with an unpredictable public health emergency, our societies did not simply try to find practical ways of managing an infectious disease: they threw everything under the bus, including concerns about the education and development of the young. When commentators refer to teenagers and young adults as 'the Covid generation', they are referring to a cohort for whom life was put on hold, and the subsequent 'return to normal' marked a re-entry into a fractured new world in which nothing could be taken for granted.

But the pandemic did not cause the normative crisis that we are currently experiencing. The fragmentation of cultural norms, moral values, and social solidarities had been taking place for decades – indeed, as we discuss in Chapter 3, since the modern culture wars began in the 1960s. That chapter challenges the conceit that cultural conflicts are a distraction from 'real' problems and politics, a media-driven indulgence that doesn't really affect people's daily lives. In fact the culture wars matter so much because they affect the fundamental relations within the intimate, pre-political sphere of education and the family.

The culture wars also, and increasingly, take a highly emotional form, operating through the realm of feeling rather than reasoned argument or political debate. The principle 'you are what you feel' dominates; at the same time, life is organised around a complex set of 'feeling rules' (Hochschild 1979, 2018) that endow some feelings with moral authority while condemning others as 'problematic'. The politicisation of personal identity and subjective feeling interferes both with young people's ability to work out for themselves what they think and with the relationships that surround them, weakening their ability to develop a rounded, grounded sense of themselves as they transition into adulthood.

The fusion of presentism and identity is expressed in the emergence of 'generational identities', whereby different generations in society are incited to view each other as mutually incomprehensible and somehow problematic. Jennie has spent many years researching and writing about ideas of generational conflict, and Chapter 4 builds on this work to ask whether we are witnessing the emergence of a new generation gap, brought about by the discombobulation of shared social understanding. The assertion of political positions as generational identities, expressed through such slogans as 'OK Boomer' and 'educate yourself', fuels the sense of a stand-off between the generations, making it difficult for parents and teachers to provide young people with a confident foundation on which they can work out their ideas and beliefs.

We are living through an historical hiatus, which is unsettling many of the norms and practices that Anglo-American culture has taken for granted over the past few decades of relative stasis and stability. This situation has the potential to create a genuine generation gap, as young people develop ideas and assumptions that seem radically different from those of their parents and teachers. As adults, we have a responsibility to engage with this situation and help young people to navigate it. This means avoiding the temptation to label young people with distinctively pathological generational 'traits' such as being emotionally damaged or work-shy. It also means steeling ourselves against the prevailing demand for uncritical endorsement of the ways in which young people see the world. Adults need to be bolder about the importance of sharing their knowledge and experience with the young, so as to provide a bulwark against the lonely insecurity of living only in the present and equip young people with the tools they need to make the future.

One institution that could go a long way towards achieving all this is education; but education systems have themselves become hopelessly mired in the culture wars. Chapter 5 explores why the university, specifically, has become the breeding ground for a censorious cancel culture where masked mobs shut down public lectures and the long-standing principle of academic freedom is regarded as a dog whistle for hate speech. We trace the changing role of the academy from an institution dedicated to integrating young adults into a common culture of shared knowledge and norms to politicised organisations that reflect and inculcate present-day sentiments of fragmentation and anomie.

One consequence is that today the purpose of universities is overtly called into question, being continually the focus of rows over the 'value for money' they provide to society and individual students, the institutionalisation and impact of diversity, equity and inclusion (DEI) policies, and the intellectual consequences of relativising knowledge via 'decolonising' and 'queering' the curriculum. Students and staff become increasingly detached from the university's traditional role of educating young people about the intellectual and practical gains of our past and training them to take responsibility for society in the present. This raises the difficult question of whether the academy has become so captured by the demands of presentism that we need to look elsewhere for the development of new ideas.

Chapter 6 extends the analysis developed in our ongoing study of parenting culture (Centre for Parenting Culture Studies 2025, Lee et al. 2023) by discussing the various ways in which childrearing has, over time, become colonised by authorities outside of the family, via the prominence of 'parenting experts'. One effect of the external surveillance of, and intervention in, the family through 'expert' therapeutic advice has been to render parents and other adults in the community increasingly insecure about exercising their authority. This leaves children uncertain and confused about the boundaries and relationships that frame their existence.

For young adults, the problem is projected into the future: fraught discussions among Gen Z about whether having children of their own is either possible or desirable reflect a prevailing struggle to see the responsibilities of adulthood and reproduction in a positive, life-affirming way. For example, what tends to be missed in angst-ridden debates about falling birth rates and the kinds of financial, emotional, or policy support that young people need in order to embark on parenthood is the importance of cultural endorsement for the idea that families, whatever they look like, are a really good thing – something fundamental rather than just another 'lifestyle choice' (Berger 2017).

In Chapter 7 we discuss why obsession with cultural identities mitigates against the development of the one identity that really matters to young people: that of becoming an adult. We suggest that the development of an adult identity is bound up with three profound dimensions of social life – work, sex, and politics – all of which are compromised by the cult of identity. The practical necessity of working for a wage, and the sense of social fulfilment this brings, have become thwarted by the narcissistic (and impossible) assumption that work should be about making you feel good about yourself. This trend negatively impacts on the stabilising effect that getting on with the job has historically had for young people, developing both the material and emotional foundation for the transition to adulthood.

For many commentators and activists, the sudden rise in young people who reject their biological sex in favour of transgender or non-binary identities is merely the next chapter in the story of sexual liberation and experimentation written during the twentieth century. Yet the dynamics here are quite different. Gender identity is a form of individual self-presentation rather than an orientation towards an intimate relationship with another person. Nor is the demand for the affirmation of gender fluidity merely the product of young people's own needs and desires: as gender-critical campaigners have revealed, its promotion as a positive attribute has been led by advocacy organisations and public institutions (Joyce 2021). Indeed, the recent backlash against transgender ideology has been provoked by the way in which affirmation processes actively push young people against the concrete relationships that provide their lives with security and meaning – their families, their potential sexual partners, and their own bodies – and towards the embrace of a symbolic self-identity that seeks meaning in the fragile, unstable ties created via social media, therapeutic diagnosis, and institutional validation.

Then there is politics: the area of public, social life that struggles to make itself heard in the mire of the culture wars. We suggest that it is neither possible nor desirable today to separate political and cultural struggles: all are bound up with a quest to find meaning in social and individual existence, and all engage with the issues that fundamentally matter to people in their everyday lives. But while the fractious polarisation of these battles is unsettling, it provides an opportunity for the young to grapple with profound questions of meaning and belonging in a way that, for some decades, has been hidden behind an uninspiring cloak of 'business as usual'.

The times we are living through are anything but usual – and, rather than retreating from the challenges they pose, we need to stand with our young people as they work their way through. This means affirming the importance of the informal bonds that tie young people to their families, friends, and communities and defending these ties that bind from the cultural forces that undermine them in the name of identity. It also means resisting the demand to affirm everything that young people say about themselves, or that is said in their name. Above all, it means being prepared to have the arguments that we need to have, even when – or rather especially when – we don't want to have them.

2

Why aren't the kids all right?

Once upon a time, children were really happy. They played outside, obeyed their parents, flourished in school and went on to create harmonious, fulfilling families of their own. Their parents knew what they were doing and their teachers ensured they had access to the best that has been thought, known, and said. Nobody cried, lied, or died, and even the weather was better.

If you think this sounds like fairytale, you'd be right. Growing up has always been hard to do. Before the twentieth century, childhood was a brief and precarious time of life, experienced by most people as 'something to be got through on the way... to something better' (Cunningham 2006: 15). Even as economic and scientific developments reduced the levels of childhood death and disease, increased the standards of living, and required children to spend their days in schools rather than mines or factories, the realities of being a kid rarely matched their idyllic, fictionalised counterparts. In any case, children's literature is replete with death, destitution, boredom, and angst.

If it was tough being a kid, being a teenager was even worse. The freewheeling teenage years that we think of today barely existed before the 1950s, when young adults were expected to contribute their labour and wages to the household and there was little time, opportunity, or money to spend on pleasure or leisure (Savage 2007). The frenzied fun of *Grease* (dir. Randal Kleiser, 1978) and its saccharine spin-offs capture the teen years more as they were idealised than as they were experienced. *The Breakfast Club* (dir. John Hughes, 1985), *Dead Poets Society* (dir. Peter Weir, 1989), *Mean Girls* (dir. Mark Waters, 2004), and countless other coming-of-age films and books dramatise the pain, confusion, and self-consciousness of growing into adulthood within peer groups where everyone feels like a misfit. 'I'm just a kid, and life is a nightmare', wailed the pop punk band Simple Plan in 2002 – bored and lonely, while 'the world is / having more fun than me'.

All this misery, when nobody had a smartphone!

From the vantage point of the mid-2020s, it is tempting to look back on the second half of the twentieth century and wonder what on earth we were moaning about. Current discussions about the plight of teenagers and 'emerging adults' (Arnett 2000, 2015) present a terrifying picture of a generation of people beset by anxiety, depression, and other mental health disorders, unable either to enjoy their youth or to grow up. We read about 'snowflakes' who crumple when they encounter an idea they don't like, 'crybullies' who marshal their hurt feelings to bend others to their will, and kids so in thrall to digital networks and influencers that they simply can't function 'in real life' (IRL).

The fickle finger of blame flicks between causes, like a game of Spin the Bottle for neurotic commentators: parents who indulge their kids, neglect their kids, or fail in myriad other ways; anxieties about climate change and the imminent end of the world; teachers who have lost the plot in education; economic pressures and political tensions; the Covid-19 pandemic and the impact of lockdowns; the insatiable development of new technologies and demands from them; intrusive and manipulative therapeutic interventions in young people's emotional lives.

It is impossible to have any kind of relationship with young people as a parent, teacher, or colleague without being aware that something disturbing is going on. It's not just the level of distress shown by the young as they grapple with growing up in society that is new; it's the form taken by this distress, and adults' reaction to it. Whereas previous generations of young people dealt with the difficulties of coming of age by rebelling, today's kids tend to respond with more individualised expressions of angry violence or introspective sadness that are often explained through the prism of mental health. And whereas previously adults would have shouted at their kids and tried to set them on the straight and narrow, today's grown-ups bend over backwards to empathise with their kids, recognise their predicament, and make exceptions and concessions.

While all this should concern us, we should resist the temptation to panic. We can look back at history and acknowledge that growing up has always involved a degree of restlessness, confusion, disorientation, and dissatisfaction on the part of the young, as their parents and other adults have looked on the process with anxiety and horror. There is a need to take a sober historical perspective on our fears about the kids today: in the past things were neither as bad nor as good as they are often portrayed, and many of the problems playing out today are neither as new nor as catastrophic as they are made out to be. Many of the overwrought claims made about the crisis of youth today, particularly in the media and policy domains, are the product of a lazy, presentist imagination, which loads anxieties about the current moment onto predictions about the fate of our children – something that has a bad effect on the kids themselves.

But we should also pay attention to what has changed. Every generation grows up in a particular social and cultural context, which shapes its members' understanding of the world and their relationships with people older and younger than themselves. This means that we can't neatly separate the prevailing fears about the state of young people from the reality of their lives: these fears, however overblown, reflect something real that is affecting young people. The fears also affect the ways in which we engage with the young and they engage with us. Much as we may want to apply to our children the rules of our own growing up by referring to practices 'back in my day' that 'never did me any harm', we can't do that without acknowledging that today, in *their* day, many of these practices will be assumed to cause harm to young people; and these assumptions form the basis of their reality.

Think, for example, of the slaps routinely doled out to children when they persistently misbehaved or messed about – say, at the side of the road as a car hurtled out. In the US and in the UK today, smacking is presented as a form of child abuse, as though it were tantamount to beating a kid with a cane – in Scotland and Wales it has been officially outlawed, and there are ongoing campaigns to ban the practice in England too. A poll carried out for the National Society for the Prevention of Cruelty to Children (NSPCC) in 2025 found that over 80 per cent of people aged between 18 and 24 'believed it was unacceptable for a parent to use force, however slight, against a child' (Telegraph Reporters, 2025). But age and experience may yield a different view: a Parentkind-YouGov poll of parents in England and Northern Ireland found that 43 per cent wanted the right to smack their children to remain legal, while 39 per cent supported a smacking ban and 18 per cent remained undecided (Lovell 2025).

Or remember the casual stereotypes and low-level bullying that surrounded kids who would now be described as 'gender non-conforming' or 'neurodiverse'. Today such behaviour is regarded as the trigger for a spiralling decline into mental breakdown; such children should be feted for their differences and continually affirmed for who they are, *or else*. Practically as soon as they can talk, children are made aware that the only acceptable way to behave is to 'be kind' – and that the price of not 'being kind' is to bear responsibility for a terrifying range of outcomes. The hit young adult novel and Netflix series *Thirteen Reasons Why* (Asher 2007), in which a schoolgirl makes a series of tapes calling out the actions of 13 of her classmates as reasons why she killed herself, encapsulates how high the stakes seem to be.

Adults torment themselves with dark fantasies about the consequences of children's suffering from the kind of insult or injury that our own parents seemed to think was a normal, if often inconvenient and sometimes regrettable, part of life. In her book *Reclaiming Childhood*, a critique of adult over-supervision of children's play, Helene Guldberg (2009: 59) recounts that, when she was a child in Norway, outdoor activities were encouraged from an early age: 'A childhood with no broken bones was said to be a "no-good childhood"'. The independence cultivated by unsupervised play was seen as positive and necessary for children's development, as it gave them the ability to navigate risks and resolve conflicts with one another. 'There were many arguments and many tears were spilt,' she writes. 'But the richness of the experience we gained from the freedom we were given above all involved a lot of fun and excitement.'

These days, in trying to prevent children from both suffering and perpetuating bad habits and broken hearts or limbs, we seem to have created a self-fulfilling prophecy. We have conjured up an impossible, idealised reality for children in which nothing should happen that makes them feel bad, with the result that, when something bad *does* happen, it has a deeper and more long-lasting impact than it might otherwise have had. An incident of playground bullying escalates into the focus of a school investigation, dragging parents, teachers, and the children themselves into a protracted process of recrimination and remorse; the pressure to achieve well in school examinations becomes internalised as carrying an unbearable level of stress.

As Abigail Shrier (2024: 244) observes in *Bad Therapy*, 'we have somehow downgraded our own children without even realizing it', by deciding that 'they couldn't possibly handle' all the things we did and experienced as youngsters; and then we wonder why they can't cope with the stresses and strains of everyday life. Worse, by routinely dramatising every slight and setback, we flail in our attempts to offer an adequate response to the tragedies that go beyond the everyday 'nightmare' of just being a kid. In a study of British students' experiences of higher education that Jennie conducted with colleagues, some academics raised concerns that spiralling rates of reported anxiety and depression among students were leading, on one hand, to increased demands that academics provide unsustainable levels of emotional support for students on everything from upset over assessment grades to serious mental health problems and, on the other, to an increasingly mechanical approach to discretion regarding concessions around assignments and the simple provision of sympathy. One university lecturer recounted their response to the standard letter sent to a student whose mother had passed away. The letter was along the lines of 'it's sad to hear about your loss, in the light of your circumstances you are given a two-week extension' and the lecturer responded, 'we can't send that, it's completely inhumane' (Bristow, Cant, & Chatterjee 2020: 116).

For the past three decades, Anglo-American culture around children has been based on a kind of magical thinking: if we practise 'gentle' or 'positive' parenting – a form of discipline modelled on the woolly principle of 'be nice' (Reece 2013) – our kids will mirror this behaviour, making the world a kinder and happier place. Unsurprisingly, positive parenting in practice turns out to make parents more frustrated and children more badly behaved, and also to inflate their interpretation of a harsh word or a quick smack, which becomes a deep, lasting wound rather than something to learn from and shrug off.

In Chapter 6 we discuss how this risk-averse, therapy-oriented approach to socialising children emerged, and its consequences. Unpicking the damage that has been done requires a lot more than bemoaning the existence of a 'snowflake generation' and developing therapeutic resilience-building techniques: it means reckoning with the crisis of socialisation itself and with our deep insecurity about the society we are bringing children into. Here our aim is simply to point to a contradiction that the current generation of kids growing up in the culture wars is navigating: the contradiction between an increasingly tumultuous present and a disorienting assault on anything we might be able to learn from the past.

Kids, culture, and technology

Discussing the problem of growing up in today's culture wars requires looking at the relationship between several distinct but connected questions. What does it mean to grow up, and why has this always posed challenges – both for individual children and for societies? What do we mean when we talk about the culture wars, and what is new about the way these conflicts are playing out today? What is the relationship between the individual life course, the intimate relations – family and friends – in which young people develop, and the wider culture of a society? What makes us into the people we are?

It is impossible to answer any of these questions satisfactorily in this short book. We can, however, make some suggestions about the problem of collapsing different trends and issues into a one-sided and deterministic view of the issues that face our children today. It has become fashionable to take a particular feature of contemporary life – social media, for example, or the Covid-19 lockdowns, or the transgender trend (among many others) – and to see these as providing an overarching explanation for why today's young people express heightened levels of anxiety or misery. While we agree that there are problems with these and other cultural developments, it is important to keep asking the questions that (good) social scientists have always asked – about cause and effect, about generalisations, and, above all, about whether the desire to make good headlines has run ahead of the claims made by research.

One good example of this critical approach is given by social scientists at the London School of Economics (LSE), in a short blog post responding to Jonathan Haidt's bestselling 2024 book *The Anxious Generation: How the Great Rewiring of Childhood Is Causing an Epidemic of Mental Illness*. The claim at the heart of Haidt's book is that the major increases in depression and anxiety registered among teenagers can be explained by 'the rapid increase in the paired technologies of social media and the mobile phone', which is the product of a wider shift from a 'play-based childhood' to a 'phone-based childhood' (Haidt 2024: 7). While other factors contribute to the rise in poor mental health, argues Haidt, '[n]o other theory has been able to explain why rates of anxiety and depression surged among adolescents in so many countries at the same time and in the same way' (p. 45).

Haidt's concerns about the proportion of teenagers who spend their lives 'almost constantly' online (p. 34) and about the social and emotional difficulties experienced by many young people today chime with the worries of many parents and teachers. In consequence, it is not surprising that the book had a major impact on discussions about the problem of social media. Since its publication, the Australian government has officially banned under-16s from using major social media services (Livingstone 2026), and the UK is considering a similar ban: despite concerns from high-profile campaigners on this issue about the potential unintended and adverse consequences of such a ban (Khalil 2026, Taylor 2024).

As parents we can see why it's beguiling to think that, if children's smartphone use were more heavily regulated, that would make them feel better about themselves. As researchers of parenting culture, we have written a lot about the problem of parental over-supervision of children's play, and there are good insights in Haidt's book about the importance of 'risky play' for developing children's independence – insights with which we agree (Lee et al. 2023). But at the same time, collapsing a range of complex sociological and psychological problems into one main cause – the smartphone – creates problems of its own.

In a pithy post for the *Parenting for a Digital Future* blog, the LSE researchers highlight 'ten problems with Jonathan Haidt's book', identified by asking the basic questions that social scientists train their undergraduate students to ask (Lebedíková et al. 2024). The first problem is that research has been 'cherry-picked': studies that support the author's claims are given prominence, those that don't are omitted or downplayed. The second is that causal conclusions have been drawn (mostly) from correlational data. Because mental ill health diagnoses seem to rise alongside increased smartphone use, it does not mean that smartphone use is *causing* this 'epidemic': indeed, the growth in adolescent mental ill health has been observed for much longer. Problem 3, therefore, is that 'alternative explanations' for the phenomenon under investigation are dismissed through a one-sided focus on smartphones.

Further problems that the LSE researchers identify are that Haidt's thesis generalises beyond the data: it does not pay close enough attention to national and contextual differences; it assumes that media effects are the same for everyone (the impact of sustained social media use on a vulnerable, isolated child is likely to be much greater than on a happy, sociable child); and it overstates the scale of adolescents' internet addiction: other studies show the prevalence of actual 'addiction' as being much more limited that Haidt's thesis implies. The researchers also challenge Haidt for assuming that adolescents are merely passive victims of a new technology rather than young people who have some agency in how they use it; and downplaying the benefits of technology. Finally, Haidt – and, more importantly, those who have used his work as a warrant to call for heavy-handed regulation – propose reforms without considering their impacts and unintended consequences, and show themselves in danger of (ouch) '[v]aluing a good story over responsible science' (Lebedíková et al. 2024).

The kind of sceptical questioning to which the LSE researchers submit *The Anxious Generation* should be used when looking at any claims about the reasons why our kids seem to be in a mess today. For example, what do we mean when we talk about mental ill health? A large body of work in sociology and psychology stretching back decades has discussed the ways in which the miseries and anxieties that were once associated with everyday life have become pathologised through the labels of 'anxiety' and 'depression'; this obscures the distinction between real and dangerous clinical conditions and equally real but actually quite normal human emotions. Or, as we ask and explore later in this book, why are young adults not having children? It is easy to reach for pat explanations, from economic struggles to fear of climate change – and these are certainly important factors to consider, but they do not provide a plausible *causal* explanation for the declining birth rates.

But while we should avoid leaping to conclusions about the causes of cultural and technological changes and their effects on children and young adults, we shouldn't dismiss their impact on growing up. Neil Postman's influential book *The Disappearance of Childhood*, first published in 1982, showed how the construction of childhood as a separate domain of life was bound up with the invention of the printing press, which demanded that children be gradually inducted into adulthood via a process of education, specifically through the skill of reading (Postman 1994). Children's illiteracy both barred and protected them from the secrets of the adult world; by teaching them to read, adults controlled the pace and level at which they were able to access certain ideas and materials.

With the advent of television, contended Postman, children's access to social culture became less mediated: childhood began to 'disappear' as the young were able to access the kind of cultural content, such as the news, advertising, or TV dramas, that dealt with themes of adult life. This undifferentiated access did not raise children to the status of adults so much as exposed them to ideas beyond their understanding, while the content itself became infantilised in order to appeal across the board, to adults and children alike. Meanwhile, as Christopher Lasch (1995 [1977]) argued, television disrupted the privacy and authority of family life by opening it up to the invasion of wider cultural forces.

Reading Postman now, his focus on television seems almost quaint. When we were children in the 1970s and early 1980s, television in the UK was restricted to a mere three channels, slowly growing to four and five; there was generally one TV set in the house, in the family living room; and attempts were made to demarcate appropriate content through the strict operation of a 9 p.m. 'watershed', after which it was deemed acceptable to screen shows with sex, violence, and swear (or curse) words. The growth of streaming via the internet has made such a differentiation a thing of the past: there is no way of controlling what channels children can watch at what time of day. Differentiations between national cultures have also waned: kids from all over the world absorb American content as if it related to their own daily lives. The overall impact is that culture becomes globalised, generic, and more detached from its location in a specific time and place.

When we consider all the other media readily available via the internet, produced and consumed by anyone with access to everyday technology, the cultural influences over children today seem to be light years away from the relatively naïve and bounded world that shaped our own coming of age.

Gatekeepers – in the form of parents, editorial controllers, and the limitations of technology itself – have faded into the background, as children seem capable of accessing all kinds of content from anywhere, wherever they are. Apart from the dark and dangerous stuff that parents and policymakers worry most about, one major effect of all this is the emergence of peer-group influencers and the development of apps (TikTok, or whatever catches on next) in which youngsters create and exist, in a symbolic universe that many adults find incomprehensible and inaccessible. This contributes to another significant trend that we explore in this book: a sense of generational detachment, in which relations between older and younger people seem strained and the generations themselves at odds with each other.

All these developments are important, and all have some difficult implications for how we socialise children. But the question is not whether technological change matters; it is *why* it matters. As Timandra Harkness (2024) argues, new digital technologies feast on current political and cultural trends towards polarisation, individuation, surveillance, and conflicts over identity. In this sense, they accelerate and exacerbate 'real world' developments. This is not all bad, though: digital technologies also provide 'new shared spaces for news, current affairs and public debate', and people do already use the internet and social media 'to reach out and forge new connections, and to seek out information that challenges our own assumptions' (p. 307). Technology is not the problem, Harkness argues: the problem is how it has intersected with prevailing cultural trends in our 'WEIRD (Western, educated, industrialised, rich, democratic)' societies to push us apart from each other (p. 246).

In Chapter 3 we identify the key trends at the root of the modern 'culture wars', and in Chapter 4 we explore why these tend to take the form of an apparent conflict between the generations. But before getting into all that, we again need to emphasise the importance of balance when considering the impact of these trends on growing up.

Growing up and the need for 'normal'

Even in less fractious times, young people have struggled with the transition from childhood to adulthood, and society has struggled to understand that experience and give meaning to it. What the psychologist Erik Erikson (1995 [1950]) famously described as the 'identity crisis' that individuals experience as they move through the stages of development, as they struggle to reconcile who they have been with who they are becoming, has long been recognised as particularly acute during the teenage years, when physical, emotional, and social changes all conspire to rip youngsters away from the protective bubble of childhood and catapult them towards the confusions and contradictions of the adult world.

Sociologists have explored this tension with reference to the already fraught relationship between the individual and society, in a context where the norms and expectations of society change from one generation to the next. Teenagers and emerging adults exist in the 'betwixt and between' of adulthood and childhood, 'growing up in a society subject to continuous change' (Giddens & Sutton 2017: 348). In this sense, the identity crisis experienced by the young is to do not only with their relationship with the (already considerable) demands of their changing sense of self, but also with the identity of the society into which they are coming of age. For, notwithstanding all the standard symbols and rites of passage that have developed to mark the key to the door of adulthood, the world that you enter at 18 or 21 is not the same as the world that your parents entered. Society has moved on – and you are expected to move with it.

In this sense, the difficulty of growing up also involves a problem related to time. Children are gradually pulled beyond the familiar, cyclical rhythms of family time, where routines are laid down, repeated, and organised within the boundaries of family life, and pushed towards a relationship with social and historical time, which has its own dynamic (Hareven 1977). This was difficult enough even during the mid-twentieth century, when social time was more regimented and regulated: for the most part, the working day took place during standard hours, weekends were for leisure, and people went to bed at night because there was little to do. But with the emergence of globalised post-industrial economies and the development of the internet, the rhythm of social time became more fluid and fragmented. Manual jobs in retail and services began to operate round the clock, and even before the working from home (WFH) explosion seen during the Covid-19 lockdowns, work had become something one could (or could be expected to) do from any place at any time. Arguably the biggest impact of this migratory, globalised dynamic was on culture, which escaped the confines of its production, to take place on the 'worldwide web', as it was known in those early days.

The loosening of temporal, cultural, and geographical boundaries has shaped the experience of everyone in our modern 'network society' (Castells 2009 [1996]). But it has had a particular impact on young people, for whom the challenge of growing up is to forge connections between and across biographical time and social time. This means, as the Italian sociologist Carmen Leccardi (2016: 16) notes, 'constructing significant connections between an individual and collective past, present and future' – connections through which meaning can be given to overall living time. When social time no longer provides a clear pattern according to which your biography can be shaped, your own biography becomes contingent and changeable, needing to flex to the demands of any given moment.

This has been described as a shift away from a 'linear' biography and towards a 'choice' or 'risk' biography, characterised by individualisation in the context of uncertainty (Leccardi 2016: 17). In other words, the onus is on young people to make continuous choices about the risks and benefits associated with every next step they might take, rather than following a clear path towards adulthood. Do you commit to your job, hoping to work your way up the company, or do you focus on keeping your LinkedIn profile active and engaging, in case you want or need to get a new job tomorrow? Do you commit to your partner, in the expectation that you will stay together forever and start a family of your own, or do you keep marriage and childbearing at arm's length, in case the relationship breaks down or your circumstances change? The choices are endless, each one fraught with danger and possibility.

The diagnosis of a shift towards a choice or risk biography captures something important in what's new about the pressures that weigh on young people today. Those of us who came of age in the twentieth century were broadly expected to follow a map towards adulthood, with milestones – job, car, partner, marriage, mortgage, kids – marking the way. It was the path laid out in Hasbro's classic Game of Life, where you might take a slightly different path depending on decisions and good or bad luck, but you'd generally be headed in the same direction. Some people would deviate from the road altogether, but they were understood to be the exceptions to the rule. In contrast, the journey towards growing up in the twenty-first century is more akin to following a SatNav: you know where you are and you look for directions to the next milestone, but you don't see the highway stretching ahead and you're aware that at any moment you may need to reroute. That's all great if you decide you want to change direction (choice biography), but when the direction is changed for you by the circumstances outside your control (risk biography), it gets quite unsettling.

Of course, there are limits to all this. For all the talk about the range of choices open to young people today – travel the world, experiment with their personal identities, or enjoy an extended adolescence of consumerism and play – in many ways their lives are remarkably constrained (France & Roberts 2015). Extended periods of education, rocketing housing costs, and insecure employment mean that, for many, the experience is not one of freewheeling freedom so much as of debt and insecurity. On the plus side, the cultural 'individualisation' described by social theorists as both an opportunity for the young and an explanation for their predicament remains, for most, limited by the concrete relationships of everyday life – with family, friends, co-workers, and communities. We shouldn't get carried away by imagining that 'real life' for young people is the same as the virtual possibilities conjured up online. A salutary lesson on this came with the Covid-19 lockdowns, where the degree of disorientation and misery observed among teenagers and young adults as they were locked in their homes with only the internet as social life revealed how much their lives remain grounded in the everyday.

Yet, online and offline, the fragmentation of social time makes the job of 'constructing significant connections between an individual and collective past, present and future' (Leccardi 2016: 16) more complicated. The sense of a collective past has, in recent decades, become subsumed to an aggressively presentist imagination, where the only problems that seem to matter are those that dominate right now. This not only traps us in a state of reactive short-termism where we seem to lurch from one crisis to the next; it also affects our capacity to remember the past and conceptualise the future.

The problem of presentism

Presentism, according to Leccardi et al. (2023: 43), describes an historical moment characterised by 'the marked accentuation of the present, or the almost exclusive concentration of our attention on the present'. This sentiment associates the future with a sense of threat 'as well as the idea of a past that does not pass: a blocked time that locks us into an accelerated but directionless present' (Leccardi et al. 2023: 70–1). A 'constellation' of social, cultural, and political elements in recent decades has led to this, they argue. One such element is 'the loss of history's end directedness, which deprives linear time of purposiveness'. We can note that, by the close of the twentieth century, Francis Fukuyama (1992) famously theorised that the end of the Cold War, which had represented the decades-long confrontation between capitalism and communism, meant that the world had reached the final stage of 'mankind's ideological evolution' and that western liberal democracy had become universalised as 'the final form of human government'. As is now starkly revealed in the turmoil of world affairs, Fukuyama's pronouncement of 'the end of history' was far short of the mark; but it nonetheless captured the millennial sensibility, certainly within the western world, which assumed that the challenge to governments and societies was not moving towards a clear vision of the future so much as managing risk and uncertainty.

In this vein, Leccardi and colleagues observe that other features underpinning the presentist sensibility associated with the *fin de siècle* 'risk society' (Beck 1992) are 'the marked expansion of the realm of the possible, accompanied by the perception of the increasing likelihood of uncontrollable social and ecological risks; and the perception of living, in more than one way, in an unpredictable age'. In recent years, these sentiments have been starkly reinforced by the '"assaults" of forces that were thought to be part of the past – viruses and war' (Leccardi et al. 2023: 70).

The sense of living in a perpetual state of emergency, where we react to one event after another, was consolidated by the response to the Covid-19 pandemic, when it seemed for a while that the world literally stopped. As societies across the world organised their economies and healthcare systems almost exclusively around mitigating the threat posed by the

SARS-CoV-2 virus, the first casualties were cultural connections with the past. Schools and universities, museums and galleries, theatres and orchestral halls, and numerous other gateways into our collective cultural heritage were unceremoniously shut down for a prolonged period of time. What made this significant was not so much the closures themselves, as the idea that *they didn't matter.* Who needs live music when people are dying? Why risk spreading infection for the luxury of learning how to read, or solve equations?

During this extraordinary moment, two well-worn phrases summed up modern society's confusion about time. The first was that the challenge posed by the Covid-19 pandemic, and the measures brought in to contain it, were 'unprecedented': a statement that immediately dismissed the idea that we could learn something from the ways in which our ancestors have managed epidemics of respiratory disease. The second was the assertion that the bizarre regime of isolation and social distancing, in which people jumped into the road to avoid breathing on a passing pedestrian and workers tried to run public services from home while juggling childcare with sunbathing and overloaded WiFi connections, would – and *should* – become the 'new normal'. What Leccardi et al. (2023: 71) describe as 'the colonization of the future by the present' was starkly revealed in the idea that the future would bring, not the passing of an epidemic and a return to normal, but a society in which we engaged with each other as vectors of contagious disease, to be managed by a public health Leviathan that prided itself on its willingness to sacrifice culture and freedom for the false promise of safety.

Fortunately, the grim prophecies of the 'new normal' were off the mark, too. The pandemic passed, having exacted a grim toll on human health and an enormous social and economic cost. But when the return to 'normal' came, it was one in which all the tensions and contradictions of our presentist moment were magnified. It turned out that, for quite a long time, we have been pretty confused about what is, or should be, normal – and we have transmitted that confusion to our kids.

Moral confusion

In the perceptive 2011 book *Lost in Transition: The Dark Side of Emerging Adulthood,* which is based on a study of young adults and moral thinking, Christian Smith and colleagues suggest that American adults 'routinely take one of two different attitudes to "kids these days"', both of which are unhelpful. The first is characterised as the Chicken Little approach: an outlook that is 'essentially one of fear. . . that "the sky is falling"', that 'all that was good in the supposed golden days of yore is now going down the drain', and that 'something decisive has recently happened that is corrupting youth today'. This is the attitude commonly associated with conservatives. The second is the '"nothing new under the sun" approach': essentially an outlook of '*complacency* – a bemused dismissal of any concern about troubles in the lives of youth', typified by phrases such as 'They'll grow out of it' and commonly associated with liberals. As Smith argues, both these simplistic reactions 'usually do more to confirm the political and moral ideologies of the adults who hold them than to take young people seriously on their own terms and consider what might actually be good and bad for them' (Smith et al. 2011: 6).

The authors propose, as an alternative, an approach of 'realistic care': an approach that is 'informed by the facts of empirical reality rather than personal memories or simplistic, prefabricated, ideological narratives'. This recognises that '[t]eenagers and emerging adults desperately need other mature and concerned adults who genuinely care for them' and who are prepared to love, engage, challenge, mentor, and enjoy the young people in their lives (Smith et al. 2011: 7). As an aspiration, this is surely right. But what does it mean in practice?

Parents, teachers, and other adults have not given up on the project of raising children. We continue to love, care for, educate, and guide our young, trying to provide a sense of stability even as society seems increasingly wrought by change and confusion. Yet individual adults cannot compensate for the disorientation engendered when a society is at odds with itself on some very basic life questions, which we explore throughout this book. Put bluntly: when we are no longer sure what it means to grow up, why families matter, what education is for, or whether work is worth the hassle, it's very difficult to mentor teenagers on the path towards adulthood.

Lost in Transition focused on young people broadly within the generation known as Millennials (Smith et al. 2011: 16). The name refers to the transition from childhood to adulthood – a reminder that the now familiar idea that 'transition' has to do with gender identity is a relatively new connotation of this term. The problem that preoccupied Smith and colleagues was the dominance of a contingent 'it depends' approach to basic moral principles such as the difference between good and bad, right and wrong, truth and dishonesty. For example, while most emerging adults reported trying to do what they believed to be, legally and morally, the right thing, one in three of the interviewees admitted that they might do certain things they considered morally wrong if they thought they could get away with it. They talked about cheating – 'with your girlfriend, or a test, or your taxes, or, you know, everything' as something that 'everybody does' and that an individualistic culture, which prizes 'getting ahead' over doing what is right, implicitly condones. 'My high school football coach used to tell me that, "if you ain't cheating, you're not trying"', said one respondent (Smith et al. 2011: 47–8).

'What we have found, in short, is that moral individualism is widespread among emerging adults and that a sizeable minority professes to believe in moral relativism', write Smith et al. (2011: 59–60). The sentiment of 'morality adrift' is captured in the way their young interviewees 'resort to a variety of explanations about what makes anything good or bad, wrong or right'. The majority said that 'they do not or would not refer to moral traditions or authorities or religious or philosophical ethics to make difficult moral decisions, but would rather decide by what would personally make them happy or would help them to get ahead in life' – and a substantial minority admitted that, for various reasons, 'they do violate or would consider violating their own moral standards and those of society if it worked to their advantage and they thought they could get away with it'.

What this tells us, Smith and colleagues argue, is that 'the adult world that has socialized these youth for 18 to 23 years has done an awful job when it comes to moral education and formation'. As a consequence, 'these emerging adults are simply lost. They are morally at sea in boats that leak water badly' (Smith et al. 2011: 60).

Lost in Transition offers powerful insight into what happens to young people when their society's moral compass starts going haywire. In the latter decades of the twentieth century intellectual, cultural, and political trends in western societies have turned against traditional forms of moral judgement on certain behaviours or principles. This is not, in itself, a bad thing: when it comes to matters of sexuality or self-expression, for example, it reflects a growing openness and tolerance, in the spirit of the liberalising sixties (to be explored in the next chapter). We would certainly not want to see a return to the criminalisation of homosexuality, or to the brutal shame meted out to unmarried pregnant women in the Mother and Baby homes that were once prevalent in various western countries. But there is a difference between accepting that social norms and attitudes have moved on to a more enlightened place, and a more thoroughgoing relativism that regards the making of moral judgements as a problem in and of itself.

What Frank Furedi (2020) describes as the pervasive ethos of non-judgementalism has had a disorienting impact on our capacity, as a society, to have even a principled discussion on right and wrong. In universities, for example, cheating and plagiarism may be formally described as 'academic misconduct', but the message transmitted to students is often that this is an understandable, if misguided, act that won't help the individual student in the long run ('you're only cheating yourself'). With the surge in the use of artificial intelligence (AI) tools, with which students can generate plausible essays in the absence of a reliable technology to identify this practice and catch them out, guidance is moving in the direction of encouraging them to use AI 'smartly' – which transforms the learning process from one of absorbing and expressing knowledge in one's own words into developing the skills to work with large language models (LLMs) and sort the wheat from the chaff. These are no doubt useful skills to learn, but little thought seems to have been given to the wider message transmitted to students by pragmatically removing from the educational process the moral opprobrium attached to cheating. What matters, it seems, is not that it is morally questionable that you are getting an algorithm to present other people's ideas as your own, but whether you can demonstrate the skills necessary to get away with it.

The problem of moral relativism extends way beyond the tacit endorsement of cheating in education. We are increasingly seeing actions that used to be regarded as crimes – such as looting, vandalism, even targeted violence against individuals – re-presented as understandable consequences of poverty or frustration or as legitimate acts of protest against 'the Man' (whoever that happens to be). Such ideas have been around for a long time within radical movements, but are now expressed by establishment figures and mainstream media organisations, with feeble calls to understand the 'context'. When climate change protesters deface paintings or anti-racist protesters defile statues, the furthest permissible condemnation takes the form of 'it's wrong, but. . .'. And in the eyes of those who support the cause in question, the wrongness of the action appears to add to its righteousness: it is an expression of just how brave you are and how passionate about the wrong you are trying to redress.

The cult of non-judgementalism, which seeks to excuse all manner of bad things if they are done for 'good' or understandable reasons, is of course highly partial in practice. The phenomenon known as 'cancel culture' is marked by an obsequious tolerance for all kinds of bad behaviours performed in the name of one cause or one view, coupled with a vicious censoriousness towards the most basic expressions of sympathy for those with a different worldview (Doyle 2022, Lukianoff & Schlott 2023). On the face of it, this binary position taking looks like the opposite of moral relativism, as anybody deemed to be 'on the wrong side of history' is swiftly consigned to its dustbin. In fact there is no contradiction. When questions of right and wrong get detached from their anchor in the principles of moral thinking developed by communities over time, they become even more arbitrary than the situation described by the authors of *Lost in Transition*. This moral arbitrariness is the context in which today's young have been socialised.

Gen Z and the war against the past

Where *Lost in Transition* focused on the generation that was coming of age around the new millennium, amid the 'end of history' zeitgeist and the sense that anything goes, today's young adults are those known as Gen Z, born around the turn of the twenty-first century and reaching adulthood in the tumultuous decade of the 2020s. (We discuss in Chapter 4 what these popular but contested generation labels mean.) We suggest that, with these kids, the trend towards moral relativism has become so pervasive that the very idea of moral norms and values is regarded not only as irrelevant, but actively harmful to their personal and cultural identities. This has partly to do with the takeover of the public realm by the unstable and divisive politics of identity, which we explore in the next chapter. But it is also a consequence of years spent in the prison of the presentist imagination, which not only colonises the future but actively works to destroy the past.

Looking at the frenzied debates on the fate of Gen Z, we can add to the two 'unhelpful' attitudes to 'kids these days' outlined by Smith and colleagues a third approach, which has come to inform not only how young people are talked about but how they frame their own experiences. This is the sentiment characterised by Frank Furedi (2024) as the 'war against the past', which positions the values, attitudes, and behaviours of the past – and the people who lived there – as the cause of all that is wrong today. From this perspective, young people are burdened with the curse of history: the knowledge, norms, and values associated with the past are cast as not only irrelevant to their future but a barrier to their becoming who they need to be. To counteract such influences, their education is 'decolonised' and 'queered'; the intention is to focus not on what can be positively learned from history but on why the old ways of thinking were wrong at the time and have made such a mess of things today.

This deep historical pessimism has an impact not only on what the young learn from the curriculum but also on how they feel about the world and their place in it. The US psychology professor and generational expert Jean Twenge (2023: 421) writes of a 'stunning' finding from a 2020 voter survey: four out of ten members of Gen Z believe that the founders of the United States are 'better described as villains' than 'as heroes'. 'Somewhere along the line, a significant proportion of young adults developed the idea that America's founders were more evil than good', she writes. This stands in marked contrast with the sentiments of older generations – the Silents or the Baby Boomers. Yet the belief that things were really terrible in the past does not translate into the sentiment that life is better today; young adults are less likely than their elders to believe that 'America is a fair society where everyone can get ahead' – in fact three quarters of Gen Zers say that 'significant changes' to the government's 'fundamental design and structure' are necessary. In effect, they think we should 'tear it all down and start over', as '[t]he old way of doing things . . . doesn't work anymore'.

As Twenge observes, Gen Z's pessimism about their personal futures cannot be simply explained away by the considerable economic and political difficulties confronting them in the present day: '[t]hey are negative not just about the current world but about a time 250 years in the past' (p. 421). Psychologically, this doesn't bode well, as it encourages the development of an 'external locus of control': the belief that 'nothing matters, because it's all up to luck and powerful other people to determine what happens' (Twenge 2023: 428–9). The conviction that 'the cards are stacked against me', evident in young people's hypersensitivity about the persistence of sexual and racial discrimination even where, on standard empirical measures, discrimination is diminishing, both undermines ongoing struggles for equality and affects young people's sense of their own agency. 'Convinced that the world is against them, some young people have decided that there's no point in trying, a viewpoint linked to failure', Twenge writes. 'Countering this view will be one of the biggest challenges of the next decade' (Twenge 2023: 430).

As we discuss in Chapter 4, there are many difficulties with generational research – particularly when it tries to make overarching claims about what a whole generation thinks about anything. Twenge's research, while better than most, also tends towards one-sidedness, overgeneralisation, and overemphasis on the impact of new technologies. Nonetheless, her insights into how young adults express the prevailing zeitgeist are valuable for understanding both the process by which abstract cultural trends are absorbed into a particular worldview, expressed by kids who grow up in these times, and the ways in which this frames how they think about themselves.

Twenge's discussion of the relationship between the tainted 'origin stories' (p. 421) into which Gen Z are socialised and a fatalistic outlook on their personal prospects and social change points to an interesting dynamic in the progressive worldview associated with today's youth. This new form of progressivism promotes a vision of the future that is directly opposed to the values, norms, and behaviours of even the recent past. Unlike previous forms of progressive thought, which imagined society as building on incremental changes in order to arrive at a better place, the new progressivism pushes for a Year Zero approach, in which the 'old ways' of knowing and thinking are dramatically superseded by new value positions, complete with a new language that encodes whether you stand on the 'right side of history'. It's no longer enough to accept that some people are trans: you have to become an 'ally', insist that transwomen are (literally) women, and police a rigorous adherence to chosen pronouns. It is not enough to be not racist – you have to be an active anti-racist, constantly checking your own and everyone else's language and behaviour for signs of bias, privilege, and unconscious prejudice.

A key requirement of the Year Zero imagination is that it queries society's traditional assumptions about what is right and what is normal. Anyone who has any relationship with a university will be aware that any word ending in '-normativity' is a red flag for something bad and oppressive. The biggest culprit is heteronormativity: the idea that heterosexuality is the normal sexual orientation and that anything outside that should be considered different. Cisnormativity – the assumption that the normal way to be is that of a person whose gender identity aligns with their biological sex, as it does for the vast majority of people – is also under attack; while homonormativity – where LGBT people adopt lifestyle markers associated with heterosexuality, such as getting married – is pernicious because it excludes those LGBT people who want to behave differently. Neuronormativity has also become a big no-no, on account of its assumption that most people don't have a condition such as autism or attention-deficit/hyperactivity disorder (ADHD); the aspiration for the modern workplace or educational institution is to celebrate neurodivergence or neurodiversity.

Sociologists, including ourselves, have long used the concept of 'normativity' critically, to show that societies reinforce conventions around how things *should be* through assertions about how things *are*. There is nothing wrong with challenging normative assumptions by showing that not everybody fits the mould, or even by challenging the confines of the mould itself. If feminism had not challenged the numerous normative assumptions about women's role in work and public life, for example, we would never have been able to write this book. But challenging normative assumptions about how things should be is very different from the current onslaught on the very idea of normality.

Social norms are not just mission statements made up by movements or institutions to reflect what they think is the right thing to do. They develop gradually over time, in the context of communities that shape expectations, conventions, and behaviours. Although designed to reflect the changing shape and outlook of their societies, they are grounded in the past and bounded by the communities that have both given them meaning and derived meaning from them (Durkheim 2002 [1925]). As we saw during the pandemic, if a 'new normal' is simply declared, the one thing we know is that this is not a norm but a prescription – and one that is likely to be highly partial and unstable.

In a similar vein, we should be suspicious of another academic *bête noire*: anything that ends in '-centric'. It has become fashionable to criticise ideas or attitudes for being (for example) Eurocentric, ethnocentric, or anthropocentric, because they privilege the assumptions held by, or about, a particular culture or species over others. But while there is clearly a problem when, for example, ethnocentric ideas about gender and sexuality are applied by Americans to discussions of traditional rural communities in Africa, the criticism of 'centricity' is now seen to extend to the view that we can make observations about any society or community without allowing for the possibility that not everybody feels that way. The very attempt to make sense of a particular society is regarded as an act of symbolic violence against the imperative of diversity. To seek the 'normal' is itself an expression of bias and a tool of oppression. The future, we tell young people, lies in rejecting every certainty of the past and simply navigating the chaos of the present – as former US presidential hopeful Kamala Harris famously put it, several times, imagining 'what can be, unburdened by what has been' (Grabien Staff 2023).

The disorganisation of the normal is most explicitly, and positively, expressed by those on the progressive side of the culture wars. As we explore in Chapter 5, it has been influential in the domain of education, which accounts for the impact of this way of thinking on young people. But it also forms a significant part of the reaction to progressive thinking by those on the 'other side' of today's conflict over cultural meaning.

Many of those who react to the excesses of Year Zero thinking draw on idealised ideas about the past which are, themselves, infected with presentist prejudices, leading to a partial and ahistorical account that sees a solution to the concerns of now in a confected sense of the security of yesteryear. For example, self-styled 'conservative feminists' look at the pressures and insecurities experienced by young women brought up to believe they should 'have it all', and hark back to a time when women could just be mothers, cared for by their husbands – paying scant attention to the fact, for many women back then, things weren't like that; and even for those for whom it was, the price paid for security was their autonomy and freedom. Those who profess to love the past without understanding it are as complicit as those who just want to 'tear it all down and start over'. Meanwhile, elements of the cultural right are little more than a mirror image of their progressive foes, promoting an identitarian and dogmatic worldview, and shutting down those who disagree.

Welcome to the culture wars. They might be a shitshow – but they are our shitshow, and it's our responsibility as adults to help the kids get through them.

Conclusion

In attempting to understand the plight of Gen Z, we should be careful not to draw too direct a connection between social and cultural problems and individual, psychological outcomes. Both sociology and psychology, in their own ways, have attempted to short-circuit the complicated dynamics involved in growing up in the culture wars by reading their own interpretations into the fate of young people. A caricature sociologist will use rising rates of mental ill health as evidence of the structural inequalities and economic problems that they have been warning about for years (see for example claims about increased levels of student anxiety that result directly from increased levels of student debt), while a caricature psychologist will present increases in mental health disorders as a consequence of the individual and interpersonal behaviours that young people are currently engaged in but weren't in the past (see for example claims about smartphones and social media use).

The relationship between individuals' sense of themselves and the prevailing mood is more nuanced. People's identities are not simply conferred by the social and cultural forces surrounding them: they are mediated through their personalities, individual circumstances, and the relationships around them.

We are social creatures, after all; part of the promise and pain of being young is learning how to become your own person while navigating these wider social relationships and cultural influences.

In this respect, we suggest that there are distinct challenges posed by the current context in which young people are coming of age. They are not caused, as is often claimed, by specific developments in technology (phones and social media), ideology (gender identity), or politics (polarisation) – although all these factors play a part. Rather they relate to a generalised sense of cultural fragmentation. Today's culture wars are characterised by a crisis of normative values that has unsettled much of what our society thought to be true, without proposing alternatives that can offer a shared sense of meaning.

They are also characterised by a crisis of time, in which the past bears responsibility for all that has gone wrong, while the future is regarded with fearful uncertainty. As Twenge (2023) indicates in her discussion of Gen Z, an exaggerated view of the evils of the past does not make young people focus on how much better things are today: if anything, it simply fuels the overwhelming sense of pessimism and powerlessness. Caught as they are between a depiction of the past as a nightmare of intolerance, discrimination, greed, and exploitation and a future imagined in terms of living out the end times on a burning planet, it's no wonder that young people are less than optimistic about their prospects.

This is not something that can be solved by simply counselling the young to adopt a different outlook, or by restricting their access to cultural material or new technologies. What we can do is to help young people make sense of the times they live in by providing a more balanced, historically informed perspective on some of the challenges that confront our present moment. To that end, the next chapter explores the characteristics of today's culture wars and how they differ from previous cultural conflicts that erupted during the twentieth century.

3

The culture wars and the crisis of socialisation

One difficulty we have in understanding what it means to grow up in the culture wars is the lack of a common language to describe what is actually being talked about. When we talk about Gen Z's struggles with questions of identity, for example, we are acutely aware of the need to define what we mean by 'Gen Z': as we discuss in the next chapter, there are wildly different and often bitterly conflicting ideas about what constitutes a generation and about the characteristics ascribed to today's teens and young adults. When we talk about identity, we are not only engaging with competing ideas from sociology, psychology, and politics about what identity is and why it's important – we are also discussing how both the meaning of 'identity' today and the language used to describe it are often quite different from those that framed such discussions in the twentieth century.

The language problem is magnified in discussions between older and younger people, where it seems that the young understand, and express themselves quite differently from those of us who grew up in the 1970s or 1980s. There is nothing new about the young having different tastes from those of their elders in music and fashion, or speaking in a language that feels barely comprehensible to their grandparents, but the current rift seems to indicate something deeper and darker. Nowadays, when we see a boy dressed 'like a girl', we are conditioned not simply to shrug it off as youthful eccentricity, experimentation, or fashion but to read it as a signal that the boy 'really is' a girl and should be acknowledged as such. When we hear young people talk about their problems in the language of mental health – 'I have anxiety', 'I am neurodiverse' – we know not to assume that this is just a new way of expressing that they feel worried or different. It is a statement of who they are.

This is often taken as evidence that conflicts around gender, race, mental health, freedom of speech, and the many other touchstone culture wars issues originate in differences of attitude or opinion between the generations. In reality, they are the product of a much wider conflict over meaning, which relates to the most basic and intimate aspects of our lives. What it means to be male or female, a child or an adult, sick or well, privileged or victimised, is constantly held in question, and the answer is often assumed to position you on a particular, pre-determined political side. For example, as gender-critical feminists have found, there's no faster way to get yourself kicked out of the progressive camp than to declare that sex is a biological reality rather than a cultural characteristic 'assigned at birth' – and if you think *that*, you presumably also think that mass immigration is a problem, that abortion should be banned, and that everyone should vote for Donald Trump. That these positions seem to have little to do with one another makes a tense, febrile situation all the more bewildering.

Yet when national elections are fought on the success or failure of 'vibes', when voters set their faces against established political parties throughout Europe, and when an exodus of readers and listeners migrate from mainstream media towards new publications that seem better able to connect with them, it's increasingly unclear what politics even is – let alone where you might situate yourself within it. Western societies have cast off from their traditional political moorings, entering a new epoch of unchartered waters.

To grapple with what this means, the present chapter first explores what we mean when we talk about the culture wars and why the cultural conflicts that are flaring today cut so deeply. Unlike political battles, which revolve around competing opinions about what people should think and what societies should do, the culture wars take the form of a symbolic clash of identities that turns on the question of how people should *feel*.

To describe the dynamic of the culture wars as symbolic and emotional is not to dismiss it. It has long been understood that there are powerful forces in social life that feel outside the scope of rational explanation and yet, to paraphrase the old Heineken advert, get to the parts that logical argument cannot reach. Sociologists such as Erving Goffman (1990a [1959], 1990b [1963]), with his work on self-presentation, stigma, and 'spoiled identities', and Arlie Russell Hochschild (1979, 2018), with her studies of emotional management and 'feeling rules', have developed powerful ways of understanding that social reality operates not only through structure and policy but through modes in which people derive and construct meaning about themselves and their societies on a personal, emotional level.

Furedi's (2005, 2018) work on the culture and politics of fear has explored how the decline of politics as a means of working through the problems of public life has led elites to interfere in the pre-political sphere. The pre-political refers to the areas of social life such as education and the family, which exist beyond the realm of politics; the authority relations that operate here are foundational and intimate. In chapters 5 and 6 we discuss how attempts to resolve the crisis of public life by intervening in these relationships has a profoundly destabilising effect on the socialisation of the young. Socialisation can be thought of as an effort to take responsibility for transmitting shared norms and morality. This has been replaced with an encouragement to defer to a professionalised, therapeutic style of managing relationships. The weakening of boundaries between the public and the private realms that results from this therapeutic orientation has diminished the capacity for both political action and private self-expression (Lasch 1985, Kennedy & Panton 2019, Jenkins 2025).

The culture wars play out in the intimate domain of life, via the language and sentiment of emotion. Stripped of the defences that the concept of private life provided against the febrile confusions of the outside world, we are incited to regard ourselves and others as mere cultural constructions, to be shaped by the whim of the moment. Meanwhile, political actors and institutions feed off our personal sensitivities and insecurities, colonising ever greater chunks of the pre-political sphere, in a bid to keep themselves relevant and shore up their own authority. Political conflicts become presented, and then experienced, as conflicts over identity, and identity politics is imported back into the political realm, thwarting the opportunity for sober, reasoned debate.

For those of us old enough to remember when it was possible to have heated disagreements over world issues followed by a convivial drink in the pub, this is disorienting enough. But today's young never had those moorings in the first place, and that's what makes growing up in the culture wars such a challenge for now. In understanding their impact on the younger generation, we first need to understand a bit more about the history of the culture wars themselves – how and why they have developed in western societies, why they flare at particular moments, and what is distinct about the cultural conflicts of the 2020s. From there we can consider how the sensibility of viewing the world through the prism of identity impacts young people, as they work out who they are in the world.

The emotional terrain of the culture wars

'What differentiates a culture war from mere disagreement is the extent to which attitudes coalesce into utterly opposed worldviews with competing visions for the future, and the perceived threat to what either side considers the right or acceptable way to live one's life', explain Bobby Duffy and Kirstie Hewlett (2021), introducing a project at King's College London (KCL) that maps the state of the culture wars in the UK. Duffy and Hewlett note that the language of our current culture wars was first popularised by the sociologist James Davison Hunter (1991), who intended to describe 'the deep-seated tension that had emerged in the US between "orthodox" and "progressive" worldviews' following the cultural upheavals of the late 1960s. The term captured not only a political struggle over cultural issues but a 'conflict over the very meaning of America – the nation's past, present, and aspirations for the future' (Duffy & Hewlett 2021).

In the twentieth century, talk of the culture wars generated intense debates about whether they actually existed and, if they did, whether they should be characterised as a squabble among intellectual and political elites or as a more pervasive polarisation across society (Hunter & Wolfe 2007). Across the spectrum of political values, the simplistic polarisations characteristic of today's culture wars debates have often been shrugged off as a silliness associated with politicians and media and a distraction from real, serious politics. The public, however, is less dismissive. In 2023, the majority of respondents to the KCL study agreed that politicians invent or exaggerate culture wars as a political tactic, yet they did not see this as a 'purely manufactured issue': 49 per cent of respondents regarded culture wars as a real-life problem, by comparison with 22 per cent, who saw them as existing only in the media and on social media. Furthermore, just over half of respondents agreed that culture wars are a serious problem for UK society and politics: three years previously, only 43 per cent thought this (Duffy & Skinner 2023, KCL News Centre 2023). A more recent study found that 'perceptions of division' in the UK have reached their highest point since trends began in 2020, with 84 per cent of the public saying that the country feels divided and 67 per cent now believing it to be divided specifically by the culture wars (Duffy & Skinner 2025, KCL News Centre 2025).

When Donald Trump won the US presidential election for the second time in 2024, the centrality of the culture wars to political debate was crushingly affirmed. Trump and his running mate J. D. Vance positioned themselves as standing for family, industry, jobs, and security against the DEI machinery of the Biden–Harris progressivist bloc. Support for Trump cut across the lines of age and ethnicity, which had been trumpeted as the new 'dividing lines' in politics: this time, cultural identities were out and national identity was back in, albeit in a defensive and protectionist form. Yet both the touchiness of the Trump camp on matters of free speech and its selective appreciation of the importance of individual rights and formal equality show that the anti-progressive is often as identarian as his or her opponent.

As we discuss below, the current culture wars form the latest chapter in an unfolding story, which began in the 1960s. But some important things have changed even since the 1990s, when Hunter and others were writing. First, there has been a notable shift in the way the reaction against the progressive culture wars camp is now described – no longer as a defence of 'orthodox' or 'traditional' values but as deviant political conspiracies coming from the 'far right' or 'hard right'. This shows that, by the early twenty-first century, a particular form of progressive ideology had become thoroughly institutionalised in western societies. This is very different from the progressivism associated with the early twentieth century, which sought democratic and professional improvements designed to enhance people's living and working conditions. It was also different from the progressive movements associated with the 1960s that, as we discuss below, pursued the ideals of equality, autonomy, and individual freedom. The twenty-first-century incarnation of progressivism privileged the management of competing cultural identities over the pursuit of equality and projected a future orientation that was aggressively hostile to the norms of the past.

While the appeal of contemporary progressive ideas stems from a radical orientation to cultural change, such ideas are promoted by institutions as the acceptable, incontestable value set that all right-thinking people share. This is represented by the institutional acronym DEI – diversity, equity, and inclusion. Whereas equality speaks to the ideal that all citizens should have the right to the same treatment, diversity and equity make differential treatment into a virtue, the demand for 'fairness' being arbitrated by a higher power such as a human resources (HR) department or policy committee. This is not only undemocratic but explicitly anti-democratic. Inclusion, meanwhile, both assumes that some groups are excluded from equal treatment and provides a warrant for the exclusion of those who don't accept the new parameters – for instance lesbian and gay people who object to the inclusion of all kinds of other sexualities and practices in the newly constructed LGBTQIA+ communities.

This approach has led to practices that many of those who would consider themselves progressive regard as dangerously regressive. For example, gender-critical campaigners have argued that part of the appeal of gender ideology, particularly for young people, is that it can speak to an internalised homophobia (Joyce 2021): somehow it has come to be seen as more palatable to believe that you are born in the wrong body than that you are attracted to people of the same sex as yourself. In this vein, attempts to ban 'gender identity conversion practices' – in which young people who seek gender affirmative care are encouraged to consider other possible reasons for their distress – have been criticised as attempts to 'trans the gay away' (LGB Alliance 2024). Feminists, having fought for so long to have women's rights and needs properly acknowledged, are horrified by the idea that it can now be considered progressive to erase the word 'woman' from policies around single-sex spaces or female health care (Sullivan & Todd 2024).

In the pursuit of inclusion, those who hold a different view are cast out for being, at best, 'controversial' and, at worst, dangerously illegitimate. This, in turn, has fuelled the problem of cancel culture. Cancel culture springs from the impulse to censor ideas that are perceived as not only wrong but a threat to the social and moral order. Unlike the censorship of old, however, which targeted ideas that were deemed a threat to national security, public safety, or conventional morality, cancel culture seeks to suppress ideas that are deemed threatening to the identity of particular groups of people. By contradicting the ideas upon which certain groups of people have based their understanding of who they are, critics of progressive ideology are seen to pose an existential threat to these individuals' very existence: in the words of some trans activists, the threat is 'annihilation'. Emotional harm is conflated with physical harm, with the logical consequence that physical harm (or even annihilation) is seen as proportionate retaliation.

We saw this most shockingly in the reaction to the assassination of Charlie Kirk, which was openly celebrated by some, including the then president-elect of the prestigious Oxford Union debating society. 'Charlie Kirk got shot, let's fucking go', posted George Abaraonye to a WhatsApp group (Badshah 2025). In the ensuing controversy, Abaraonye deleted the messages, saying that he 'reacted impulsively', with words that 'did not reflect my values'. Yet Abaraonye's explanation used a rhetorical, sorry-not-sorry loop that has become familiar in violent protests around gender, Gaza, and Black Lives Matter:

> At the same time, my reaction was shaped by the context of Mr Kirk's own rhetoric – words that often dismissed or mocked the suffering of others. He described the deaths of American children from school shootings as an acceptable 'cost' of protecting gun rights. He justified the killing of civilians in Gaza, including women and children, by blaming them collectively for Hamas. He called for the retraction of the Civil Rights Act, and repeatedly spread harmful stereotypes about LGBTQ and trans communities. These were horrific and dehumanising statements. (Quoted in Badshah 2025)

Because cancel culture speaks to the problem of emotion, it is more expansive and arbitrary than censorship. It does not only call on officials to censor 'bad' ideas but mobilises groups of people to act directly, whether through monstering or ostracisation on social media or through physical intimidation. As a result, things can very quickly get out of control.

Another novel feature of today's culture wars is what the journalist Hadley Freeman (2024) has described as 'the Omnicause': 'every cause you must care about if you're A Good Progressive rolled into one, because everything in the world is connected'. Freeman gives the example of a *New York Times* article (Peters 2024) that leads with this standfirst: 'In many students' eyes, the war in Gaza is linked to other issues, such as policing, mistreatment of Indigenous people, racism and the impact of climate change.'

The *New York Times* journalist talked to a Cornell student who claimed that 'climate justice is an everyone issue', which 'affects every dimension of identity because it's rooted in the same struggles of imperialism, capitalism – things like that' – and that the same is also true of 'the genocide in Palestine'. He also interviewed a first-year student at Emory who uses non-binary pronouns (they/them) and 'acknowledged not having followed the conflict in Gaza especially closely, but said there was considerable overlap between the movement for greater justice in policing and pro-Palestinian sentiment' (Peters 2024).

'Gender, environment, Gaza: they're all the same, even though LGBT people live under the threat of death in Palestine, and I haven't heard too much from Hamas about the environment', thunders Freeman. But they are 'magically connected' through the Omnicause, a 'fatberg' glued together by a combination of western narcissism – 'idiots who cannot fathom the idea that their issues are totally irrelevant to other people's issues' – and conspiracy theories. She notes that, for the past decade, 'progressives have been obsessed with finding a single source for all oppression. For a while it was "patriarchy". Then it was "white supremacy". For the hardcore there was "heteronormative cis supremacy". And now it's "Zionism".'

Freeman's frustration with the sloppy thinking that ties one fashionable cause to another without considering the contradictions between them is understandable. But how many of us have found ourselves trapped in arguments that start in one place and end somewhere on 'the wrong side of history', because we don't think that, say, supporting abortion rights for women can be reconciled with a moral imperative to give experimental puberty-blocking drugs to children? Politics has always involved some types of omnicause, to the extent that people situated on 'the right' or on 'the left' would be drawn to take particular positions on a range of issues; yet these debates could at least be understood and argued out intellectually. Because the omnicauses of the 2020s develop in the realm of emotion and identity, they have a very different dynamic.

Cancel culture and omnicauses are not, of course, merely a feature of the progressive side of the culture wars. One 'right-wing' version connects a desire to restrict abortion rights with claims that the contraceptive pill is responsible for the demise of the family, the emasculation of men, and the emergence of 'trans kids', plummeting birth rates and the emotional struggles of women to reconcile their desire to be mothers with their engagement in paid work. Another rests on anxieties about migration, which see a direct connection between increased migration and an upsurge in terrorist violence, the costs of welfare provision, confusion over western values, and the problems of drugs, rape, and paedophilia. Conspiracy theories have abounded among people who are trying to join the dots between the Covid-19 lockdowns, the power of Big Pharma and Big Tech, and the trajectory towards increasingly digitalised and 'cashless' societies, which leads to some concerning reactions against modern food, vaccination, and scientific knowledge.

The idea that it might be possible to defend abortion rights *and* the institution of the nuclear family, or accept certain levels of migration without reorganising western societies around the sensibilities of hardcore Islamists, or oppose population-wide lockdowns without rejecting the scientific knowledge that lies behind so many significant medical advances, falls outside the narrow meme framing of the culture wars battles. But while this does make having sensible discussions quite difficult, it is not enough to mock these omnicauses as being irrational, because rationality and logic is not what gives rise to them. Rather they are the outcome of a more visceral and symbolic sensibility, which centres on a culturally induced feeling about what is right and wrong in the current moment, and script feeling rules, be they tacit or explicit, to signal how one should respond to a particular issue, whatever the empirical facts of the matter at stake.

Deep stories and feeling rules

The touchstone culture wars issues represent a messy battle between competing visions of society, played out in the emotional domain. This makes them no less real than the more straightforwardly political struggles of the past – in fact arguably more so, to the extent that they cut deeply into people's sense of self. This point is skilfully drawn out in Arlie Hochschild's (2018 [2016]) book *Strangers in Their Own Land: Anger and Mourning on the American Right*, which seeks 'a full understanding of emotion in politics' (p. 15). *Strangers* is based on a five-year ethnographic study that took the author from Berkeley, California to Louisiana – a 'red state' wracked with poverty and pollution. Hochschild aimed to 'scale the empathy wall' (p. 10) between people in her own milieu – highly educated liberals who live in coastal states, eat organic food, recycle their garbage, use public transport, and work in public or non-profit sector jobs – and those on the other side of the political, cultural, and economic divide.

Hochschild's method builds on the insights of Max Weber to understand the relationship between the wider social context and how individuals make sense of that context in shaping their own lives. The main concepts that she uses – empathy walls, feeling rules, and deep stories – are not about reflecting people's misery in order to show why they make what some would see as the wrong choices, but are designed to help us understand how social conflicts are internalised and mediated. What drives people to take sides in political conflicts today, argues Hochschild, goes much deeper than a particular view on, say, immigration policies, or the extent of environmental regulation. It is how a particular view of the world connects with people's sense of themselves and where they are headed, or whether it is experienced as an assault on their way of life and sense of self. At play here, she explains, 'are "feeling rules", left ones and right ones' – rules according to which '[t]he right seeks release from liberal notions of what they *should* feel – happy for the gay newlyweds, sad at the plight of the Syrian refugee, unresentful about paying taxes. The left sees prejudice' (Hochschild 2018: 15–16).

By dismissing people's rejection of contemporary feeling rules as mere prejudice, the left fails to understand 'the emotional core of right-wing belief', which is rooted in social, economic, and cultural factors that are far more significant in framing people's outlook. These factors include the realities of life for many working-class Americans: insecure jobs, stagnant wages, and debilitating working conditions. But more than that, they include having little control over the world around you and being despised for doing your best to support your family and community. This is the core of right-wing belief that Hochschild approaches through her pursuit of what she calls 'a "deep story", a story that *feels as if* it were true', and one that would take her to 'the shoulds and shouldn'ts of feeling, to the management of feeling, and to the core feelings stirred by charismatic leaders' (Hochschild 2018: 16).

The 'deep story' narrated by Hochschild's interviewees is essentially one of loss, as 'people like you' – white, Christian, working and middle class – suffer a sense of 'fading honor', as you move from being the embodiment of society's mainstream to being a problematic reminder of the norms and values of the past (Hochschild 2018: 144). Your values and feelings are out of sync with the rules that instruct you how you should be thinking and feeling. You feel betrayed, cut out of the American Dream.

The stock progressive response to this deep story would be: so what? Western societies have spent far too long being organised around 'people like you', with the kind of twentieth-century moral values and work ethic associated with the problems of that time. If the feeling rules in operation today make them feel insecure, defensive and excluded, isn't this just how women, young people, and marginalised groups have been forced to feel for centuries? Isn't it beyond time that the old white guys moved out of the way, to make room for the future?

Identity politics has marshalled a bitter sense of victimisation and grievance, born out of a sentiment of injustice and exclusion felt not only in the present day but across historical time. In this sense, the deep story of the American right is a confrontation with the deep story held by the progressive left. Both sides genuinely feel a profound sense of alienation from the attitudes and values that they perceive to be dominant in their country today, framed as they are by a particular cultural imaginary of the past. The trouble is that feeling rules and the sensibilities of grievance and exclusion don't operate according to a zero-sum game.

Unlike ideals such as equality, where there is at least a formal resolution at the level of equal rights, the problem of feeling aggrieved or excluded has no resolution. That people previously denied equal rights and inclusion in society's mainstream may be doing better on formal democratic measures than ever before does not lead to a celebration of the present circumstances. Rather, the history of oppression is imprinted as an explanation for a wider social discontent: the sentiment that something is *still* not right. The society in which oppressed and marginalised groups have become 'included' is not necessarily one of which they want to be a part. This collapsing of time means that the wrongs of the past are seen to be continually infecting the present and the future.

The backlash, from the identitarian right and some conservative voices, transmits a similar sensibility. The assumption that formally marginalised groups have the upper hand – for example, that girls 'rule the world', but not in a good way – triggers narratives of exclusion and victimisation. These also express the idea that the heart of society is somewhere else, pushing people to become 'strangers in their own land', estranged both from mainstream culture and from those around them. As Furedi remarked, following discussions with 'Groyper' supporters of the young US activist Nick Fuentes, 'it became evident to me that my interlocutors were the unconscious inheritors of the latest version of western identity politics'. The contemporary version of white nationalism, he argued, 'is founded on the sensibility of unbounded grievance', whose proponents perceive themselves as 'put upon white Christian men who have been systematically victimized by a political order that structurally discriminates against them':

> They uphold a narrative of reverse victimhood – a mirror of woke complaints about the structural oppression they face. To the feminist and the anti-racist rhetoric of intersectionality they counterpose a white nationalist version of a hierarchy of oppression. (Furedi 2025)

The phrase 'nobody wins in the Oppression Olympics' has come to capture the divisiveness of progressive thought, as it pitches identities against one another and undermines any common cause. But it can equally be argued that nobody wins in the Grievance Games: when the sentiment of being an 'outsider' is embraced by the one-time mainstream, nobody is able to claim society as rightfully theirs.

Across the political spectrum, the foot-soldier feelings of the culture wars are a bitter sentiment of alienation and a yearning for belonging. These take root within a deep-seated insecurity about what it's possible to belong *to* and about whether integration into the present society is either possible or desirable. On the progressive side, this feeling rests on an inflated sense of historical wrongs: the deep pessimism about the past and the present outlined in the previous chapter. On the other side, it rests on a sense of dispossession and resentment – about the undermining of the values, principles, and ways of life with which one has grown up – and harks back to the past as a way of resisting the current direction of change.

The ensuing battle between competing cultural imaginaries of the past and the future is captured by the imperative to stand on 'the right side of history'. While this is essentially a nonsensical phrase, implying that history has already happened rather than being something that is continually being made, it speaks the temporal crisis at the heart of the modern culture wars.

Reimagining the sixties

Cultural conflicts come to the fore when there is a distinctive and rapid shift in the social order, meaning that the established ways of thinking about social problems and solutions no longer seem to hold purchase. Historians can point to many periods in which cultural conflicts have dominated, but the 'modern' culture wars, the latest chapter of which we are battling today, are generally dated back to the 'cultural revolution' of the late 1960s (Marwick 1999), when the norms and conventions that had defined western societies throughout the earlier part of the century were dramatically challenged by a permissive counter-culture that promoted the virtues of individual self-expression and personal freedom over the more collectivist values that had previously dominated both the trade union movement and the conservative right. What the journalist Christopher Booker (1992 [1969]) described as the 'neophiliac' momentum of the sixties, with its excitement about youth, novelty, freedom, and personal identity, was an economic as well as cultural force, which provided a narrative for the trends of consumerism, deindustrialisation, and deregulation as the century went on.

In *Baby Boomers and Generational Conflict*, Jennie explored the ways in which political and policy debates raging in the early part of the twenty-first century around questions of 'generational inequity' are framed by an attempt to reckon with the legacy of the sixties (Bristow 2015). While those on the cultural right tend to blame leftist academics and hippies for the promotion of social irresponsibility and moral relativism, those on the cultural left pin the blame on economic neoliberals for promoting individual freedom and social atomisation. In seeking easy targets, both sides miss the point about the sixties culture wars, which were more to do with the fragmentation of meaning than the construction of a radical new way to be.

The spirit of the sixties was to question everything, from the authority of church and state to the sanctity of the family and the promise of romantic love. The desire to free individuals from the conventions and constraints that prevented them from 'being themselves' led to a critical reappraisal of fundamental social institutions. Through the Civil Rights movement and the campaigns against the Vietnam War, the nation state was challenged for its racism, imperialism, and violence: to be 'born in the USA' meant, as expressed by Springsteen's famous anthem of 1984, a conflicted kind of patriotism, where national pride was tainted by self-doubt. Feminism exposed the 'dark side' of the family as a site of domestic violence and abuse, and education was reimagined as a 'Wall' of oppressive and often cruel conformity. 'We don't need no thought control', shouted Pink Floyd (1979). 'Hey! Teacher! Leave them kids alone!'

It is tempting to draw a straight line from the sixties counterculture's critical questioning of core values and institutions to the current progressive demonisation of the past. That is why many conservative critics of contemporary progressivism default to the argument that the rot set in with liberalising legal reforms, and delude themselves that the cure lies in rowing back on these developments, for example by restricting access to abortion. This misses the fact that the counterculture was a reaction to the crumbling of conventions and institutions, rather than its cause. 'The order is rapidly fadin',' sang Bob Dylan (1964). The injustices and inequalities highlighted by feminists and civil rights campaigners were real and entrenched, and even the guardians of the old order were finding them difficult to defend.

This was indicated in the swathes of legislation passed during this period on both sides of the Atlantic, to outlaw racial segregation and discrimination, make abortion legally available, and protect against sex discrimination in the workplace.[1] The notion that legislative change drives cultural change, as seen in the policy push for 'trans rights', is a much more recent conceit: traditionally, changes in the law have been brought after sustained periods of political campaigning and transformations in social attitudes. The new order of equal rights ushered in by the legislation of the 'permissive sixties' not only ratified the social changes that followed the end of the Second World War; it pointed to an optimistic vision, in which people were to be free to make their own way in a society that was striving towards a brighter, wealthier, more democratic future. The openness of those times contrasts sharply with the fearful, defensive posturing of the current progressivist vision, which marshals censorious imperatives to 'be kind' against an overwrought assumption of everyday nastiness and injustice.

But in this moment we can see the beginnings of the identitarian turn, which is causing so much tension today. The 'spirit of '68', with its focus on personal liberation, marked a turn away from the politics of the traditional left and towards the terrains of culture and identity as primary sites for self-actualisation and change. The counterculture, as the name implies, expressed a deep cultural critique of the norms and institutions of modern capitalist society; the result, as we discuss in Chapter 5, was the emergence of an 'adversary culture' (Bell 1979: 40) that came to dominate cultural and educational institutions. The movements associated with the counterculture promoted a critical orientation that foregrounded the experiences of historical oppression and present-day alienation and demanded greater recognition for, and validation of, personal and group identities.

This approach was encapsulated in the idea that 'the personal is political'. This idea captured, in its early stages, the blurring of temporal and personal boundaries that we find in modern identity politics, as it aspired to address 'a fundamental schism in the American experience: the gap most people feel most of the time between their daily lives and history' (Whalen & Flacks 1989: 9). 'The personal is political' was, famously, the title of a contribution to the Women's Liberation Movement by Carole Hanisch in 1969, a paper that spoke both to excitement about the possibilities for individual self-realisation and to disenchantment with the ways in which established collectivist political frameworks, such as trade unions, often downgraded, in pursuit of their overarching goal, the struggles and experiences of oppressed groups. The demand for the integration of personal experience and political action foregrounded the importance of emotions and interpersonal behaviours and ushered in a therapeutic approach that saw activism as consisting not only in doing good for society but in feeling better about oneself.

Hanisch's article was a response to the charge, from 'women who consider themselves "more political"', that the women's groups in which she had been participating were 'personal' and about 'therapy'. Maybe they are, she responded – but that's what is needed. Hanisch refuted the idea that the groups were about therapy in a clinical sense. 'Therapy assumes that someone is sick and that there is a cure, e.g., a personal solution', she wrote. 'I am greatly offended that I or any other woman is thought to need therapy in the first place. Women are messed over, not messed up!' But they did have a therapeutic dimension in the sense of what Hanisch preferred to call 'political therapy': getting rid of 'self-blame' and looking instead at the social circumstances of women's oppression, which was 'what the black movement is doing in its own way'. 'Can you imagine what would happen if women, blacks, and workers . . . would stop blaming ourselves for our sad situations?' she wrote. 'It seems to me the whole country needs that kind of political therapy' (Hanisch 1969).

From the vantage point of the 2020s, it might seem that Hanisch got her wish. Her assertion of the power of 'the personal is political' as a way for oppressed groups to think about their social position and work towards equality has strong resonances with what has now become the everyday language of identity politics, with its focus on lived experience: an individual's subjective understanding of the problems they face, magnified to explain the broader social problem. The language of trauma and healing, and demands for others to 'educate yourself' about the impacts of the microaggressions provoked by living in a culture of 'whiteness', 'heteronormativity', and 'everyday sexism', take the integration of the personal and the political to the point where it is increasingly difficult to see the separation between the two. Political debates or causes are cast into the domain of personal life, while debates about national issues of policy and politics – even Britain's relationship with the European Union, or America's geopolitical interests – are refracted through the sensibility of how we feel about the personalities involved and how it might look to question the consensus of our tribe.

Yet even early proponents of the removal of the distinction between the personal and the political are worried that things may have gone too far. Talking to Timandra Harkness in the 2020s, Hanisch remarked that a more apt description now would be 'the political is personal', and she expressed reservations about the direction taken by contemporary identity politics. The individualistic character of identity politics 'invites us to escape the real world by "living in our heads"', she says, allowing us to believe that, 'if we can change ourselves and/or just a few people, everything will be fine, which is, of course, nonsense. You can't "identify" yourself out of oppression, though over the centuries people sure have tried!' (Hanisch, quoted in Harkness 2024: 309).

The conceit that individuals can identify out of oppression seems to lie behind some of the most disturbing manifestations of current identity politics. The idea that, for example, the problems of being a woman can be evaded through gender transition, or by battling 'everyday sexism' through the rejection of expressions of sexual difference, results in a brittle and censorious war on language, images, and interpersonal behaviour. There seems to be a notion that, if people stop talking about women as female beings, sexual inequality will melt away. Not only does this have a chilling effect on public discourse and interpersonal behaviour; it also burdens the individual with the need to perform who they should be and police those around them in a quest for affirmation. The very 'political therapy' that was initially hoped to support oppressed groups in their struggles for equality has become the vehicle through which individuals are encouraged to magnify their grievance and isolate themselves further from the people around them.

In the twenty-first-century culture wars, the imperative to identify oneself out of oppression effectively leads to its opposite: the self-conscious adoption and performance of an oppressed identity, which does not seek inclusion into mainstream society so much as demands a constant affirmation of one's exclusion from it. While this was not what the protagonists of sixties liberation movements intended, it is a consequence of both the ideas set in motion 50 years ago and the reaction against them.

Post-sixties pessimism and the beleaguered self

The liberationist spirit of the 1960s contrasts sharply with the reaction that followed it. A decade after publishing *The Neophiliacs,* Booker wrote a 'portrait' of the 1970s, in which he wryly observed that '[t]wo unfolding barometers of cultural optimism' in the twentieth century were 'the height of buildings and the height of girls' hemlines'. 'Never', he wrote, 'did skirts rise so high, nor was there such a universal frenzy for building tower-blocks as in the Sixties: and never, in either case, was the reaction so complete as it has been in the Seventies' (Booker 1980: 6).

In *Decade of Nightmares,* the US historian Philip Jenkins (2006) charts the relationship between the end of the sixties and 'the making of Eighties America'. While mention of 'the sixties' carries 'multiple possible meanings', he observes that it usually invokes 'the radical and liberal values of that era, a package of beliefs and values that Europeans characterize as "'68ism"' and that include 'personal and social liberation and the imperative need to challenge laws or social mores that restrict those goals'. From sexual liberation to experimentation with drugs, from anti-war movements to campaigns for racial and gender equality, from environmentalism to radical activism and esoteric spirituality, 'all have powerful associations with the upheavals of the 1960s' (Jenkins 2006: 3).

But by the mid- to late 1970s, explains Jenkins (2006: 4), a 'marked change in the national mood' had occurred, 'bringing with it a much deeper pessimism about the state of America and its future, and a growing rejection of recent liberal orthodoxies'. The conservative backlash, in its fearful obsession with casual sex, gay sex, latchkey children, race, drugs, crime, subversive teachers, and the rest of the cast of the 'folk devils' (Cohen 2011 [1972]) that starred in the moral panics of the period, cast the extension of personal freedom as the cause of social and moral crisis. Politics became 'dominated by questions of gender roles and relationships and of sexual exploitation and restraint, by concepts of normality and perversion, by the definition of masculinity – in short, by exactly those issues of virtue and morality that not long before had seemed inappropriate for mainstream political discourse' (Jenkins 2006: 108).

The biggest fear dominating the cultural backlash, observes Jenkins (2006: 133), was 'the various threats to children – sexual, chemical, criminal, and religious'. The projection onto children of competing ideas about the direction of society is as much a feature of the culture wars today as it was back in the 1980s. The controversies over 'Drag Queen storytime' and the proliferation of 'trans-inclusive' books, teaching materials, and gender-affirmative health care arise from the suspicion that progressives are sexualising young children and indoctrinating children into their own aspiration for a non-binary future.

In the UK, local communities have reacted to the placing of illegal migrants in hotels and placement centres by focusing on the threats posed to their children when unknown young men are roaming the streets: the paraphernalia of these protests speak both to a sentiment of patriotic solidarity (the Union Jack and St George's flags) and to a desire to 'protect the children'. On a recent protest in our hometown of Faversham, Kent, some of the chants focused on the migrants ('Send them back!') but others targeted a reckless, degenerate left ('Leftie scum off our streets!' 'Never trust a leftie with your kids!') (Bristow, 2025a). Middle-class counterprotesters escalated the tensions to a national level, writing an anonymous article to the *Guardian* that fantasised about the return of fascism (Anonymous 2025a). They also launched a 'de-flagging' campaign under the slogan 'Faversham Community Clean up' that called on people to 'remove litter [i.e. flags] from street furniture' and to bring back 'our town . . . to the inclusive haven we know and love' (Anonymous 2025b). In the course of writing this book, the saga spun out to the extremes of both sides of the culture wars, with our sleepy market town becoming a magnet for journalists, activists, and commentators (Glover 2025, Sculthorp 2025, Woods 2025).

In the 1970s as now, those in the conservative or 'orthodox' camp of the culture wars were as guilty of collapsing the distinction between the personal and the political as their progressive foes. As we discuss in subsequent chapters, both sides looked for answers at the institutions of socialisation: education, the family, and the church. Yet it soon became apparent that neither camp spoke for the majority in society, nor could it project a confident vision of the future. The cumulative impact of the culture wars was a defensive turn towards shoring up personal identity in a society that seemed increasingly hostile and unstable.

This vindicated the bleak insights offered by Christopher Lasch's (1984) book *The Minimal Self*, which argued that the belief that political action can create a better world had given way to an inward-looking focus on personal survival, the primary ambition being 'to hold one's own life together' in the face of the mounting pressures of the present day and a fearful orientation towards the future. The consequence, argued Lasch (1984:16), was a 'beleaguered' sense of selfhood, which displayed 'a kind of emotional retreat from the long-term commitments that presuppose a stable, secure, and orderly world'. The therapeutic turn in culture, society, and politics was already normalising a fragile, 'narcissistic' understanding of identity formation (Lasch 2018 [1979]), in which emotional self-protection came to be regarded almost as a moral virtue.

The resulting tension between a yearning for security and a desire for personal freedom set the scene for the confused narratives that are now playing out around identity, exclusion, and identity. Caught in the eye of the storm are young people coming into adulthood, who are trying to make sense of themselves – and of their place in a society that is palpably at odds with itself.

Anomie and anti-social socialisation

The focus on emotion gives the fights of our current moment an intimate and inescapable quality. It is one thing to argue that transgender men are women; it is quite another to experience as a threat to one's very being the question whether individuals can change their biological sex, as captured by overwrought transactivist slogans such as 'Stop Killing Trans Kids'. This is a particular problem when the issue at stake is presented, and experienced, as one of personal identity and when social questions of injustice, inequality, and unfairness are presented, and experienced, in terms of a failure to affirm people's feelings about themselves.

The concept of identity politics fails to capture the prominence of identity in the way people understand and talk about themselves and their beliefs – which is characterised by the shift from 'I think' to 'I feel' and by a change from the aspiration to fit into the world to the expectation that the world should fit around you. This is particularly the case for young people, whose orientation to the world is not generally political or motivated by a sense of societal injustice, but rather to do with how they fit into it. Parents and teachers of teenagers and young adults will be only too familiar with the way this plays out in disagreements ('you're hurting my feelings'), expectations ('I want to work the hours that work for me'), and demands ('respect my pronouns!').

That young people have taken on board this 'look at me' vernacular is not surprising; and it is not entirely new either. Part of the condition of being young is that you are self-obsessed, you don't know very much, and you have a lot of feelings. This is not to decry the intensity and authenticity of young people's emotions, or the creativity and energy that these bring to culture and politics. Think of the iconic songs, poems, and novels centred on the joy and pain of coming of age, and the energetic idealism of radical political leaders, whose inexperience has provided a buffer against the cynicism and self-doubt that tend to come with having been around the block. But these contributions are tempered by their interaction with established ways of thinking about and doing things – in short, their socialisation by older generations into the norms of society.

Society has historically encouraged young people to manage their feelings; it has done so by educating them in the world beyond the self, by socialising them into wider norms about how to behave towards others, and by grounding them in realistic expectations about life and work. This is far from straightforward, and has long been a difficult and contested process. Adults don't have all the answers – and in that sense the 'culture war over socialisation' (Furedi 2021) is as much about adults' confusions about social norms and roles as it is about young people's struggles to work themselves out. But until relatively recently there was at least an understanding that adults should strive to offer stability and security to their young.

Today the problem of socialisation has become magnified through the wider cultural conflicts that society is undergoing. The politics of identity rests on a contradiction – feeling excluded from the mainstream while rejecting the mainstream ideas and values as oppressive – that has contributed to a more profound normative crisis within western societies, where the very idea of what is 'normal' becomes confused and contested. The normative crisis described in the previous chapter means that we are no longer sure what we are socialising young people into. This, in turn, impacts the development of identity itself – how people come to know and define themselves in the context of their societies.

In a confident society that knows what it is about, people work out who they are in relation to the prevailing social norms and values. This has never been a perfect process, and the integration of most people into society has relied on the exclusion of others. This was Goffman's (1990b [1963]) insight in his seminal study *Stigma*. Goffman showed how people make sense of social position not only in relation to the laws and moral codes, but in relation to a wider set of characteristics, behaviours, and conventions that measure outsiders against 'the normals'. Those who don't 'fit' are forced to develop what Goffman termed a 'spoiled identity'.

In his time, Goffman identified broadly three features that constituted a spoiled identity: body (disability); character (for example dishonesty, criminality, addiction, homosexuality, unemployment); and tribe (race, religion, national origin) (Goffman 1990b: 14). Half a century on, the terrain of 'stigma' has altered substantially. By and large, western societies no longer regard homosexuality as deviance, or one's racial or religious background as 'other', and this is a very good thing. A greater acceptance of individual differences is progressive in the sixties sense of the word, and has brought the possibility for people to live more equal and fulfilling lives. When a society has a shared understanding of 'normal', it is possible to tolerate, indeed welcome, difference.

But the same forces that have given rise to the current orthodoxy of non-judgementalism have also transformed the understanding of stigma. As a sociological observation, stigma refers to the ways in which a society draws boundaries around what it deems to be normal and acceptable. For the most part, the progressive movements of the sixties challenged the idea that people should be stigmatised by their sexuality, race, or physical abilities, arguing for a more expansive and tolerant understanding of what should be considered normal characteristics and behaviours in modern western societies. In more recent times, progressive arguments have tended to focus on the problem of stigma *itself*, as though any judgement about difference were inherently discriminatory and unkind. This has led to a perplexing, unstable, and contradictory situation, in which material differences between people are recast as competing identities that should be flattered by affirmation.

According to this perspective, welfare claimants should not be stigmatised by the assumption that it is better to have a job. Disabled people should not be stigmatised by the idea that it would be better not to have a disability. Criminals should not be stigmatised by moral judgements about the wrongness of their behaviour; instead, we should be more understanding of the personal and social difficulties that have led them to stray. Migrants should not be stigmatised by the provision of rights and services that are different from those afforded to citizens of their host country. Trans people should not be stigmatised by the acknowledgement that most people do not consider themselves to have a 'gender identity' that is at odds with their sexed body. And so it goes on.

Proponents of the 'be kind' approach argue that this soppy, sloppy approach to the concept of stigma has resulted in a more inclusive situation, where people's diverse identities can be nurtured and celebrated. In reality, it has had two perverse consequences. The first is that it washes over the social or physical problems that give rise to certain forms of difference, presenting them almost as a lifestyle choice that should be accepted rather than tackled. It is one thing to call for a better understanding of the social, economic, and personal circumstances that might result in somebody being unemployed or committing a crime, when this leads to attempts to change those conditions. It is another thing entirely to claim that unemployment or criminality should be 'destigmatised' as a feature of modern life, and that people should just have to put up with it.

Attempts to destigmatise disability through the use of inclusive language provide another example of the problem. Definitions and identities of disability, particularly in the arena of mental health, have expanded to the point where the corresponding conditions have become de facto 'normal', often to the detriment of those individuals who have serious physical or mental health conditions and find that the social attention or resources directed at helping their specific difficulties are lost in a slew of policy and verbiage designed to promote 'wellbeing' (Clements 2026). In recasting disability as an identity to be affirmed rather than a difficulty to be managed, the celebration of difference runs alongside a wilful refusal to acknowledge, and make sensible provision for, the very specific differences and difficulties that disabled people experience when participating in society.

For example, VisitBritain, Britain's official tourism quango, has reportedly advised tour guides that the phrase 'able-bodied' now constitutes harmful language: the phrase 'non-disabled' should be used instead (Sigsworth 2025). In another example, the British theme park owner Merlin Entertainments had planned to tighten the eligibility rules for its Ride Access Pass (RAP) by excluding people with conditions such as ADHD, autism, and anxiety from the scheme. It was forced to backtrack as a result of complaints that tightening the rules would create barriers to access by neurodivergent customers. The RAP scheme was originally designed to reduce queues for those with physical difficulties who struggled to stand; but it has increasingly been used by people whose conditions mean that they have 'difficulty with crowds'. We can sympathise with this latter group, of course; but when increasing numbers of people are diagnosed with such conditions and were therefore claiming the special pass, some disabled theme park visitors were facing longer waits than those in the main queue – which, as Merlin Entertainments reasonably said, is 'not the experience we want for anyone' (Witherington 2026).

A similar problem lies at the heart of what has become known as the 'gender wars'. The recognition of material differences between men and women has formed a key part of legislation and social provision designed to support equality. This is why gender-critical feminists, many of whom spent their younger years battling against the various derogatory terms used to describe women, have reacted with fury to the current trend for trans-inclusive language, in which women become described as 'not-men', 'persons with breasts', 'pregnant people', and so on. Here, collapsing the time-honoured biological distinction between women and men on the grounds that the very idea of a 'binary' forms the basis of the oppression and exclusion of trans people has led to a terrifying situation: individuals' healthcare needs are obscured by language that pretends that men have vaginas, and women's equality rights are eclipsed by the demand that they 'include' the desires of men to choose their own gender.

This aggressive destabilisation of the 'cis-normative' has been a considerable cultural accomplishment, to the point where we can no longer be confident of understanding how many women and men there are in the UK, let alone with which 'gender' they identify (Melley 2024). As the sociologist Alice Sullivan has argued, the muddling up of sex and gender by organisations that gather social statistics has led to a situation where it becomes increasingly difficult to identify and address the different needs of men, women, and trans people. Collecting accurate data on sex is 'both a scientific and an ethical imperative'; failing to do this has a negative impact both on society's understanding of the differences in the lives of men and women, girls and boys, and on research addressing outcomes for trans people. Rather than removing data on sex, we should collect data on both sex and gender identity, 'in order to develop a better understanding of the influence of both these factors, and the intersection between them, on people's lives' (Sullivan, Murray & Mackenzie 2024: 119).

Sullivan is right – and it has been shocking how weak the defence of this position has been from mainstream social scientists, who fundamentally rely on categorisation and data collection to understand the social world. But in an era where any form of categorisation is attacked as oppressive and empirical studies are trumped by claims about 'lived experience' and 'My Truth', we should perhaps be less surprised. If society is indeed in a state of anomie where there are no agreed norms or moral standards, the task of truth seeking becomes reframed as irrelevant, if not actively harmful. The only task ahead is for individuals to navigate the contradictions and seek to protect their beleaguered selves from pressure to be held accountable to the same rules as everyone else.

This reveals the second perverse consequence of attempts to destigmatise difference via the language of inclusion. This has not encouraged more groups of people to feel part of 'normal' or mainstream society; rather it has fuelled the fragmentation of the idea of normal society itself. The liberalising trends that began in the 1960s have morphed into the wider crisis of normativity discussed in the previous chapter. The result has been a proliferation of spoiled identities, where increasing numbers of people feel detached from, and antagonistic to, the mainstream. This includes those spoiled identities highlighted by Goffman back in the 1960s – people who are pressured to accentuate their particular needs and grievances in order to summon recognition and resources. But it also includes, increasingly, the 'normals' of Goffman's time: the white working-class men and women interviewed in Hochschild's *Strangers in Their Own Land*, who found themselves cast into Hillary Clinton's infamous 'basket of deplorables' (Reilly 2016), or the female nurses in the UK, penalised for daring to insist on single-sex changing rooms (Leatherdale 2026).

The attack on the concept of normal has not made stigma disappear. Stigma persists in a diffuse and unacknowledged form, and operates in a more arbitrary way – who knows when they will suddenly find themselves othered as a Karen, a Gammon, or even a Normie? To refer back to another famous sociological text from the early 1960s: when Howard Becker (1997 [1963]) wrote *Outsiders*, the subtitle was *Studies in the Sociology of Deviance*. Today it seems that we are all 'outsiders' and lack any social consensus on what is deviant. This creates a very unstable situation for young people trying to develop a grounded social identity.

Conclusion

The fragile, hypersensitive identities that dominate public discourse today are the outcome of cultural developments that began in the late 1960s and gradually gained influence during the later twentieth century, to the point where we began to socialise young people into these ways of thinking and acting. Kids did not invent the cult of pronoun declaration: not so long ago, English language teachers struggled to get them to understand what a pronoun even was. Rather, they have absorbed the deeper message – transmitted by educational, cultural, and political institutions – that gender identity is something you should feel, express, and have affirmed. The bemusement that some older people feel about youngsters who declare their pronouns is matched by the bemusement of some younger people about why you *wouldn't* declare your pronouns. This is their 'normal', and those who scoff are the deviants.

This means that many of the young people growing into adulthood now often seem better equipped to navigate this de-normalised cultural terrain than older generations. Even if they don't declare their pronouns at every conceivable opportunity, they get why it's considered important to do so. They seem to understand, implicitly, the politically coded ways of speaking and self-presenting that are meant to demonstrate that they are on 'the right side of history'; and they mount impassioned and lucid accounts in defence of arguments that seem quite bewildering to their elders – such as why J. K. Rowling's opposition to transactivism means that genuine fans of *Harry Potter* should reclaim the true spirit of the books from the author who created them (Lewis 2020).

Young people's apparent ability to sit comfortably with the zeitgeist, in all its contradictions and excesses, reveals the success of a decades-long project of *antisocial socialisation*, in which cultural elites have compelled young people to adopt an oppositional orientation towards their society. Rather than encouraging young people to grow up and adapt to the existing social norms and structures, the institutions of education and the media have drip-fed the message that the role of today's young citizen is to act as a critical reflector on everything that is wrong with 'your own land' and to force through change by insisting on the primacy of personal identity: freedom *from* society, rather than freedom *in* society.

Young people are caught in the confusion as well, on a hamster wheel of 'reflexivity' and self-evaluation that means they have to be prepared to renegotiate their identity positions in line with the next new way of thinking. This is satirised brilliantly by the Millennial comedian Bo Burnham (2021). In *Inside,* a one-man Netflix special produced during the 2020 lockdown, Burnham self-flagellates about the 'vaguely shitty' jokes he told as a 'sheltered kid'. All of it was 'perfectly lawful', just 'not very thoughtful' – and for that he needs to be punished. 'The times are changing and I'm getting old', he wails. 'Aren't you gonna hold me accountable?'

Trapped between the past and the future, the young are incited to view their former, childish selves with the kind of disgust with which they are trained to look at their elders – and to regard those younger than themselves as a threat. As Burnham muses on turning 30 in lockdown, he confesses how he 'used to make fun of the boomers, in retrospect, a bit too much / Now all these fucking zoomers are telling me that I'm out of touch'. His snipey riposte to Gen Z is that 'your fucking phones are poisoning your minds, okay?' and putting them at risk of developing 'a dissociative mental disorder' – a recurring theme in his rants about the internet and Big Tech.

In its extreme forms, the linguistic reprogramming of our ideas about what is 'normal', associated with the progressive side of the culture wars, has provoked a backlash among some older folk, who may otherwise have situated themselves within this camp. For all that it has become fashionable for transactivists to denounce gender-critical feminists as fascists, it's fair to say that few of them would self-identify as 'hard right' – or, given the backdrop of radical feminism and the women's liberation movement, would identify with particularly 'orthodox' ways of thinking.

The age profile of this backlash fuels the idea that the culture wars are, at root, a conflict between old and young; that young people are the embodiment of progressive thought, while older generations act as a block to the realisation of a more enlightened future. But, as we see in the next chapter, this is an overblown conceit; young people are far from uniform in their attitudes, and the current process of cultural fragmentation is pulling members of younger generations in all kinds of directions. As the pushback from populist movements is gaining momentum, the millennial idea of a settled progressive consensus is being rapidly unsettled. The desire for a better future means understanding that there is no 'right side of history' that can simply be legislated for – rather that future depends on the part we play in the history that is currently being made. This is unsettling and fraught with difficulty: but it is also exciting, carrying the opportunity for change. The unresolved question is what we will make of it.

4

Hostile generational identities and the making of Gen Z

In the early days of the Covid-19 pandemic, a nasty little meme trended on Twitter that labelled the SARS-Cov-2 virus a Boomer Remover – combining the age-related morbidity profile of Covid-19 with the pre-existing fashion for blaming the Baby Boomer generation for everything. It was horribly tasteless and didn't land well in the cauldron of panic and fear that was March 2020. But the bizarre thing is how much attention it received.

In different times, the name Boomer Remover might have been dismissed as a silly gesture propagated by thoughtless kids online: indeed, that was how many young people saw it (Tenbarge 2020). Back in the real world of infection and death, there were more pressing and practical things to worry about, such as hospital capacity, protective equipment, and treatment protocols. When Jennie and her daughter Emma wrote *The Corona Generation* during the first UK lockdown of summer 2020, young people's concern about the impact of the virus on the elderly and their compliance with the extraordinary restrictions brought in to curb its spread – including the closure of their social and educational spaces and the periods spent 'locked down' with their families – were notable (Bristow

& Gilland 2020). As the Covid restrictions in the UK and elsewhere dragged on, studies indicated that the young became more fed up with the restrictions than their elders and were less likely to observe all 'the rules'. Yet they still demonstrated little open rebellion and remarkably high levels of compliance overall (Ibbetson 2021, Strömmer et al. 2022).

But the online rage generated by the BoomerRemover meme revealed how quickly the pandemic became assimilated into the wider culture wars, taking the form of a clash of identities between older and younger people. (In classic culture wars fashion, the definition of 'old' and 'young' varies according to whatever claim is being made.) This identity clash is often grandly referred to as a 'generational conflict', encapsulating the idea that social, cultural, political, and economic problems today can best be understood as problems of generations.

In this framing, climate change is a problem caused by the greedy consumption of older generations. Older people's longevity and housing wealth are restricting the opportunities of younger generations. Poverty, worklessness, and traumatic events get passed down through the generations. Voting patterns increasingly show a generational divide. The Covid-19 lockdowns were a policy designed to protect the older generations at the expense of the younger ones; indeed their legacy is a distinctive 'Covid generation' indelibly scarred by this experience. And on it goes. Critics refer to this lazy narrative as 'generationalism' (Ryder 1965, White 2013, Purhonen 2016, Elliott 2021) and point to its divisive consequences: it fuels ageism against the elderly and a standoff with the young.

Much of Jennie's research has focused on the problem of generationalism and on debunking the dubious claims about generational conflict that excite current media and policy debates (Bristow 2015, 2016a, 2016b, 2019, 2021a, 2025b). This chapter builds on these observations to understand the peculiar mythology that has developed around the cohort known as Gen Z – today's young adults, and the subject of this book. To return to the question introduced in Chapter 2: is the current 'crisis of youth' about the predicament of the kids themselves, or are adults projecting their own fears and concerns about society and how they fit in onto the handy cultural script of the 'generation wars'? Does it even make sense to talk about Gen Z as a particular group with a distinct identity? Are we witnessing the emergence of a generation gap – and, if so, what does this really mean?

Boomer Remover and the generation wars myth

The BoomerRemover meme went viral because it fitted neatly into a fashionable trend known as 'Boomer blaming'. The idea that the major problems we face today – economic and political turmoil, war, climate change, inequality, failing welfare states, even a respiratory infection that reserved its worst effects for the elderly – are the result of the bad attitudes and decisions of an older and powerful 'generation of sociopaths' (Gibney 2017), who simply cannot empathise with the predicament of the young, has become a go-to diagnosis; and it is obviously attractive to young people, who have always tended to feel misunderstood and blame their parents for everything. But in the twenty-first-century culture wars, the range and depth of this grievance has been magnified and institutionalised by a parasitic policy class, which struggles to provide a positive direction for society and instead puts its energies into finding scapegoats from the past.

As noted in the previous chapters, overblown anxieties about the state of a nation's youth are nothing new. But in more political times it was understood that any solution had to lie in tackling the social problems that gave rise to those fears, be they unemployment, living standards, drugs, crime, or anything else. Many of these are the kinds of 'wicked problems' that cannot simply be resolved with better policy; but the aspiration to do so sent a powerful message to the young, namely that they were part of both the problem and the solution to complicated issues that affected their society as a whole. Youth does not last forever, and the young would soon grow into adults with the capacity to change their circumstances, both individually and collectively, whether through political participation or simply by taking their share of responsibility for their communities.

The twenty-first-century approach to youth and politics is different in two key respects. By popularising the idea that young people's struggles can be explained by the claim that older generations have taken more than their 'fair share' of power, wealth, and resources (i.e. by appealing to Boomer blaming), and that the situation can be resolved only by taking some of that away from the old and giving it to the young (say, via policies pompously framed as promoting 'intergenerational equity'), parasitic policymakers have sought to replace the dynamic idea of youth – a temporary state with the future in its grasp – with a fatalistic generational determinism, which assumes that particular cohorts – first the Millennials, and now Gen Z – will forever be disadvantaged. Moreover, they use this narrative as a warrant for the kind of policies they want to achieve.

For example, a briefing produced for the European Parliament in December 2020 wasted no time in shoehorning concerns about the impact of the pandemic on the young into their existing desire to provide 'generation-fit' policies that 'reflect the youngest generation's concerns in the first place and not that of older generations' and their projections on the young' [*sic*] (Milotay 2020: 9). Titled 'Next Generation or Lost Generation? Children, Young People and the Pandemic', the briefing offered the following sweeping generalisations about Generation Z:

> This generation is described as self-aware, persistent, realist, innovative and self-reliant, in contrast to the Millennials, who

> have been found to be self-centered, entitled, idealist, creative and dependent. Generation Z is claimed to be the best educated proportionally, as well as liberal-minded and open to emerging social trends. (Milotay 2020: 2)

The author presumably didn't think the impact of months of school closure and disrupted education worth considering. Nor did the briefing entertain the possibility that, by 2025, sizeable sections of Gen Z would terrify the liberal-minded by supporting populist political causes and parties.

Self-serving policy bullshit is bad enough. Far worse is that, by attempting to reframe social, economic, and political problems as cultural issues attached to people's sense of identity, 'generational conflict' narratives transform age-old sentiments of youthful frustration into a hardened sense of grievance and personal harm, which really does inflame the perception of conflict between the generations.

All of this was apparent in the Boomer Remover spat. Youthful tweeters excused their nastiness on the grounds that they were the real victims of the historical injustice of being born in the present era. One tweet contrasted the allegedly dismissive attitude shown by the Boomers to Millennials and Gen Z – who are 'dying from depression, homelessness, non-living wages, mass shootings, poor healthcare, etc.' – with their snowflakish reaction to the BoomerRemover meme (Whalen 2020). Another shouted:

> BREAKING: The generation who caused the climate crisis & killed the housing market & privatised public services & crippled the NHS & enabled austerity & Windrush & every other post-war outrage . . . are absolutely furious ungrateful kids have dubbed #COVID19 the BOOMER REMOVER! (Elliott 2022: 82)

Rebecca Elliott's (2022) astute analysis shows how such tweets fit into a script of 'intergenerational discounting': that is, 'a description of breakdown in reciprocal moral obligations of care, giving rise to accusations of hypocrisy, expressions of resentment and rage' that are focused in particular on the suggestion that COVID-19's disproportionate effects on older people are 'a kind of karmic retribution for their failure to address climate change' (Elliott 2022: 75). In other words, for the Boomer Remover brigade, Covid-19 represented a warped kind of accountability for the elderly, on the grounds of having caused the young to suffer so much.

The unapologetic ageism behind Boomer Remover – and, indeed, behind other forms of 'generationalized rhetoric' around the pandemic (Rudolph & Zacher 2020: 139) – has been widely criticised in the academic literature (see e.g. Lichtenstein 2021, Skipper & Rose 2021, Meisner 2022, Plastina 2022). As an article in *Newsweek* observed at the time,

> Since all generational narratives assign stereotyped attributes and flatten massive demographics into loose age categories, the trending use of Boomer Remover as a nickname for coronavirus inevitably involves sweeping statements and attacks, guaranteed to leave everyone feeling aggrieved, misunderstood and ill-used. (Whalen 2020)

This sentiment of all-round grievance was revealed by the Boomer backlash on Twitter, which combined sanctimony with spite. 'Let's see if these kids think it's so funny when they kill off a beloved grandparent because they thought the whole COVID-19 issue was a joke and [they] infected their grandparent', thundered one, while another proposed: 'The Boomers referred to in the #BoomerRemover hashtag should think twice about where they leave their money and property . . . If your kids and grandkids think the hashtag is OK then perhaps it's time to leave it to charity' (Skipper & Rose 2021: 4). The age-old phenomenon of kids being silly in the face of tragedy was escalated into something existentially darker: wait 'til their grandad gets it, and let's disinherit the ungrateful brats in the meantime.

As the tit-for-tat Twitter-spat revealed the old to be as mean and childish as the young, the official social distancing policy and messaging gave legitimacy to the presentation of Covid-19 as a battle between the generations. Government campaigns targeted young people with the message that they should not consider themselves 'invincible' in the face of this coronavirus and that failure to heed social distancing regulations could result in 'killing granny' (Nebehay 2020; Bristow 2021b). In the UK, this was part of a deliberate strategy on the part of behavioural scientists, who regarded ramping up 'the perceived level of personal threat' as part of an effective, evidence-based strategy for 'increasing adherence to social distancing measures' (SAGE 2020).

Governments worldwide deliberately overstated the danger that the virus posed to young people and their own ability to limit its spread – causing unwarranted levels of fear and guilt among sensitive kids. Well-placed concerns about the effect of prolonged school closures and young people's isolation from the social world ignited some bitter arguments about whether we were sacrificing the needs of the young to the wellbeing of the old, or prioritising the demands of the present emergency over the needs of the future (Bristow 2021b, Cole & Kingsley 2022). In a context where the whole society was organised around the need to mitigate the devastating effects of a novel virus, it is hard to think of a more irresponsible intervention than one that set the needs of the old and those of the young against each other in this way.

But the real impact of generationalised pandemic rhetoric came afterwards. With national populations around the world cowering fearfully in their homes and spending way too much time online while officials assumed extraordinary powers over the regulation of everyday life, the lockdown years provided fertile ground for the consolidation of the culture wars. The suspension of the taken-for-granted features of the social contract – that one should routinely go to work or school, that communities should engage with one another in physical space, that families' care for their elderly should mean more than an occasional Zoom call – intensified the sense of disorientation, atomisation, and estrangement that was already bubbling and gave it visible and visceral form via social media.

The dynamics behind, say, the Black Lives Matter (BLM) protests, the surge in transgender identification among teenagers, and the rise of a cancel culture were clearly present before the pandemic, but they erupted from 2020 onwards (Lukianoff & Schlott 2023, Bowles 2024). While these were distinct phenomena, they had in common a focus on identity and emotion, a preoccupation with the symbolic realm of language and imagery, and an orientation around the sentiments associated with young people.

In reacting to these events, people – of all ages – ended up coming down on a particular 'side' of the culture wars, fuelling the development of now familiar omnicauses. But their reaction also had a notable generational dimension. For example, it is the middle-aged mother (the figure defended by Victoria Smith (2023) in *Hags: The Demonisation of Middle-Aged Women*) who appears as the most vocal critic of gender identity; it is the older person using the 'wrong' kind of language that generally becomes the target of cancellation. This in turn sharpens the sense that we now experience the world from the vantage point of rigidly defined *generational* identities, which set us at odds with those whose outlook developed at a different moment in history. But how true is this, beyond the symbolic polarisation of social media?

Generational identities: labels in search of meaning

For those on all sides of the culture wars, the idea of a rift between old and young is beguiling. In a political context where the dominant, progressivist ways of thinking have become associated with the outlook of the young, older generations often find themselves positioned on the defensive. Positions that would have been considered 'orthodox' back in the 1990s are now framed as outlandish outliers from the current consensus (the keyword here is 'out-'). Attitudes, opinions, and an understanding of the world on the basis of the norms and conventions of the recent past are literally cast as being on the 'wrong' side of history, while the 'right' side of history is the future and the young people who will grow up there.

A toxified view of the past as the place where all bad things began, as discussed in Chapter 2, coexists with a peculiarly selective and rose-tinted view of how great things were for those who were lucky enough to grow up there. Amid all this nonsensical revisionism, a conceit has emerged that the battle of our times is 'generational' (Bristow 2015, 2019). When those on the 'wrong' side of history reject the progressive narrative of reality, they often accept the claim that its protagonists are young people; then they draw up their defences accordingly.

Yet, as we discuss in what follows, the idea that political attitudes are determined by age or by generation is way too simplistic. Empirical studies of attitudes and voting trends reveal big differences *within* generations, and challenge the assumption that differences *between* generations are as stark as they are made out to be. This is especially apparent now, as mainstream political parties across the US and Europe are finding themselves challenged by populist movements that appeal to young people (especially, although not exclusively, young men) and to older voters alike (Grasso & Smith 2021, Mehring, Off, & Wojnicka 2025, Milosav et al. 2025). While this trend certainly challenges the cosy assumption that the 'voice of youth' is a vote for progressive politics, it does not warrant the hysterical warnings that Gen Z has turned into the twenty-first century version of the Hitler Youth (Bristow 2025c). Rather it reveals the problem with substituting cultural categories such as generation for political understanding.

When commentators and policymakers talk about generations such as Baby Boomers, Gen X, Millennials, Gen Z, and so on, they are not really talking about people. Rather they are making use of cultural categories that were developed by social scientists and popularised by marketers to illustrate shifts in the zeitgeist – the spirit of a particular age. These shifts are internalised by young people as they come into adulthood; and they are (to some extent) expressed by them in cultural products such as poetry, literature, film, music, or social media and in certain attitudes and characteristics. This gives rise to the commonly used generational labels summarised in Box 4.1.[1]

When one looks at these labels, several problems jump out, all of which are well known in the field of generational research and have been written about at length elsewhere (Kingstone & Bristow 2025). The most obvious problem is that labels reduce entire cohorts to crass stereotypes, which capture something about an historical period and map it onto everyone who happened to be born during that time. Social class, sex, ethnicity, and geographical location – all have a powerful effect on people's experiences of life, arguably much more so than their generation.

North American labels are applied to countries with quite different social experiences and memories, in an attempt to capture some kind of 'universal' temporal experience. The Greatest Generation, which helped the Allies win the Second World War, is remembered quite differently in Germany and in parts of Europe where this cohort is tainted by association with fascism. Even in an Anglo-American context, the stereotypes are clearly one-sided and slightly weird; most Baby Boomers were not cool countercultural '68ers, and there are a

Box 4.1 Generation labels and what they stand for

Common label	Approximate birth cohort dates	Formative historical period, and ascribed characteristics
First World War Generation *aka the Lost or Forgotten Generation*	1896–1910	Through their bleak expressions of moral and spiritual alienation, the writers and poets of this era gave voice to the sense of crisis and confusion that dominated the early twentieth century.
Greatest Generation *aka the Second World War Generation*	1911–1925	Born during the Depression years; came of age to fight in the Second World War. In the Allied countries, they are imagined mostly as brave fighters for good against evil, returning from war to build a peacetime based on prosperity and freedom.
Silent Generation	1926–1945	Marked by the Depression and the Second World War. Coming of age in the 1950s, they have been represented as a conformist, apathetic generation.
Baby Boomers *aka the Sixties Generation*	1946–1964	The products of two simultaneous 'booms' – a sharp rise in birth rates as soldiers returned from the war and got busy making babies, and an economic boom that began in the 1950s and continued throughout the 1960s. These babies were initially considered to symbolise peace, freedom and optimism, but went on to turn against the values, conventions, and institutions of the post-war world, spawning a radical countercultural movement.
Generation X	1965–1980	Gen X is generally depicted as a small, coolly embittered generation born in the shadow of the Boomers and growing up through the crisis-ridden seventies and the 'end of history' eighties, as the Cold War was coming to an end.

Box 4.1 (*continued*)

Common label	**Approximate birth cohort dates**	**Formative historical period, and ascribed characteristics**
Millennials *aka Generation Y, and the Echo Boomers*	1981–1996	In place of Generation X's grimly self-destructive nihilism, the kids who came of age at the turn of the twenty-first century were described as anxious and stressed, entitled and desperate to please. Millennials were also the 'Boomer echo', the diminished children of that vast and glitzy sixties generation. Their coming of age was marked not only by a change of century but by the terrorist attacks of 9/11 and the global financial crisis of 2008.
Gen Z	1997–2012	Gen Z are styled as the children of economic hardship and austerity policies, the 'digital natives' lost in communication and incomprehensible to those for whom a phone is a useful device rather than an extension of the self, and the 'Covid generation', whose coming of age was heavily impacted by Covid-19 restrictions.
Alpha Generation	2013–	The narrative around these young people is still being formed. There is emphasis on the experience of living one's early years under lockdown and on the further reach of social media, especially generative AI.

lot of youngsters in Gen Z who are not crippled by anxiety and addicted to their phones. Meanwhile the birth dates accorded to each cohort vary slightly according to who is writing about it and the points that the writers are trying to make: a further indication that the generations are social and cultural constructs, not fixed and determined entities.

The fashion for slicing society up into birth cohorts implies that it is both possible and desirable to find deterministic explanations for why people think and behave the way they do. At its crudest, this notion is based on the biology of birth dates: why should somebody born right at the end of 1980 (a Gen Xer) be so different from somebody born right at the start of 1981 (a Millennial)? The answer, revealed in empirical studies of social and political attitudes, is that they are not: and members of completely different generations often have more attitudes in common than is assumed. For example, as Bobby Duffy (2021) demonstrates in *Generations: Does When You're Born Shape Who You Are?*, the attitudes of younger and older people in the UK on key social issues such as climate change are fairly well aligned; and when it comes to ideas about gender roles, attitudes have changed across every generation, reflecting deeper changes in women's position in society. For example, in 1987, '48 per cent of the British population believed that "the job of the man is to earn money, the job of the woman is to look after the home and family". Now only 8 per cent of people say they hold this view' (Duffy 2021: 178).

Meanwhile, attitudes to issues that tend to be highly polarised politically, such as abortion, depend less on generation than on national context. Duffy (2021: 181) explains that long-term generational trends on attitudes to abortion in the US show that, from the 1970s onwards, 'around half . . . of Americans have consistently said that a married woman should *not* be able to get a legal abortion just because she does not want more children', and over 40 per cent of Gen Zers still hold this view. This issue 'splits the country down the middle, regardless of generation'. In Britain, by contrast, with the exception of the very old, 'pre-war generation', only a quarter of the population said in 2016 that 'a woman should not be allowed to have an abortion if she simply did not wish to have the child'.

Individuals' attitudes are shaped not by some pre-given generational identity, but by changes in the wider social and cultural context that frame them. They are also shaped by their age and their position in the life course (Woodman & Wyn 2015, Rudolph & Zacher 2020, Duffy 2021). Particularly when trying to make sense of younger generations such as Gen Z, it is difficult to disentangle the extent to which their attitudes to, say, sexual and gender fluidity derive from their absorption of contemporary cultural trends around 'queerness' or from their engagement in sexual experimentation, which has long been associated with youth. Whereas our generation, Gen X, characteristically expressed this in a penchant for 'casual sex' with other people (a cause of much handwringing among older commentators back in the day), today's youngsters characteristically play with identity categories to express how they see themselves.

For example, the 'traits' that Jean Twenge ascribes to Gen Zers include a tendency to identify as gender fluid or bisexual or both (and, to a lesser degree, gay or lesbian) and to have less sexual activity overall.[2] In a context in which identifying with a 'diverse' sexual and gender identity has cultural cachet, it is easy to see why young people would express such a tendency, particularly if they are not actually having sex, with all its messy, physical consequences. The negative effects highlighted by gender-critical feminists that 'trans inclusion' has on women's spaces, health services, and sense of identity as 'women' may not become apparent to young women until they age into somebody who wants to have children or an abortion, confronts a diagnosis of breast cancer, or finds herself having to swap the abstract identification with a gender for the very concrete demands of motherhood. Something also worth noting is the inherent instability of cultural self-identification categories based on present feelings: by 2025, some were suggesting that trans and queer identities may be 'in decline' among young people (Kauffmann 2025).

The problem of trying to define young people in terms of their generational attributes is particularly marked when thinking about the kids who are nowhere near adulthood – and therefore a long way from being able to craft a particular 'generational' understanding of their experience, let alone make this understanding carry the zeitgeist. This goes for the so-called Alpha Generation and the subsequent cohort, which consultants are already labelling, unimaginatively, Gen Beta (McCrindle 2025). Attempts to ascribe a common worldview and set of characteristics to children barely old enough to know what, individually, they think about anything show the extent to which so much generation talk is less about engaging with some kind of generational identity than it is about constructing one according to the prejudices of those who come up with the labels.

A decade ago, the journalist Chloe Combi (2015: loc. 29) interviewed dozens of young people from across the UK. They were from the cohort known as Generation Z, which she defined as people born between 1995 and 2001. She presented a familiar picture of the context in which they were growing up, noting that these kids have 'never known a world without the internet' and have 'grown up with violence and porn at their fingertips via an object unknown just one generation before: a smartphone'. But Combi resisted the temptation to put a label on it, despite the pressure to declare one. 'Are they the Internet Generation, the Sex-Mad Generation, the Social-Media Generation, the Celebrity-Obsessed Generation or the Not-Much-To-See-Here Generation?', she asked, noting that the young people to whom she had talked ranged from some whose lives are painfully distressing and chaotic to others whose lives 'are so achingly normal that they worry if it rains too much' (loc. 64, 40). In contrast to the dramatic generationalist claimsmaking visible elsewhere, Combi offered a sober summary:

> There was a temptation to string together all the most shocking and affecting vignettes, but this would have been disingenuous. The mundane is as much a feature of being a teenager as the fantastic. (Combi 2015, loc. 40)

A similar point could be made about all the other generational categories. While most people are familiar with the stereotypes of Gen X, Millennials, and so on, they do not actually identify with them. In this sense, generational identities are not expressed by people so much as ascribed to them and imposed upon them by commentators on the lookout for shorthand explanations to difficult problems.

In 2021 a group of demographers and social scientists wrote to the US Pew Research Center, one of the front-runners of generational research, to criticise generational labels for being divisive and based on 'pseudoscience' (Cohen 2021, Elliott 2021). Pew acknowledged that the field 'has been flooded with content that's often sold as research but is more like clickbait or marketing mythology', and announced that it would take a new approach to generational research going forward (Parker 2023). Even before this, its own research found that, for all the obsession with generational identities, these don't have much purchase among people themselves. In 2015, only 40 per cent of the US adults categorised within the Millennial cohort considered themselves part of the 'Millennial generation'; 33 per cent considered themselves rather to be part of the older Generation X. With the exception of Baby Boomers, generational identity was weak. Only 18 per cent of members of the so-called Silent Generation – people aged 70 to 87 at the time – regarded themselves as belonging there; they were more likely to place themselves either in the older Greatest

Generation or among the younger Boomers (Pew Research Center 2015).

When teaching, Jennie always asks her students whether they see themselves as part of a particular generation. The earlier cohorts, formally Millennials, were scathing about the Millennials, whom they regarded as entitled, arrogant, and generally quite old, and saw themselves as different from their younger siblings and cousins, whom they perceived as disturbingly in thrall to their mobile phones and other electronic devices. A few years later, Jennie asked a group what they thought of the climate activist Greta Thunberg, who was about their age at that time and was widely talked about as the 'voice' of the younger generation. They reacted with a snarl: not because they objected to Greta's politics or activism, but because they felt that they were constantly being compared unfavourably to her. When members of a more recent cohort were asked whether they identified with the Gen Z 'traits' identified by Jean Twenge, they said no – these traits were 'a bit negative' and 'mainly about America'.

As authors of a book that is about the predicament of today's young people or Gen Z – categories that we have tended to use interchangeably – it might seem strange that we raise so many problems with talking about people in generational terms, and then proceed to do so. The overuse and abuse of generational labels have become a big problem for the ways in which we talk about people in our society and about the shared issues that confront us. But this is precisely why we need to engage with both.

Generation talk has become so prominent in the current culture wars *because* generations are a symbolic and cultural concept rather than a reflection of the way people actually think of themselves or behave in everyday life. When the dynamics of the culture wars are increasingly understood in terms of a clash of hostile generational identities, it is important to remind ourselves that 'real life' encounters are more mediated than this and that young and old are not at loggerheads in the way one might assume if one never got off social media. At the same time, the construction of hostile generational identities in the cultural domain bleeds into the way we try to make sense of events and of one another. In these febrile times, generational identity becomes one frame through which the battle for meaning and sense of self is played out in cultural debates. This cultural identity is then mapped back onto the people it purports to describe, which makes things very personal – and, consequently, damaging.

What generation talk *can* tell us

We don't have to take the claims about generations and about the differences between them literally to acknowledge that there is something useful in the concept of a social generation. We are all a product of our time: both the time in which we grew up and the time in which we live now. We might agree that the traits Twenge ascribes to Gen Z paint a one-sided picture of this cohort, even if we look no further than the US; but anybody who spends significant amounts of time with young adults will surely recognise that they capture something about the cohort in general. Twenge, like Haidt, sees advances in technology as explaining why different cohorts relate to the world in different ways.[3] In these accounts, technological developments are used as a symbolic proxy for historical developments, and this leads to a rather brittle and deterministic result.

Yet for all these problems, Haidt's insights on the 'coddling of the American mind' (Lukianoff & Haidt 2018) and the 'anxious generation' (Haidt 2024) have drawn much needed attention to some significant problems with the ways in which our society is failing in its responsibility to young people. In her years of paying close attention to cultural dynamics, Twenge has been able to make some astute and pithy observations about the orientation of young Americans towards their society. For example, Twenge's (2006) book on Millennials was titled *Generation Me: Why Today's Young Americans Are More Confident, Assertive, Entitled – and More Miserable than Ever Before.* Her 2017 book *iGen* bears the subtitle *Why Today's Super-Connected Kids Are Growing Up Less Rebellious, More Tolerant, Less Happy – and Completely Unprepared for Adulthood – and What That Means for the Rest of Us.* In their unflinching negativity, such accounts reveal just how much of a mess Anglo-American societies have made of socialising our kids.

Generations are best understood as symbolic concepts that help us to make sense of social time; and generational labels, rather than being literal representations of experience, are constructions born out of an attempt to give meaning to cultural trends. Understanding this balance between history and biography (Mills 1970 [1959]) is a problem that those who work with the idea of generation have grappled with for centuries. Within sociology, the most systematic attempt to theorise this phenomenon was developed by Karl Mannheim (1952 [1928]) 100 years ago, and to get there he brought together two different ways of thinking about generations. One emphasised the qualitative experience of people in particular birth cohorts; the other, positivist approach abstracted from this experience, looking at generational change as a pure expression of social progress. Both approaches were important, but neither was sufficient to explain the question at the heart of the 'problem of generations': the ways in which events of the present time impact upon, and are shaped by, the coming of age of young people.

For Mannheim (1952: 293), the question at the heart of the generations problem was about knowledge and meaning-making. Thinking about generations is a way of trying to understand how young people make sense of the world in which they grow up and do it differently from their elders, but also how they absorb and bring meaning to the wealth of knowledge and understanding that is passed down through families, communities, and the institutions of education. The young are not merely passive recipients of the wisdom, practices, and commonsense assumptions of 'the past'; by forming 'fresh contacts' with it (Mannheim 1952: 293), they interpret the knowledge of their elders in ways that help them to understand the world as it appears to them right now. They do all this within an active and ongoing relationship with older generations, whose own formative years brought a certain orientation to the world, and with people around their own age, whose shared experience of events as they grow up together can shape them into a 'social generation' (Bristow 2025b).

This idea of social generations lies behind the now ubiquitous labels used to describe particular birth cohorts. It should be noted that the people who came up with these labels tend to be marketers, not the likes of Mannheim – and he would have been horrified by the crass way in which assumptions and prejudices about social generations are bandied around today. In marked contrast to the sweeping generalisations made about Baby Boomers or Gen Z, as though everyone in those cohorts is the same across the world, Mannheim stressed that the making of a generation did not simply come from the passage of time, but from experiencing a significant historical moment in early adulthood and within a shared geographical, often national, context. Later on some academics referred to such a moment as a 'traumatic' social event (Edmunds & Turner 2005).

Mannheim also stressed that the members of a social generation would not all make sense of their experience in the same way. Rather, different 'generation units' would emerge that worked up their experiences in different ways. The ideas that would later come to be associated with the generation were those that best captured the zeitgeist of that time. If we apply this understanding to the generation known as the Baby Boomers, for example, we can see how the cohort born directly after the Second World War was in part formed by the 'cultural revolution' of the sixties and came to be associated with the permissive culture of ''68ism' ('free love', protest, psychedelic drugs) – even though most of the people who were young at the time had nothing to do with any of that.

The same goes for the cultural assumptions made about Millennials and Gen Z as the warriors of 'woke'. The characteristics ascribed to particular generations tend to reflect a particular, middle-class outlook: in Mannheim's terms, they capture the cultural zeitgeist as expressed by those in a position to shape it, not as experienced by the daily lives of most people. This is why the caricatures of the 'entitled' Millennial or the 'gender-fluid' Zoomer are more likely to be found on Ivy League campuses or in publishing companies than among young people working in retail or construction – and why they tend to be sympathetically reproduced for mainstream media organisations, by journalists who have carefully curated their own images in line with such caricatures.

In other words Mannheim's theorisation of social generations can be seen to provide the underpinning for the labels currently used to express generational differences and identities. But it also challenges the use of such labels to define whole cohorts, by explaining why the historical forces that can give rise to a particular expression of generational identity also give rise to competing attitudes within groups of people of a similar age. During periods of social upheaval, members of the same generation 'work up the material of their common experiences in different specific ways' (Mannheim 1952: 304); and until things have settled, it is impossible to predict which of these ways will come to be seen as defining the spirit of the generation.

We have seen this with the making of Gen Z. When Combi struggled, back in 2015, to put a label on this diverse group of kids, it was partly because the context in which they were growing up differed too little from that surrounding the Millennials, who had come before: 'a world shadowed with economic uncertainty, shrinking job prospects, widening social inequality and political apathy' (Combi 2015: loc. 29). Five years later, the Covid-19 pandemic would rock the experience of their formative years, leading to a wave of hyperbolic predictions about what the 'Covid generation' would be like – none of which accounted for the explosion of the culture wars. The BLM protests and the explosion of trans ideology provoked commentators to settle on the assumption that Gen Z would be radically 'woke'; yet this cosy narrative is already being unsettled by the populist backlash.

Any attempt to work out how Gen Z might personify the zeitgeist is made impossible by the fact that, right now, the spirit of our age is up for grabs. With this in mind, we can consider the problem of the generation gap.

Generational estrangement and gaps

The most significant problem with generational labels is that they overemphasise the influence of contemporaries and downplay the interaction between different generations. A focus on generations should remind us that we live in a set of relationships with our families and communities, in constant interaction with people older and younger than ourselves. When we talk about generations in a vertical sense, as in generations in the family, we ground ourselves in an intimate relationship with the past and the future. Grandparents are a living reminder of the world as it was and of how it has changed. Through children, we take responsibility for the world as it is now, so that it may become something else. When people throughout history have talked about generations, they have been talking about history and what it means to them; the people and the principles we care about beyond the present day.

At a time when western societies are in thrall to a culture of presentism, it is not surprising that these labels are in vogue: it seems far easier to explain away the plight of Gen Z, for example, in terms of what others in this cohort are doing than to discuss the more subtle and powerful process through which Gen Zers are socialised by adults, who bring their own understanding and experience of the past into play. However, as we discuss in the next two chapters, the logic of presentism means that vertical relations between generations have come under sustained cultural attack. This is most destructive in relation to education, which has now become an institution geared towards encouraging young people to reject the wisdom of the past, and in relation to the family, where the young are counselled not only to reject the common sense of their elders but to doubt their own desire and capacity to have children. This assault on the basic generational transaction is a far more significant source of disorientation for today's young adults than the popularity of transactivist or alt-right influencers on TikTok.

Our oversensitivity to generational differences speaks to our experience of the fragmentation and age segregation that are visible in everyday life. The sense that young people live much of their lives online, in social media communities in which their elders are neither interested nor invited, is magnified by the visibility of statements of self-imposed cut-off when out in public: the headphones and ear defenders, the constant one-sided chatter via iPods. The extension and expansion of education means that young people spend relatively longer grouped with people their own age; in the UK, the school-leaving age is 18, and around 36 per cent of school leavers go on to university (Bolton 2025: 5). One effect of this, as we discuss in the next chapter, is that a substantial proportion of young adults spend their formative years cloistered together rather than interacting in the workplace with people of all ages, as fellow employees.

This increasing age segregation is not just driven by trends among young people. The fashion for working from home (WFH), widespread among the professional classes and accelerated by the Covid pandemic, also contributes – along with the increasing proportions of retired people in our ageing societies. None of this, in itself, leads to hostility between the generations. But much of it does contribute a sense of estrangement and mutual incomprehension – which can open the door to nasty stand-offs such as the Boomer Remover. At its most extreme, this sense of estrangement gives rise to fears that we face the prospect of a generation gap, in which older people somehow inhabit a different reality from that of the young.

'Generation gap' is a term that trips neatly off the headline writer's tongue. It is often used to describe banal differences between older and younger people in matters of cultural taste, approaches to work, political opinion, and myriad other features of social life. The generationalist narratives discussed above have often stoked fears of a new generation gap in order to maximise the dramatic effects of their arguments. For example, the cult of Boomer blaming emerged from claims that the different economic circumstances experienced by Baby Boomers in the 1960s and by their Millennial children during the global financial crisis (GFC) were leading to an economic gap (Howker & Malik 2010, Willetts 2010). This claim was exacerbated by allegations of an empathy gap according to which the Boomers, as a 'generation of sociopaths' (Gibney 2017), did not care enough for their children to remedy the situation through policies designed to promote generational equity and somehow solve the climate emergency (Elliott 2022).

During the political turmoil of the Brexit referendum in the UK and the election of Donald Trump to the US presidency, both in 2016, it became fashionable to talk about age and generation as the new 'dividing line' in politics, on the basis of the assumption that all older people would vote to the right and all younger people to the left (Bristow 2019, 2021a). Alarmist claims about kids and social media have often been framed by the simplistic assumption of a 'digital divide', as though anybody over 45 barely knows how to turn a mobile phone on, and anybody under 30 is incapable of navigating the difference between social media and 'real life'.

Talking up generation gaps in this way has two bad consequences. The first has been to consolidate the assumptions about hostile generational differences discussed above. The second has been to make commentators insensitive to the circumstances in which the emergence of a genuine generation gap does seem like a possibility, and one with quite serious consequences. Fixation on the differences between Gen Z and everybody else means that more difficult discussions can be avoided about what distinguishes our current historical moment from previous moments in time. The decisive shift isn't to do with smartphones and social media, lockdowns, or political polarisation, although all these factors are important. It's to do with Anglo-American societies' aggressive cultural turn against the past and with their deep pessimism about the future. And this is where the experience of the Covid-19 pandemic and all that follows from it is important to reckon with.

Historically, generation gaps are very rare. They express moments of intense cultural dislocation, brought about by far-reaching external events that affect everybody, but have different and often polarising impacts on the young (Bristow 2023). The UK's last experience of one was during the sixties, when the 'cultural revolution' (Marwick 1999) that consumed Western Europe and North America led to an explosion of books and articles trying to make sense of the apparent gulf between the generation that won the war and the kids who were growing up in the peace. We can also talk about a generation gap emerging in the hiatus between the two world wars – the period in which Mannheim was grappling with his theory of the conditions that gave rise to 'social generations'. As we discuss in Chapter 6, generation gaps also preoccupied those who wrote about parental authority during the interwar period.

Generation gaps such as these two are not simply the result of the passage of time or changes in technology. They are the outcome of a far more profound and rapid shift in the social order, one that throws established norms, values, conventions, and institutions into disarray, without a consensus about what new form of order should replace them. Those in authority find themselves contested, while newer potential forms of authority jostle tetchily for position. Caught up in this are the young people coming into adulthood, who, as we have previously noted, are trying to make sense of themselves and their place in a society that is palpably at odds with itself.

Mannheim observed that periods of accelerated social change give rise to distinctive forms of generational consciousness, in which people on the cusp of adulthood develop a different orientation to the world from that of their elders. In these circumstances, what we might call a 'generation gap' marks a break in continuous time, forcing an abrupt re-evaluation of how we understand our society and what we can take for granted. This temporal dislocation can result in a schism between the generations, as young people, being closer to the problems of their time, 'are dramatically aware of a process of de-stabilization and take sides in it', while 'the older generation cling to the re-orientation that had been the drama of *their* youth' (Mannheim 1952: 301). To the extent that there is a generational dimension to the current culture wars, this is an important observation.

There is always a degree of friction between the generations, as the young try to apply the social rules and conventions they have been passed down by their elders, in family and school, to a present that might look quite different. A young person coming into adulthood today is confronting a different reality from that which greeted those of us who grew up in the 1990s – and from that which, in turn, greeted our own parents. This friction doesn't necessarily result in conflict; by being in a state of constant interaction, members of different generations learn from one another and are able to share a social space. But when significant events cause time to speed up, this process is short-circuited. As the sociologist Kingsley Davis (1940: 523) suggested in his discussion of 'parent–youth conflict', 'within a fast-changing social order the time-interval between generations, ordinarily but a mere moment in the life of a social system, becomes historically significant, thereby creating a hiatus between one generation and the next'.

It is this sense of 'hiatus' that seems to characterise the historical moment we are currently experiencing, as we hurtle from the end of the post-war liberal order into a period of dramatically destabilising social change. From international conflicts escalating abroad to the cultural conflicts ripping western nations apart at home, the old order is clearly unravelling, but what comes next is far from decided. The historian Robert Wohl (1980: 1) described the First World War generation as 'wanderers between two worlds'; a century on, to some extent, it feels like we are walking in their shoes.

The catalyst for this shift was the Covid pandemic, alongside its abrupt suspension of normal social life (Bristow 2023, 2025b). The disruption of social time and the upheaval of taken-for-granted ways of living and interacting gave social distancing measures an intimate quality that impacted every dimension of life for a substantial period. This had distinctive implications for those coming of age: right at the point where they were 'really questioning and reflecting on things' (Mannheim 1952: 300), they found that those rites of passage that had previously been considered all-important stages on the path to the personal futures of the young now simply disappeared in a cloud of anxiety about the problem of the present. In particular, the closure of schools and universities as core institutions of education and socialisation, followed by attempts to substitute online learning of curriculum content, raised some profound questions about the value that contemporary society places on the transmission of our accumulated knowledge and wisdom to the young.

The pandemic restrictions were not justified merely as a pragmatic response designed to slow the spread of a novel coronavirus. They were legitimised by hyperbolic statements about living through an 'unprecedented' emergency, which the knowledge and experience of the past could not help us to understand, and about the need to establish a 'new normal' based on the priority of maintaining our distance from one another in order to remain safe. In this way pandemic rhetoric positively embraced the normative collapse discussed in Chapter 2. It demanded that whole societies let go of the values and rules of behaviour they had hitherto taken for granted and start living according to a hastily constructed 'new normal', based on obeying a bewildering array of arbitrary social distancing rules given authority by 'the science'. The imperative to go to work or school unless you were really sick was replaced by the imperative to stay at home unless you could prove you were 'well'; and the imperative to care for your elderly was replaced by the imperative to stay away. The internet and social media were suddenly recast from being the thing that was making children thick and sick to becoming the saviour that would allow them to 'educate themselves' and 'stay connected' when locked down in their bedrooms.

The junking of time-honoured norms and values provided fertile ground for the acceleration of the culture wars. The attempt to construct an artificial new social 'normal' within the chaos of a public health emergency transmitted the message that there was no such thing as a moral code: all that mattered was what was expedient for the present, right now. At first this took the form of compliance with bizarre behaviours allegedly mandated by 'the science'; but, as people grew restive and frustrated, it became explicitly anomic.

The first flashpoint was the wave of protest that took place after the murder of George Floyd, a Black American, by a police officer, on 25 May 2020. As Thomas Chatterton Williams, author of *Summer of Our Discontent* (Williams 2025a), argues, this horrific event would always have gained attention; but it had a particular impact because people were stuck at home glued to the internet. The ensuing BLM protests became globalised in a way that was highly symbolic – through the posting of black squares on social media as expressions of solidarity, the pile-ons against those who failed to perform in this way, and the adoption of slogans such as 'defund the police' in countries such as the UK, where they make no sense.

As locked-down people spilled out onto the streets, public health officials – who had been quick to condemn those who protested against stay-at-home orders for spreading infection – welcomed the response to BLM on the grounds that racism is also a pandemic, against which people have a moral duty to protest. As the protests turned into acts of vandalism and looting, 'crimes of opportunity' – even among those with no activist agenda – became legitimised as the 'language of the unheard', a way of 'liberating' Black, Brown and Indigenous people. As Williams (2025b) explained in an interview,

> I can't overstate what effect that had ... on the rest of the country, saying, 'Wait a minute, I didn't bury my dad. Now you're saying that anybody, in defence of racial justice, can just walk into Walmart and take a washing machine?'

Nellie Bowles' (2024) *Morning after the Revolution: Dispatches from the Wrong Side of History* provides an account of how the extremes of progressive politics flourished in the normative void of the pandemic. From the chaos and instability of Seattle's police-free Autonomous Zone, constructed by the calls to 'defund the police', to the 'seamless' transition on social media from 'Black Lives Matter' to 'Trans Lives Matter', her snapshot of this moment captures how the destabilisation of the normal conventions of living and being during this period opened the door to an aggressive cultural reconfiguration, led by activists but endorsed by erstwhile 'mainstream' institutions. As we will see in the next chapter, which focuses on the crisis of the university, this process has much deeper roots: the pandemic didn't cause it so much as bring things to a head.

In their attempts to fumble back to some semblance of 'normal', western societies have not truly reckoned with the disruptive and destructive impact of our response to Covid-19, particularly as it relates to the socialisation of the young. In this regard, for all the difficulties with the concept of social generations, a balanced understanding of it may have an important role to play in our coming to terms with our current historical moment and its implications for the future. This is less to do with the experience of the pandemic itself than with the meaning that our societies have attributed to it, as an 'unprecedented' event requiring a decisive break from the social, economic, and cultural conventions that hitherto framed our social existence. It seems that the upheavals provoked by the pandemic were no mere historical blip after which everything could return to normal: they represented part of a much wider process of accelerated social change, in which wider social forces would come forcefully into conflict, driving a schism between past and present.

The current hiatus creates a very destabilising situation for the young, who are having to make sense of what's new without a clear anchor in what went before. But recognising this does not mean that we have to catastrophise it, as we did with the bleak prognosis offered for the 'Covid generation'. It means that we should take our responsibility as adults seriously, by trying to provide a bridge between the world we have known and the sentiments of nihilistic novelty that characterise so much of the progressive worldview. This requires, in part, being prepared to argue with our kids and socialise them into the real-world communities of working life, rather than giving them up to the symbolic cultural networks that appear to offer a beguiling alternative.

As we discuss in Chapter 6, for all that the zeitgeist pushes young people to reject the advice and guidance of their elders, they are crying out for it – not least as something to argue against. It has long been understood that pushing against boundaries is fundamental to children's development, yet parents and teachers are increasingly warned that boundaries threaten a child's self-esteem and identity, and that what they should be doing instead is affirming how children feel about themselves. Though presented as an act of compassion and understanding, the culture of affirmation is better understood as a rationalisation of neglect. Shying away from their responsibility to guide their children, adults place the full burden of fleeting choices upon immature shoulders. It's easy to flatter ourselves that we are being nicer, kinder adults by avoiding confrontation, but confrontation is sometimes exactly what the young need from us.

We can only give them that so long as we keep ourselves grounded and open to the possibilities presented by a changing world. Life in communities does not conform to the shrill dichotomies of the online culture wars, and our physical everyday interactions counter the relentless cultural pessimism of the current political moment. In the midst of a punishing economic crisis, escalating international tensions, crumbling infrastructure, a health service on its knees, and an incoherent education system, we are surrounded by people who try to make things work. We should be encouraging our young to acknowledge this and engage with it – to see themselves as part of our world as it is now, rather than as aloof 'critical thinkers' as to how society should be. This strange temporal dislocation is a storm that we will all have to weather, not something that we can blame the kids for – or leave them to resolve.

Conclusion

When looking at the problem of generations today, we can make three observations. First, social generations are, as they have ever been, cultural constructs. They can tell us something about how people make meaning out of the times in which they grow up, but this is far from a blueprint instructing us in the characteristics, attitudes, beliefs, and behaviours of entire cohorts. Yet we have become so used to generational generalisations that these prejudices have gained currency and are used to drive commentary, research, and policy. For example, Google's AI overview of 'what Gen Z wants from work' informs us that

> Gen Z values work–life balance, flexible work arrangements, and a strong sense of purpose and meaning in their jobs. They also seek opportunities for growth and advancement, technological advancements, and a commitment to diversity and inclusivity. (Accessed 19 June 2025)

Tell that to the kids stacking shelves, building houses, or languishing on welfare. The idea that your location in a particular birth cohort both determines what you think about key political issues and provides you with more interests in common with those of your own age than with anybody else is ridiculous to anybody who stops to think about it for two seconds. So we should pay less attention to the excitable generation chatter and do more stopping and thinking.

Second, social generations have a much weaker impact on people coming of age than do 'vertical' generations – that is, the relationships of responsibility and care exercised by adults towards children in families. The way in which young people's understanding of the world is developed in relation to the knowledge, norms, and values with which they have been brought up continues to shape them in far more profound a way than their identification with people of the same age. Again, this is not a new observation. Mannheim (1952: 299) stressed the impact of the 'automatic passing on to the new generations of the traditional ways of life, feelings, and attitudes' by the family and the community, which he regarded as more important than 'conscious teaching' in education, although this too plays a role. Relationships between young people and the adults in their lives, through communities and work, also remain powerful in shaping how young people think – powerful both for providing a guide to what's important and for giving the young something to rebel against.

Third, the intersection of generationalism with the wider dynamics of the culture wars shows us that the process at play is not really about generations but about something else. Attempting to reduce the dynamics of the culture wars to a clash between the outdated values of the irrelevant 'old' and the future-oriented 'young', or between the innate characteristics of Gen Z and those of Gen X, is not only empirically flawed. It also seeks to construct hostile generational identities in the political domain that encourage old and young alike to treat each other with suspicion and bad faith.

Here, at least, there are signs that things are changing. As the culture wars' touchstone conflicts around gender and race have erupted out of the university and into mainstream discussion, they are being dragged into a more explicitly political domain. This is not the insular world of parliamentary committees and polite elite wrangling that we have become used to over the past 30 years, but a vibrant, engaged, and difficult battle between the 'deep stories' discussed in Chapter 3: the professional-managerial class, which feels at home in a globalised, fluid world and is fighting to protect its privileges, and the dispossessed working class, which has its roots in communities where its families have lived and worked for generations, and which is exercising its voice.

This by no means represents some kind of return to the class politics of the twentieth century, but it is also a far cry from the managerial depoliticisation of the 1990s and early 2000s. It is a complicated, dynamic, and often incoherent moment, in which principles and prejudices are all in play and where people on all sides feel their very sense of identity to be at stake, which makes the tensions deeply personal and often visceral. But the divisions evident in these conflicts are not generational, and they are not about who wins the meme wars. They are about moral values, social positioning, and the question of whose voice counts. As we see in the next chapter, the institutions of the centrist 'old order' are spectacularly ill equipped to deal with this moment.

5

An education in fragmentation

Jennie's daughter recently graduated from a well-regarded 'redbrick' university in the UK. The sun was shining, proud parents were beaming, and the event was charmingly, slickly organised, from the marquee selling Pimms and university merch to the thoughtful provision, in the ladies' toilets, of emergency bits that panicky graduands could use for free (deodorant, tampons, sunscreen, safety pins, hair grips). The setting was the old hall, an ornate and impressive domed building that spoke of the grandeur and ambition of the original university. It was lovely.

The ceremony itself, by contrast, was a discombobulating fusion of traditional trappings and infantile identity politics, floundering somewhere between formal ritual and pantomime. The academic staff walked in procession, suitably clad in their academic gowns; the graduands, also in gowns and mortarboards, filed in to be presented with their scrolls. But ceremonial decorum was unsettled by design. The families (referred to throughout as 'supporters') were instructed by the senior academic leading the proceedings to 'make as much noise as you can' in cheering on their kids, which resulted inevitably in a rowdy two-hour popularity contest. 'That's my sister!' screamed one young woman, and the audience laughed indulgently. 'I did it!' shouted some of the graduands, with fist pumps that earned them additional rounds of applause.

The programme had carefully explained the traditional significance of the academic garb. But a few graduands sported a keffiyah on top of their gowns, and one unfurled a Palestinian flag after collecting his scroll. There were cheers, but also boos, in sympathy with the Jewish students present and in recognition that this really wasn't the way to behave at a graduation ceremony. Gesture made, the proceedings continued; palpable waves of relief emanated from the organisers. A luminary was introduced as the 'first Black woman' to have done many things, which had the effect of overshadowing her actual achievements. Another luminary told us that cleverness was overrated, before rapidly reassuring us that she didn't mean that all that tuition fee money had been wasted. In closing, we stood for the British national anthem but nobody was expected to sing; the band skipped through it and then struck up a rendition of Pharrell Williams' 'Happy'. We stumbled into the Pimms tent, proud but bemused.

This ceremony, like many similar ones across the UK, captured the contradictions of the university experience for young people growing up in the culture wars. On one hand, it remains, for many individuals, a voyage of intellectual discovery and self-discovery marked by living away from home, learning a lot about your chosen subject, making new friends, and achieving a degree. On the other hand, it's increasingly difficult to know what being at university actually *means* beyond your own personal 'journey'. And that is a tragedy, not just for the kids but for all of us.

For us as senior academics and parents of college-aged children, this is a difficult chapter to write. It presents a bleak picture of the state of the university in the UK and the US. The task is made even harder by the fact that we are personally invested in wanting it not to be so bad. And we should emphasise the caveats to the culture wars caricatures of universities. The crisis of higher education does not necessarily make it a bad experience for the young people who go through it: university may not be what it used to be, but the kids don't know what it used to be. It does not only affect a privileged group of teenagers: the integration of higher education with the domains of work and politics impacts the opportunities and aspirations of all young people. Not all academics are over-promoted warriors for woke, not all administrators are faceless bureaucrats, not all managers are evil and incompetent. As in the other failing institutions of western societies, there are good people who are trying to make things work and who defend the importance of something.

But their efforts are hobbled by dominating, fragmentary trends of the culture wars, and we are writing this book during the endgame of the university system as we know it. Over the past four decades, the academy has become detached from its moral purpose as an institution dedicated to the transmission and development of knowledge and parasitical upon the economic and cultural crisis of society as a whole. Universities feed off the aspirations of young people and their families to maintain their financial bottom line, and feed off the contradictions of the culture wars to maintain their status within a chaotic, moribund political elite. In their quest for institutional survival, universities are chewing up everything that makes their existence worthwhile. The question is, will anything positive emerge from the rubble?

The present crisis of higher education

In the UK, angst over the university sector currently takes the form of a catastrophic funding crisis, as perverse financial models constructed to bloat the higher education sector by selling lower-quality courses to increasing numbers of students implode. Panicked universities have been shedding staff and degree courses in a bid for institutional survival, heedless of what the institution is likely to become. The Labour government, which the sector assumed would step in with a bailout and a plan, is standing back and watching the whole thing happen.

The US higher education system is much more complex, in terms of both organisation and funding (Hillman 2024). Here too, cuts to federal funding and spiralling tuition fees are biting hard, leading to college closures and staff redundancies, while enrolments fall partly as a result of demographics and partly because young people are deciding that they would prefer to do something else (Perna 2025). The battle over universities has become overtly political, as President Trump has clamped down on student protests and DEI initiatives and threatened to withhold funding from colleges that refuse to comply with the administration's demands (HSS, Department of Education & GSA 2025, Lukianoff & Goldstein 2025, Niederhelman & Rai 2025).

The aim of this chapter is not to review all the ways in which western societies' once proud commitment to the higher education of young adults has spiralled into decline. Many excellent studies of this have been published, which Jennie and colleagues reviewed in their 2020 book *Generational Encounters with Higher Education* (Bristow, Cant, & Chatterjee 2020). Here we explore why universities find themselves so deeply mired in the cultural conflicts that are ripping through society at large and how the degradation of university education contributes to the predicament of young people who are growing up in the culture wars. Moral confusion, the crisis of normativity, the fostering of hostile generational identities, the undermining of the family both as an institution for socialisation and as a set of relationships that give meaning to young people's lives – all these trends have their most explicit expression in the contemporary project that calls itself 'education'.

This situation impacts all levels of the education system, and arguably its deepest corrosive effect is on children in schools, because they are more impressionable and spend more time in the classroom than college students ever do (Furedi 2009, Shrier 2024). But, apart from the fact that every bad idea in schools will have been incubated in the first place by academics in universities, there is another reason to pay particular attention to what is going on with young adults in post-compulsory education.

University students are situated at a point in their own development where, as Mannheim (1952: 300) put it, they are 'really questioning and reflecting on things'. They are not passive recipients of received ideas, but active participants in the cultural process. They elect whether to go to college, where to go, and what to study; and in doing so they bring their subjectivity with them, shaping their environment as it shapes them. In recent decades, this subjectivity has been appropriated by universities, through attempts to boost student numbers and approval ratings by organising curricula and institutional practices around the consumerist principle of 'what students want' (Williams 2013). This creates a feedback loop in which young adults' understanding of the world, as it is and as it should be, receives institutional flattery and is weaponised as the driving force for change.

Examples of this problem abound on both sides of the Atlantic. We find it in practices such as grade inflation, where academics are discouraged from failing student work – or even from awarding it a lower grade than the one the student feels they deserve – because it impacts badly on the students' sense of themselves and on the university's reputation for 'excellent' student outcomes. We find it in the proliferation of 'safe spaces' and other therapeutic mechanisms of 'student support' where the role of academic programmes is reconfigured as helping students to feel good about their achievements rather than training a new generation of brilliant minds to solve the intellectual and technical problems of our world (Hayes & Ecclestone 2008, Furedi 2017). We find it in the tacit endorsement of cheating, referred to in Chapter 2, where students are encouraged to 'work smartly' with AI and other technological tools rather than waste their time reading books and expanding their minds. Above all, we find it in the free speech crisis that has exposed our institutions of higher education as crucibles of corporate group-think, where the primary 'graduate attribute' is knowing what to say in order to get ahead.

In this scenario, the adults who are (literally) 'in the room' – those academics who have an historically grounded knowledge of their subject and consider their job to be to challenge the superficial assumptions of fledgling scholars in order to enrich and deepen their understanding – are cast as the problematic barrier to the future. By presenting a critical challenge to young people's understanding of their 'lived experience' and of the ideas they were taught in school, subject-based academics are accused of undermining students' levels of satisfaction and self-esteem and of standing in the way of the processes deemed necessary to navigate the technocratic landscape of the present world.

As we have discussed elsewhere, the 'student voice' used in policy documents and institutions to drive through change is a construction, curated to mimic institutional agendas (Bristow, Cant, & Chatterjee 2020). The student voice that wants more books, more teaching time, and fewer restrictions on freedom of speech is rarely heard. But we should also acknowledge that the student voice that warns about the stress of academic study and its impact on mental health, the need for degree classifications to represent 'value for money' and to reflect effort over achievement, and the threats posed by offensive words, images, and behaviours to individual students' self-identity is not entirely made up. Young people are products of their times: they have been raised to understand the trials and tribulations of growing up in these ways. They are also pragmatic:

few young people have ever demanded that their exams should be harder or their coursework more demanding.

The privileging of the student voice thus leads to a downward spiral in academic expectations and a clamour for easily digestible content, which should be 'relevant' to students' lives and future careers. It is the job of adults, as educators, to raise their expectations beyond the banal everyday, to push them beyond what they want from their immediate university experience and towards what they need to learn to master a subject and take forward the stock of human knowledge. This idea has become unfashionable because our institutions of higher education have lost faith in the transformative qualities of knowledge and regard it instead as an inconvenience to be navigated.

In the present hiatus, it is becoming increasingly clear that institutions of higher education have also become detached from the reality of young people's lives and the problems and opportunities that confront them. This is why we should not mourn the passing of the legacy university system, even though it has difficult implications for those working and studying within it right now. On both sides of the Atlantic, reports abound that public confidence in universities is declining – largely because of the growing mismatch between what students spend in order to gain a degree and what they earn at the end of it, alongside a growing suspicion that universities have become laboratories for 'brainwashing' students into progressive ideologies. 'The public is alienated from the university's mission and feels shut out from the benefits it supposedly provides', reports one article (Bogost 2025). This might not seem something to welcome; but in the context of the current culture wars, it probably is.

The post-war university system was able to thrive because the university moved gradually out of its rarified role as an elite institution dedicated to the pursuit and transmission of knowledge, to become a public institution concerned with the socialisation of a significant section of the young and an important plank of the welfare state. This was not a conspiracy designed to downgrade educational standards and to indoctrinate young people: it emerged from an optimistic projection of the social and cultural benefits of providing higher levels of education for all. But, once the university started to play an active and eager role in political and economic machinations, it lost its independence and authority.

Caught up in the fads and pressures of the immediate moment, higher education lost interest in educating young people and started to focus on preparing them 'for life': not life as it is, but life as the insulated policy class deemed it should be. With the rise of the populist sensibility and the crumbling of the technocratic order, a different kind of life begins to be imagined – and one that at least, and at last, presents aspirational young people with a meaningful sense of choice about their future.

The promise and the problem of education

What motivated us to become academics, several years ago, was the belief that the development and transmission of knowledge is one of the most important things a society can do for itself and for its young. No society can survive unless it continually reminds itself of what it knows already, and strives to understand that which it does not yet know. Education is not merely the transmission of 'skills' that individuals need to survive in modern work and life; it is a rich cultural heritage that takes us beyond the limitations of our individual selves and the mundanity of our everyday lives, into the shared realm of knowledge, values, and new ideas.

As the political philosopher Hannah Arendt (2006 [1961]: 193) put it, education represents a society's love both for its children and for the world in which they are growing up. If we didn't love our world, we wouldn't trouble ourselves to ensure that it is preserved and renewed through the endeavours of younger generations; we could simply consume what it has brought us in the here and now, and let it rot. And if we didn't love our children, we would not bother investing the time, money, and intellectual energy in ensuring that they have the tools to take themselves and their society forward: we could let them play forever, comforting ourselves with the conceit that the future doesn't matter.

It is impossible to understand the central role of education in any society without understanding its purpose in the process of cultural reproduction. We do not take for granted that our cultural gains, the knowledge we have gleaned over the centuries, will simply survive as the world moves forward. Societies are always renewing themselves, both through generational change – people die, as others are born – and through social and technological change, where new problems and opportunities continually present themselves. This means that societies have to invest considerable energy into ensuring that we don't forget what we have learned, but that we reproduce it. And we do that by inducting what Mannheim (1952: 292–3) called 'new participants in the cultural process' into their cultural inheritance – that is, enabling our societies both to remember what we need to and to forget what we don't. (In discussing this with students, Jennie often refers to the classic English saying 'don't reinvent the wheel'. It is telling that recent cohorts, schooled in the prejudice that knowledge gleaned from the past is irrelevant, seem never to have heard this phrase before.)

An educated society is progressive in the true sense of the word: it doesn't rest on its laurels, but strives to build on the wisdom of the past to create a better future. As Robert Nisbet (1994 [1980]) argues in his *History of the Idea of Progress*, this speaks to a belief in the human capacity to develop not just technologically but also morally, into a better version of ourselves and our societies. Advances in science, medicine, and engineering are a result of this process – but so, too, are advances in sociological, political, and philosophical thought. Only by standing on the shoulders of giants can we reach for the stars.

But, thanks to the culture wars, the giants have been cut down to size – disparaged as 'dead white European males' (DWEMs), who became influential only because other people were oppressed and other voices 'silenced'. Of course, we don't always know what these other voices might have said; the battle is not between competing giants but between an historically influential thinker and a void. All that women's literature that women never actually got to write! The curriculum is 'decolonised' – not to add in the rich intellectual contribution of thinkers from the Global South, but to replace established knowledge with 'critical' perspectives written in the present day, which foster cynicism in students about the things they have been brought up to believe are true. Complaints that the curriculum is too 'exclusive' of Black students, working-class students, neurodiverse students, LGBTQ+ students, and the endless list of other identity categories have resulted in a focus on 'lived experience' that should be measured by 'authentic assessment': not an essay about what you have learned, but some kind of portfolio expressing how you feel.

Without the giants to stand on, students have to reach much further for the stars; but that doesn't matter, because all they have to do is reach their own 'potential' and get a decent job. Here again, to return to Abigail Shrier's (2024) phrase, we have downgraded our kids and sacrificed the future to the present. But why?

Those on the cultural right blame the infiltration of liberal–left academics and teachers into the institutions of education – people on a mission to indoctrinate the young with an array of fashionable ideologies such as 'critical race theory', 'queer politics', 'cultural Marxism', and a host of other ideas that they find objectionable. There is some truth to this complaint, at least to the extent that it reflects what certain educators might aspire to do in their pursuit of 'social justice' – a term that has come to stand for organising society around progressivist definitions of equity and fairness. But, as an explanation, it misses two other key drivers that have turned our universities into the polarised mess they are today.

The first is the philistinism of the political right, which has for decades regarded education primarily as a means for training a workforce, and the pursuit of knowledge as both a distraction from this goal and a vehicle for dangerous new ideas. The second is the authoritarianism of the technocratic centrists, who have shamelessly appropriated progressive language as a cover for bureaucratic takeover. Cultural reproduction has been subordinated to the goal of institutional reproduction, enabling the survival of something that looks like the university even when, at its core, it has become something entirely different.

In *The Voice of Liberal Learning*, the political thinker Michael Oakeshott (2001 [1989]) warned of the dangers of substituting 'extrinsic' purposes, focused on immediate social goals, for education's 'intrinsic' end – the transmission of knowledge, and a central part of the transaction between the generations. 'There are those who would frustrate education by seeing it in terms of socialisation, either to produce a workforce or a race of men with the correct political and social attitudes, or a combination of both', writes Anthony O'Hear (2001: 47), in an astute summary.

This captures the narrowing framework within which policy around higher education has been developed since the 1980s. Broadly speaking, those on the left regarded the purpose of the academy as one of cultivating a more liberal, critical disposition in an increasing number of young people before they had to knuckle down into what was regarded as the limiting and dehumanising world of work. Those on the right looked at higher education as a means to improving the skills of the workforce. In the UK, the massive expansion of the university sector in the early 1990s, via the 1992 Further and Higher Education Act, was explicitly justified by the then Conservative government as removing the 'increasingly artificial distinction' between universities, focused on academic knowledge, and polytechnics, focused on the development of vocational skills (DES 1991: 4). The upshot, as one academic commentator later noted, was that, 'for all the talk' about polytechnics having engaged in 'academic drift',

> over the past 20 years the 'pre-1992 universities' have become as much like former polytechnics as the other way around. 'We are all polytechnics now', perhaps? The socially engaged and entrepreneurial university that has become the model for twenty-first-century higher education – alongside a scattering of world-class universities – is their monument. (Scott 2012)

The removal of the 'binary divide' between the knowledge-focused university and the skills-focused polytechnic was a hugely destructive reform for British higher education, paving the way for subsequent policy initiatives that would focus increasingly on the 'extrinsic' purposes of education and would sow the seeds for the present funding crisis. It would quickly prove detrimental both to the development of academic knowledge and to robust training in vocational skills, as employers outsourced their responsibilities, on the assumption that certificated students could be considered to have been trained (Wolf 2002).

However, these reforms alone would not have reduced the university sector to the shell that it is today. That required the other dynamic of the 'socialisation' mission: the focus on producing young people with the 'correct' political and social attitudes.

The idea that the institutions of higher education should be directed primarily at socialising young adults into becoming a particular kind of person was built into the expansion of higher education after the Second World War, via the GI Bill in the US and the Robbins Report in the UK. Formally titled the Servicemen's Readjustment Act of 1944, the GI Bill was a package of measures designed to assist veterans with adjusting to civilian life and included funding for tuition and living expenses for education. In the UK, the post-war expansion of higher education in the early 1960s was justified in part by a desire to guard against the ideologies of fascism and communism by promoting education as a vehicle for democratic thinking and 'the transmission of a common culture and common standards of citizenship' (Robbins 1963: 6–7).

Both these developments brought about a subtle but significant shift in the role assigned to the university. No longer would it be a rarified, elite institution focused on specialist subject knowledge; the post-war academy would be the engine of a more highly educated, technically skilled, and democratically enlightened society.

In the immediate post-war period it was hard to see this as a bad thing. The aspiration to educate a greater number of young people to a higher level, particularly in the context of a post-war economic boom – fuelled in part by the 'white heat' of scientific and technological advances that demanded more expert knowledge – represented an optimistic and (relatively) egalitarian commitment to take forward societies ravaged by half a century of war and to treat their citizens as thinkers rather than mere soldiers or workers. By comparison with the 'massified' higher education systems that were to take off from the 1980s and into the 2000s (Trow 2010, Bolton 2025), only a relatively small section of the youth in both the US and the UK studied for a three- or four-year university degree. Educational expectations were high and campuses buzzed with ideas and energy.

But from the vantage point of today we can see how these developments contributed to the moral and institutional corruption of the academy over time. In the UK, once autonomous universities became enveloped by the welfare state, subject to the instrumental demands and political whims of policymakers as they sought to solve wider social and economic problems through higher education. The Conservative government's 'widening participation' initiatives of the 1980s and early 1990s were widely understood at the time as a response to deindustrialisation – 'dole schools' designed to get people out of the unemployment figures and into a more palatable category. In the US, enrolments in public universities soared for similar reasons, and tuition costs of private colleges ratcheted upwards, as escalating credentialism became the prerequisite for landing a middle-class job.

By the late 1990s, the then New Labour Prime Minister Tony Blair had upped the ante still further, by putting 'education, education, education' at the heart of his government's policy agenda and demanding, as part of this, that 50 per cent of the teenage cohort go to university. To facilitate this, student tuition fees were introduced, along with a regime underpinned by government-issued loans designed to cover both tuition fees and students' personal maintenance; these are to be paid back by graduates when they reach a certain level of income. New Labour's justification for expansion was couched less in terms of benefits to the economy than in terms of 'social inclusion', the assumption being that young people who were not socialised through three years at university would find themselves left behind in the twenty-first century (Bristow, Cant, & Chatterjee 2020).

Critics of the 'McDonaldised' turn in university education – whereby the latter is rationalised around the logic of 'efficiency' and packaged as a 'spectacular' consumer experience rather than an educational relationship between academics and students (Ritzer 2002) – highlight the corrosive effect of orienting higher education around economic demands measured by silly metrics of efficiency, student satisfaction, and employability skills. Some counterpose this move to what they view as the worthier role of universities: to foster social goals such as 'inclusion', 'equity', and 'social justice'. Yet the 'social' purpose of universities, often lauded by leftists as a rationale for increased funding and expansion of student numbers, is, arguably, even more corrupting than the cold 'economic' imperative. The result was an unholy marriage of convenience between the corporate logic of marketisation and the politicised imperative of social justice.

As universities mobilised to 'include' increasing numbers of students, academic standards declined and the bills went up – both for individual students, who were forced to take on more debt, and for the state, as it became apparent that large numbers would never pay off their loans. This trend is also apparent in the US. Subsequent reforms by the Conservative government cemented a system in which universities were forced to compete directly with one another for student numbers. This pushed them to find a 'market' among young people who had neither the desire nor the ability to study for a degree; it also incited a scramble to recruit international students, who pay much higher fees. Unsurprisingly, the university system came to be perceived as a magnet both for migrants who aspired to move to the UK and for young British people who didn't really want a higher education but were attracted by the maintenance loans. Lost in this welfarist mess were the kids who simply wanted to go to university to study their chosen subject.

By the early twenty-first century it had become clear that, simply to enter the labour market, more and more was expected of young people in terms of the time they spent in education, and the debt they incurred to pay for it. What was expected of them *as students* was progressively less. This is not to say that today's students work less hard than the cohorts 'back in the day', though it does seem that, year on year, universities expect less reading, writing, and thinking, inanely flattering themselves that students are 'over-assessed'. Indeed, things have gone so far in this direction that students are beginning to push back and demand more rigorous assessment. In 2025, students at the prestigious KCL penned an open letter against the university's reduction in the word length expected for written assignments, arguing that such lowered expectations will not: provide sufficient preparation for postgraduate study; allow them to compete effectively with their peers in future endeavours; enable them to engage as meaningfully with their subject(s) of interest; or reduce academic stress (Goddard 2025). This change has been brought in alongside moves to introduce forms of 'inclusive' assessment that 'focus on ideas, not grammar' and 'reward the use of culture, language and identity'. As Edward Skidelsky, director of the Committee for Academic Freedom (CAF), said, '[t]hese attempts to dumb down assessment in the name of "inclusivity" are being pushed by university managers against the will of academics and students themselves, the best of whom hunger for an education that is deep and rigorous' (Henry & Harding 2026).

The KCL assessment controversy reveals that the problem is that students' role as scholars – the rising generations charged with claiming and renewing their society's cultural heritage – has been eclipsed by the *process* of being a student. This means, in part, having to play the credentials game in order to get a job. More insidiously, it has come to mean having to play the values game in order to avoid social ostracisation.

The behavioural imperative has been most visibly revealed in the promotion of 'inclusive' language – an act of institutional overreach that has catapulted the free speech crisis on college campuses into the spotlight. British universities routinely require students to take modules that instruct them in how to relate to other members of the university 'community' and in how to think about the materials on their course. For example, the compulsory online Expect Respect module introduced by the University of Kent in 2021 – the kind of 'values training' initiative that has become ubiquitous elsewhere – aimed to instruct students in 'a range of issues from racism and bias to sexual harassment and consent, supporting everyone to ensure all members of our community are treated with kindness and respect', and making them aware of how to 'report any incidents' of transgression from the appropriate code. The module included a quiz built on examples of problems such as white privilege: 'I can swear, or dress in second-hand clothes, without having people attribute these choices to the bad morals, the poverty or the illiteracy of my race' (Warren 2021).

The promotion of inclusive language is backed up explicitly by university policies and by a range of implicit pressures. Students are invited to declare their pronouns on profiles and email signatures, and even when they eschew this opportunity they get the message in lectures and seminars, where a 'microaggression' or an act of 'misgendering', be it deliberate or accidental, will attract anything from a sharp intake of breath to an official complaint.

Even before setting foot on a university campus, students have been incited to think of themselves as free-floating gender categories, who can and should control how other people relate to them. The national university admissions service UCAS encourages applicants to declare their gender and sexuality, and a report published in collaboration with Stonewall stated that 1 in 13 university applicants declared themselves to be LGBT+ (UCAS 2021). Regardless of what this might show about the actual sexual orientation of 17- and 18-year-olds, one has to ask the questions: why do universities want this data? And why, as a prospective student, *wouldn't* you tick this box, given the pressure to boost your DEI credentials? In 2024, UCAS introduced a 'non-binary option', where applicants were able to select from 'man / woman / I use another term / I prefer not to say' when asked for their gender identity (UCAS 2025).

In many respects, this kind of institutionalised values training has become inseparable from the instrumental 'employability' agenda that has long been favoured by the political right. It has been justified on the grounds of developing the kind of 'graduate attributes' that will enable young people to get ahead in the world, once they were packaged up with vague 'soft skills' such as teamwork, communication, and problem-solving. For universities to focus on fostering generic skills and attitudes corrodes their true educational purpose by pushing subject knowledge further out of the curriculum, by undermining students' commitment to their studies, and by tapping into students' anxieties about life beyond graduation.

Equally troubling, as we discuss in Chapter 7, is the fact that the attempt to socialise young people into the 'attributes' needed for modern employment effectively disenchants and deskills them *as workers*, teaching them that the most important thing is how they should present themselves, and not how they do the job in hand. From school to university graduation, young people are bombarded by the message that their career path is all-important: the basis for gaining qualifications, maximising future earnings, and achieving self-actualisation. Yet this goes alongside a cultural message of disdain for the actual jobs that people do – including those that young people are already engaged in. Many universities self-consciously organise their teaching schedules and expectations around the reality that undergraduates hold part-time jobs but give increasing emphasis to the development of 'employability' skills that place those jobs in an unfavourable light when contrasted with graduate-level careers. The latter apparently require vaguer attributes, such as flexibility and adaptability, and a commitment to values such as sustainability and social responsibility.

This leads to a paradox: mass higher education is continually justified as the basis for a more skilled workforce, yet employers complain that graduates lack concrete skills, knowledge, and a robust work ethic (ISE 2024, Jack 2025). And students are instructed to value their education in narrow employability terms, while their thinking about present and future employment is mystified by the increasingly artificial distinction between 'graduate' and 'non-graduate' jobs (Brant 2018).

Cultural void and the adversary culture

Many academics are critical of the instrumental, consumerist turn in higher education and complain, rightly, that the focus on getting a high-earning job has downgraded the value attached to creative and 'critical thinking' subjects in the arts, humanities, and social sciences. But what they often miss is their own culpability in transforming these subjects into vehicles for ideological socialisation: this is not critical thinking in its original sense, but a sceptical, if not downright cynical, attitude to knowledge. What began, in the 1960s, as an attempt to push the boundaries of established thought through the development of self-consciously 'critical theory' became institutionalised over subsequent decades as the standard intellectual approach promoted in universities.

Sociology, which began as an attempt to understand the problem of social order, became one-sidedly focused on the problem of social inequality (Dingwall 2021). It is in our subject in particular that 'normativity' has become a dirty word. But the drive to replace the object of study with a critical disposition towards the subject itself has galloped ahead in other disciplines too. When Jennie studied English literature at university in the 1990s, seminars engaging with a literary text were already fading out, in favour of a focus on theories that trumpeted the 'death of the author' and questioned the very notion of a literary canon. History, geography, politics, music, and a host of other subjects, including those in mathematics and the sciences, now cultivate in students a relativistic appreciation of the limits of existing western knowledge over and above the understanding that such knowledge has brought.

Some educational theorists have drawn attention to the pendulum's swinging too far. In the US, Neil Postman (1971 [1969]) wrote *Teaching as a Subversive Activity*, followed a decade later by *Teaching as a Conserving Activity* (Postman 1979). In the UK, in the early 1970s Michael Young produced the influential critical theory anthology *Knowledge and Control*, which focused on the ways in which education systems reproduce power relations; then in the early 2000s he wrote a powerful book that made the case for 'bringing knowledge back in' (Young 1971, 2007). More recently, an important collection of essays has focused on the centrality of academic disciplines, subjects, and the 'pursuit of truth' in engaging with the question 'what should schools teach?' (Sehgal-Cuthbert & Standish 2021). But such balanced pedagogical arguments tend to be ignored by those engaged in the battles over the politics of education.

For the cultural right, it has become fashionable to explain this problem in terms of criticality itself. If universities could do away with 'airy-fairy' subjects such as sociology or literature and stop talking about intellectuals like Foucault (who seems to attract particular ire), western societies could rescue 'real' knowledge from the lefty progressive disruptors who apparently rule the academy. This facile assumption misses the point. The transformation of a critical disposition towards subject knowledge into an orthodoxy of cultural self-abnegation has not come about because of the strength of critical thinkers, but because of the weakness of the defence of society's cultural heritage.

The problem isn't that students complete their degrees knowing nothing about their subjects – although the amount they know has clearly diminished, thanks to the trends described above. It is that they graduate with a suspicion of the knowledge of their forebears and an insecure, self-deprecating orientation to what they know themselves. No wonder, in this context, that artificial intelligence holds such an attraction: when you can't be confident about what you know, you default to checking that you are saying the right thing.

The roots of this decline were exposed back in the 1980s, with the publication of Allan Bloom's (2012 [1987]) bestseller *The Closing of the American Mind: How Higher Education Has Failed Democracy and Impoverished the Souls of Today's Students*. Bloom, a philosophy professor, drew on his experience of teaching university students from the 1950s to the 1980s to tackle the problem of cultural relativism and moral non-judgementalism. Whereas earlier cohorts of students had arrived at college with firm convictions but an enthusiasm for intellectual challenge, those whom he taught during the 1980s possessed only the conviction that all cultures and ways of life were equally valid and that the primary virtue of the modern student lay in being 'open-minded'. This attachment to 'openness' had the paradoxical effect of closing their minds. Because they believed in no truth that was superior to any other opinion, they had lost the aspiration to develop themselves through education, content instead to view cultural and moral questions as matters of personal preference.

For Bloom as for many conservative intellectuals involved in the culture wars of the 1980s, the closing of the American mind had begun in the late 1960s, as the culture of ''68ism' swept through college campuses. By expanding the ideals of liberty and democracy to include the 'democratisation' of knowledge and the freedom to be whoever one wanted to be, the counterculture had perverted them. If all ideas were to be considered equal, there was no particular value attached to the knowledge of western civilisation: indeed, to the extent that this knowledge made claims about the superiority of one type of knowledge over another, it became perceived as a barrier to the quest for equality that propelled the radical countercultural movements of the time. In this way the democratisation of the university led to its politicisation: as the academy shifted from being a bastion of the elite to being a socially useful institution, it began to attack the very cultural heritage it was charged with preserving.

That the university – an institution essentially designed for the conservation and transmission of a society's stock of knowledge – could become a hotbed of radical politics revealed that something fundamental had changed. By transforming itself from an ivory tower into a socially useful institution dedicated to fostering a meritocratic expert class, the academy had moved out of the sacred focus on knowledge to the profane terrain of everyday affairs, subject to the political and cultural currents swirling elsewhere. Rather than bringing society's bright young people into a common culture, the academy would become a major player in what the American critic Lionel Trilling (1965) described as an 'adversary culture': a culture that, as Daniel Bell explained in the 1970s, became 'detached' from the bourgeois structure of society and 'self-determining', regarding itself as being under attack even as its ideas came to be dominant (Bell 1979: 40).

In his discussion of the influence of the adversary culture on the arts and the emergence of a 'distinct cultural class', Bell explained that the protagonists remained a relatively small group of people but, because of the cultural fragmentation of the times, this group was able to gain significant influence. The cultural class was large enough to operate not as a 'bohemian enclave' but as an institutional group, 'bound by a consciousness of a kind' and dominant in the cultural institutions of the time. This could happen not so much because of the strength of the adversary culture as because of the weakness of mainstream or majority culture. 'Bourgeois culture has been shattered', he wrote. The consequence for young people, observed Bell (1979: 41), was this:

> Today, each new generation, starting off at the benchmarks attained by the adversary culture of its cultural parents, declares

> in sweeping fashion that the status quo represents backward conservatism or repression, so that, in a widening gyre, new and fresh assaults on the social structure are mounted.

Fifty years on, the absence of a confident 'bourgeois culture' that proudly boasts the gains of western civilisation is simply assumed, leaving a void that has to be continually filled with new ideas. As museums apologise for their exhibits and universities denude their curricula of 'colonial' knowledge, cultural institutions are forced ever outwards in their search for meaning and purpose. The technocratic centrists look to 'employability skills', the progressive leftists promote identity politics, and the populist right grows disaffected with higher education altogether. This creates a challenge for educators who want to teach their subjects and for students caught in the crossfire. Do we carry on fighting the good fight, to return universities to their proper focus on knowledge and education? Or do we concede that things have gone too far and that new ideas will have to come from elsewhere?

Politicisation of the university

The most corrosive aspect of values training is the way in which it draws its legitimacy from identity politics, cloaking itself in the garb of radicalism and a particular interpretation of the idea of social justice. This allows it to appear less as a managerial tool for the promotion of conformity than as an idealistic mission to make the world a better place. It is an agenda supported by academics who style themselves as passionate, critical thinkers, and it holds an attraction to young people whose thirst for ideas is barely sated by the paltry, apologetic provision of subject knowledge on offer.

The Closing of the American Mind is an erudite reflection on the way in which the modernising, future-oriented spirit of the sixties would rapidly become an assault on the accumulated cultural wisdom of the past. Bloom's descriptions of his interactions with students show him to be a thoughtful, educated teacher for whom expanding minds and horizons through the great ideas developed in the humanities was a passionate vocation. The book is a marked contrast to both the irresponsible anti-intellectualism of some leftist educational reformers of his time and the instrumental, skills-based philistinism that characterised right-wing policy around higher education in the 1980s.

But, as Jacob Hamburger (2017) noted in a perceptive commentary, the arguments made by those attempting to save the soul of the academy from its politicisation through speech codes and the imperative of 'diversifying' the curriculum would politicise it still further. The critique offered by Bloom – an unapologetic academic elitist – would become part of the cultural right's attack on the present academic elite. In the early 1990s, right-wing complaints about the effects of political correctness on the university 'helped forge common ground with the traditionalist and religious populism of the Reagan coalition', as 'college students and professors became a common enemy of the right, a "liberal elite" to blame for America's cultural decline'.

By the time of Trump's election as US president in 2016, just as the fragmentary, censorious trends identified by Bloom had become more advanced and embedded in universities, so too had the idea that the university itself was a problem. 'In the context of this right-wing fury, Bloom's attacks on the university may seem to only reinforce what has by now become a widespread anti-intellectualism', concludes Hamburger, observing that, 'in the age of Trump, Bloom's suggestion that elite education has a role to play in saving democracy from itself may nonetheless be worth returning to'.

As the present culture wars rage through memes and soundbites while thinking is downgraded to a luxury that impassioned keyboard warriors cannot afford, widespread anti-intellectualism has indeed become a problem – across both the progressive left and the cultural right. But the old post-war trope that democracy needs 'saving from itself', particularly by a highly educated elite, fails to understand the extent to which the politicised university now plays an actively anti-democratic role in public life. As we discuss below, this has been sharply revealed by the rows over academic freedom and free speech that have come to prominence especially since 2020.

Universities have been captured by a technocratic vision that regards 'expertise' as an effective way of keeping the lid on social tensions. In this regard, the populist 'anti-intellectualism' alluded to by Hamburger is less a reaction against professors and their abstract ideas than a reaction against the arrogance of the managerial 'expert class' that has for decades boasted its superiority in social and political affairs over the less educated public. This dynamic has been starkly revealed in the horror with which the university sector reacted to the Brexit referendum and the Trump election in 2016; in the arrogant positioning of the 'scientific expert' during the Covid pandemic; and in the role played by the academy in promoting gender ideology.

In all these cases, there are legitimate differences of opinion to be argued out about the issues themselves – that is not a problem. The problem arises when universities – in their mission statements, policies, and practices – decide that they are going to behave like political parties and adopt a particular stance on contested social issues by affiliating themselves to organisations such as Stonewall, supporting causes such as BLM, flying Pride flags and promoting rainbow lanyards, and making research funding contingent on meeting 'inclusive' criteria. These performative gestures send a clear signal to staff, students, and the public that the academy no longer sees itself as a community of scholars with a wide diversity of thought, but as a political institution dedicated to the protean cause of 'social justice'.

Having spent decades demanding restrictions on academic freedom in the name of DEI, progressives are now making a fuss about the US government's clampdowns on campus free speech. The assumption that Donald Trump – and, by association, right-wing populism as a political and cultural force – presents a unique threat to academic freedom has become an article of faith among academics and others in the cultural class. Even Bruce Springsteen, who has built his career on the plight of the working man in deindustrialised America, is in on the game. In his 2025 UK tour, the Boss's histrionic tirade against Trump's 'corrupt, incompetent and treasonous administration' included his outrage that 'they are defunding American universities that won't bow down to their ideological demands' (Beaumont-Thomas 2025).

Clearly, Trump is no friend of academic freedom, and his incursions on free speech on college campuses are very troublesome (Lukianoff & Goldstein 2025). But the idea that the crisis of free speech on campus has come about only now, and that this is because of attempts to roll back the DEI regime, takes us into the realm of *Alice through the Looking Glass*.

Over the past two decades, academic freedom campaigns such as the Foundation for Individual Rights and Expression (FIRE) in the US and Academics for Academic Freedom (AFAF) and CAF in the UK have highlighted and fought some egregious attacks on academics' and students' freedom to voice dissenting views around gender, race, climate change, the Covid pandemic, and many more issues. Even when such 'dissenting' views – for example on gender, or Brexit – reflect what the majority of the public think, they are flagged as controversial and polarising. Meanwhile, as we discuss below, those on the progressive left, led by academic trade unions, have tacitly redefined the very term 'academic freedom' as a dog whistle for hate speech.

Academic freedom and the diseasing of knowledge

At first sight, the spectacle of academics railing against the concept of academic freedom seems perverse. Academic freedom is the historical foundation of universities: it is what allows staff and students to pursue their research and gain correction and clarification through discussion. It is crucial for all subjects and disciplines, from the humanities to the sciences. If discussion is restricted, ideas cannot be tested – and this has negative intellectual and practical consequences, both for individual academics and for the pursuit of knowledge. The point of becoming an academic – rather than, say, an educational administrator – lies in the degree of professional autonomy accorded to us to work out how our ideas are developed and how we should teach our subject to our students.

The idea that such freedom is dangerous because it might allow particular academics to teach the 'wrong' ideas is understandable, albeit objectionable, when it comes from authoritarian regimes whose aim is to indoctrinate students into a particular way of thinking. It is no less understandable or objectionable coming from university managers who want to protect their 'satisfaction' metrics by avoiding situations in which students become upset. But when it emanates from other academics, and in particular from academics' unions, whose purpose should be to protect their members from incursions by management into their professional role, the driver comes from somewhere else. First, it comes from the narcissism of the 'right side of history' brigade, whose worldview hinges on the assumption that progressive ideas have been pre-ordained as the only ones that could possibly be correct, and that it is only by restricting criticism and other ideas that a tidal wave of prejudice can be held at bay. Second and more importantly, it comes from the ingrained belief that 'bad' ideas – whether spoken, written, or even thought – represent a tangible harm, akin to an act of physical violence.

In this regard, what Furedi (2017) has termed 'the diseasing of speech' propels the obsession with identity directly into the domain of censorship and cancel culture. The progressive assertion that questioning somebody's sense of identity is an act of violence and erasure fits neatly with the wider sense of vulnerability and powerlessness that has been cultivated among young people. The naïvely arrogant notion that it is possible and desirable to have free speech for ideas that you agree with, but not for those that you don't, has tended to gain the support of many students, who have taken on board the messages they have been given about the importance of emotional safety, the dangers of words, and their own consumer power in relation to the university.

For example, a 2022 report from the UK Higher Education Policy Institute (HEPI) titled *You Can't Say That!* found increased levels of support for campus cancel culture by comparison with a previous survey in 2016 (Hillman 2022). Seventy-nine per cent of students said that students who feel threatened 'should always have their demands for safety respected', up from 68 per cent; and 61 per cent of students said that, 'when in doubt', their own university 'should ensure all students are protected from discrimination rather than allow unlimited free speech', by comparison with 37 per cent previously. One third of students – double the proportion in 2016 – agreed that, 'if you debate an issue like sexism or racism, you make it acceptable'. Most striking was the students' suspicions of academics: 77 per cent believed there should be 'mandatory training for all university staff' on understanding 'other cultures', and 36 per cent thought that academics should be fired if they 'teach material that heavily offends some students'.

As the culture wars have deepened, so has the appetite for violence – both on and off campus. In its most recent annual 'college free speech rankings', the US FIRE found that 34 per cent of students are of the view that using violence to stop someone from speaking on campus is acceptable, at least in rare cases: a record figure. Actively preventing discussion by shouting down a speaker on campus is seen as sometimes acceptable by 72 per cent of students; while around a quarter of students say that they 'often self-censor' in discussions in class or with other students (FIRE 2025, UnHerd Staff 2025).

Findings such as these tend to fuel claims that the big enemies of academic freedom are the students, who insist on restricting what academics can talk about in case it makes them, or others, feel 'unsafe'. Certainly, it can seem like that; who can forget the scenes at the UK's University of Sussex in 2021, when a baying mob of masked students objecting to the gender-critical ideas of the philosophy professor Kathleen Stock led a concerted campaign to hound her off campus, to the horror of many philosophers, legal scholars, and other academics? (Sex Matters 2025). Most academics will hold a subconscious list of identity-related issues in their heads, around which discussions need to proceed with care; and even basic academic practices such as providing critical feedback are softened by concerns about students' hurt feelings and propensity to complain.

But the chilling effect of campus cancel culture is rarely propagated by actual students, who, as Stock herself has argued, could be 'a largely untapped asset to the project of detoxifying the current discourse around identity politics'. Young people do not, by and large, arrive on campus with a host of fully formed prejudices that they demand others to take on board. Students' relative youth means that 'they tend to be sensitive, curious, idealistic but not fanatical, and genuinely want to understand the world,' as well as 'to play – with ideas, with jokes, with each other' (Stock 2023). There are generational differences in ideas about the value that should be accorded to free speech, as younger people tend to emphasise the need for 'sensitivity' rather more than their elders (Duffy et al. 2022: 3). But the conceit that the power behind cancel culture lies with woke youth is both mistaken and irresponsible.

In addition to being maligned as a cover for prejudice, academic freedom is portrayed as something that protects only the academics' ability to say what they like, as opposed to being a precondition for a genuine conversation between teacher and student. In acknowledging that students are young adults who have the capacity and responsibility to think for themselves, the principle of academic freedom positively asserts that staff may disagree with one another, students may disagree with one another, and staff and students may disagree with each other – but that this is what makes for good and thoughtful conversations and learning. Far from endorsing all opinions or prejudices as equally valid, it puts the responsibility on academics and students alike to argue about what's right, as opposed to passively accepting a script that has been handed down. Historically, this has applied primarily to arguments within subjects, where disciplinary boundaries have limited where debates should happen in class: a seminar on mathematics, for example, should not turn into a fight over the rights and wrongs of a particular social issue. But in the context of the culture wars we probably need to think more broadly.

The transformation of the university into an institution designed to socialise young people into a particular set of attitudes and attributes has meant that all subjects have become, to a greater or lesser extent, infected with contentious political ideas. The drive to 'decolonise' curricula and promote 'gender-inclusive' language has ridden roughshod over disciplinary boundaries and both forced and encouraged academics to become ambassadors for a particular outlook – at the very least, by impressing upon students the need to comply with modules such as Expect Respect and to use people's preferred pronouns. This has blurred the line between education and politics to the extent that it becomes increasingly difficult to insist that 'academic freedom' applies only to those discussions that take place in the seminar room. To put it another way: if academics are expected to police students' language around, say, race or gender, they – and their students – should at least have the freedom to express reservations about doing so. Administrators and activists can't get away with politicising the classroom and then castigating the objectors for airing their political views.

Or at least they can't get away with it anymore. In universities as in politics, the flaring of the culture wars has ignited a questioning spirit around assumptions and practices that, for years, had been presented as incontestable features of modern society. By swaddling ideological positions in the cloak of education, institutional 'values', and desirable 'graduate attributes', the academy has for a long time managed to embed itself in the political domain while insulating itself from contestation. Now it stands exposed as a political actor and has no idea what to do. This is the true basis of its present crisis. The question is, what will this state of affairs mean for the young adults engaging in higher education and for those charged with the responsibility of educating them?

Conclusion

In their previous study of the academic–student relationship and the university experience, Jennie and colleagues concluded with the hope that students and academics would have the confidence to challenge the prevailing cultural script, which presented university as consumer good rather than an educational endeavour, and to put 'the pursuit of knowledge back at the heart of the Higher Education system' (Bristow, Cant, & Chatterjee 2020: 154). This remains a laudable aspiration, and one that is especially important given the further incursions on knowledge-based education and academic expertise that have happened over the past five years. But that book was published in 2020, just as the Covid pandemic was breaking out: an event that, as discussed in the previous chapter, exposed the weakness of western society's commitment to education and accelerated the culture wars around questions of identity, freedom, and authority. It was not so obvious, back then, that the legacy university system would rapidly become quite such a desperate shell.

As we write now, it does not seem enough to demand that universities return to their focus on knowledge and attempt to insulate themselves from further politicisation. We have noted how the line between knowledge and ideology has become increasingly blurred, as the project of teaching is cast as an attempt to arouse in students a suspicion of everything they have ever learned and to inculcate in them the skills and attitudes they allegedly need for life and work. We have also suggested that the debates ignited by the culture wars, including those related to the purpose of education and the role of the university, bring a sense of openness and energy to the student experience that the technocratic higher education system sought to squash. If teenagers are encouraged to think twice before they go to university, and then forced to think more about difficult questions when they get there, this is a good thing. The prospect may be terrifying for the institutions of higher education focused on their status and survival, but not for those of us genuinely concerned about the younger generation and what they will become.

In *The End of Education*, which is focused on the problem of schooling in the US, Neil Postman (1996) explained the book's 'ambiguous title'. '"End", of course, has at least two important meanings: "purpose" and "finish"', he wrote – and '[e]ither meaning may apply to the future of schools, depending on whether or not there ensues a serious dialogue about purpose'. Here is his suggestion:

> [W]ithout a transcendent and honourable purpose schooling must reach its finish, and the sooner we are done with it, the better. With such a purpose, schooling becomes the central

> institution through which the young may find reasons for continuing to educate themselves. (Postman 1996: xi)

For all that the present crisis of the university is unsettling for the students currently going through it, it presents a much needed opportunity for this kind of 'serious dialogue about purpose' – and for young people, as students or prospective students, to be a part of it. While one camp of the culture wars clings to the technocratic order and the other declares war on the very project of higher education, the young will be forced genuinely to consider what they want out of university – and any educator worth their salt should rise to the challenge of thinking more deeply about what exactly we are doing.

Universities, as educational institutions, should unsettle students intellectually. They should take these young minds beyond their daily lives and experiences and put them under pressure to think, question, and argue. Yet the trends described in this chapter have turned this purpose upside down, presenting high educational expectations and open academic enquiry as a threat to students' mental health and wellbeing, and demanding instead that young people's immediate concerns and experiences are flattered and affirmed, so that they achieve maximum 'satisfaction'.

At the same time, the *non-educational* experience of university – living away from home, developing a dubious set of 'graduate attributes', and performing a cynical orientation towards everything one has ever learned – works to weaken students' ties with their families and their confidence in the norms, values, and ideas with which they grew up. This paradoxical situation perhaps accounts for the fact that the more universities try to make students less stressed and more satisfied, the worse the mental health crisis on campus seems to become.

If we are neither educating young people nor making them happy, how can we defend the demand that they take several years out of their lives and large sums of money out of their future incomes simply because this is what they are expected to do? And how does our society expect the process of cultural reproduction to be accomplished, when the main thing we seem to be teaching is a sense of disenchantment with the knowledge developed and passed down over the generations?

6

Disenchanting the family

When considering what it means to grow up in the culture wars, it's easy to get distracted by the symbolism and rhetoric around the latest hot topics and assume that these alone frame young people's understanding and experience of their world. The reduction of complex debates to facile, polarising memes is not only a feature of social media; it has become the way people are encouraged to express themselves and think about each other. The rules of the game are intricate and constantly changing, and even the most committed adherent to a position, cause, or identity is likely to slip up at some point.

To many people, especially from older generations, the demands of this relentless exercise in cultural self-presentation seem arbitrary and often silly. But, as we saw in the previous chapter, social institutions take them very seriously indeed, to such an extent that keeping up with the latest linguistic fads and intellectual distortions has become the backbone of so-called higher education. The crisis of the academy contains an obvious contradiction: you cannot socialise young people into an anomic situation, which celebrates normlessness and fragmentation. As became evident during the Covid-19 pandemic and the elite's squawking about the need to embrace a 'new normal', norms cannot simply be dreamt up and imposed on a society. They develop over many years, in specific national and local contexts, gain legitimacy through shared acceptance, and are transmitted to new generations as the conventional and commonsense understanding of the way things are.

That's why, in social terms, the family really matters. Even before educational institutions became enthralled to identitarian psychobabble, attempts to socialise children through education were subject to cultural fads and political whims. The family, by contrast, provides a much more stable source of social continuity and intimate meaning than that provided by other social institutions or membership of a birth cohort.

Anyone who looks at the history of the family will know that what is taken as 'tradition' – in terms of family form, practices, or values – is far more flexible than is often imagined. As Elisabetta Ruspini (2013: 4) writes, 'although the family is seen as a social institution most resistant to change, it is, in fact, as deeply embedded in the historical process as any other institution'. Families have changed 'dramatically' over time as a result of economic, demographic, cultural and political factors and should not be considered as static '"building blocks of societies", but, rather, as products of social forces within societies'. At the same time, the *meaning* that societies and individuals attach to the family has changed with its social context. Val Gillies (2011), whose insightful work on the changing relationship between the family and the state has informed our own, observes: 'Despite widespread predictions of its demise, family, as it is experienced in everyday life, has shown itself to be a remarkably resilient and flexible set of meanings.'

Gillies is right to insist that the intimate relationships and practices of everyday family life remain an important source of meaning. And Ruspini is right to suggest that the changing form of the family is neither new nor inherently problematic. Over the twentieth century alone, the 'ideal type' of nuclear family – mom, dad, and '2.4 children' – has been criticised for its misrepresentation of larger and extended families of the past and for its failure to speak to the diversity of family forms that are around today: single parents, blended families, gay parents, adoptive families, 'childfree by choice' couples, and so on. Yet the construction of ideal types by sociologists such as Max Weber and Talcott Parsons was, by definition, not a literal representation of how people lived, but as a way of understanding an institution's role in society. It is the question of meaning that drives the culture wars over the family – with far more serious implications than culture warriors on either side generally realise.

Those on the cultural right often situate their concerns about the crisis of the modern family within a discussion about the problem of these acceptable new family forms, along with the reproductive technologies (abortion, contraception, IVF) that have made them possible; but they do so without fully engaging with *why* these should be a problem. The cultural left tends to deny that there is any problem at all with the transformation of the family into a network of diverse and intangible relationships – a constantly evolving 'lifestyle choice' (Berger 2002). In these ways, both sides express the assumption that the politics of the family turns on the question of how people live and what choices they make, rather than on the fundamental question of what the family as a social institution is expected to *do*.

Throughout history and across cultures, the family has been the foundation on which human societies raise and socialise their children. Different family forms and practices reflect not only what individuals want to do, but what their societies need and expect them to do. Over time, this has meant having many children so that everybody could work to sustain themselves in a farm or cottage industry; having somewhat fewer children but ensuring that they were healthy and capable of working outside the home; or having two or three children (the statistical '2.4') but investing the necessary time and resources in their becoming skilled and productive citizens in a complex modern society. But the family has always relied on adults to have the authority and take the responsibility to transmit the knowledge and conventions of the community to their children, gradually bringing the latter into their own world.

It is this process of socialisation that now stands in question – and with it the authority and responsibility of adults. In *100 Years of Identity Crisis*, Furedi (2021) explains that 'the culture war over socialisation' begins in the nursery. While the relationship between the culture wars and battles over abortion or changing family forms is well recognised, what tends to be far less acknowledged is the existence of long-running conflicts over adult authority, as embodied by parents in the family and very young children. These conflicts are now becoming increasingly stark and require urgent attention.

As we saw in our discussion of education, a society that doesn't know what it stands for or what it's doing will necessarily struggle to socialise its young in a meaningful way. The existence of the family provides a bulwark against this confusion, at least to the extent that most parents are less confused about the basics of life than are educational administrators, and ties between the generations are thicker. By loving their children and living with them day after day, from infancy until adulthood, parents build a relationship with them that is not conditional or transactional; it is an affective, intimate bond of care and responsibility, a love relationship that goes beyond choice, where the practices of getting through life – from playing and celebrating to feeding and disciplining – are tacitly bound up with moral questions about who and how to be.

The solidity and intensity of family relationships provide children with the foundations upon which they can develop into themselves. This does not mean, of course, that everything that happens within families is wonderful, or that children are simply 'mini-mes'; an integral part of growing up is pushing against the boundaries, restrictions, and assumptions made by parents, and the very thing that makes family ties supportive is also what makes them stifling and annoying. But the fact is that, as a 2015 song by the country singer Kacey Musgraves puts it, 'friends come in handy, but family is family'.

Unfortunately, as we discuss below, the cultural dynamics that have derailed other social institutions have also impacted the family in significant ways. The development of a prescriptive, individualised, expert-led parenting culture over the past 30 years has undermined parents' confidence in their own authority and in the informal wisdom gleaned over generations of childrearing, pushing them to 'parent' according to the latest expert-led fads. The disorienting effect of this trend fuels the self-conscious adoption of particular parenting 'styles' or identities, in which how one looks and feels as a parent comes to outweigh what one is actually doing with one's child, and why. Bringing up children has developed into a parenting lifestyle, overseen by advisors on the best style to pick. As the culture wars deepen, the rationalisation of parenting as a set of processes or practices designed to make the family adapt to the demands of the present is leading to an all-out assault on the very institution of the family and the relationships within it.

Parenting culture and problem of socialisation

The focus of this chapter is on the ways in which the current culture war over the family speaks to an ongoing sublimation of the problem of socialisation. In discussing why the term 'socialisation' has fallen out of favour in the discipline of sociology, Guhin, Calcaro and Miller-Idriss (2021) observe that its use became more common at the end of the nineteenth century, in line with the rise of sociology itself. For classic theorists including Durkheim and Simmel, the word was used in the sense of 'social reproduction', and clearly included an idea of morality, in the sense of normative values that are developed and passed on in a modern society characterised by change. This hinges on the question of what moral virtues a community should transmit to its young – how we think about what to conserve and carry forward and how, as we appreciate the need for creative engagement with change (Furedi 2021).

Furedi (2021: 3) notes that in recent decades, socialisation has 'tended to be discussed as a technical matter', with confusions about the meaning of this concept 'self-consciously ignored'. Instead of understanding the term as a category of moral action, socialisation has come to be associated with other, more narrowly psychological, meanings. This results from 'the lack of clarity that adults possess about how to exert their authority to the benefit of young people'. The crisis of socialisation is intimately linked to the problem of adult authority; and both these problems are given expression in twenty-first century parenting culture.

The obsession with 'parenting' – the techniques people use to feed, discipline, and manage their children – reflects what sociologists describe as an increasing 'individualisation' and 'demoralisation' of western culture. Parents have always had a strong degree of individual responsibility for their children: societies rely on the family as the basic source of care and socialisation, and children's fortunes (or otherwise) are closely tied to those of their parents. 'Feckless fathers' and 'irresponsible mothers' have long been held to blame when their kids turned out to be poor or criminal, and this has often been rather unfair. But parents exercised their responsibility to be good – or at least good-enough (Winnicott 2021 [1964]) – parents against a backdrop that saw the family as something that was important to society as a whole.

In *Parenting Culture Studies* (Lee et al. 2023), we examined how the transformation of the age-old societal project of childrearing into the more recent and individualised endeavour of 'parenting', in which mothers and fathers are tasked with cultivating their children in particular ways, according to the latest expert advice, presents childrearing as a terrifying risk-management exercise that should be embarked upon only when you are *absolutely ready* and prepared to do whatever it takes to optimise your child's life chances. In this way parenting has been recast as a set of complex skills or 'competences' that individual parents need to learn and practise. This, in turn, has created a warrant for governments and others to intervene more and more directly in the emotions and relationships of intimate family life; and the 'diversity' of family forms is celebrated alongside the intensifying prescription of appropriate parenting practices. 'Governments', observes Gillies (2011, n.p.), 'have come to see families more in terms of their practices than structures, with "what families do" readily translating into a new ideology of family competence'.

The repositioning of family life as a 'public rather than private concern', in which parents are instructed on the latest, officially endorsed childrearing imperatives, represents an attempt to construct a direct relationship between the state and the child, as '[f]amily has taken on a whole new political significance as the formative site through which "competent personhood" is cultivated' (Gillies 2011). The problem of socialisation, which is fundamentally a moral question pertaining to values and their transmission across generations through families and communities, has been recast a tangle of ever disputed rules for parents. And parental authority, as the key to this process, has been undermined and destabilised by the intervention of political and cultural forces bent on establishing a twenty-first-century 'parenting regime' (Macvarish & Martin 2021) that aims to counter the fragmentary dynamics of the current period but ends up consolidating and reproducing them.

Western societies have struggled for a long time to maintain a working theory of socialisation that understands socialisation as a *social* process related to generations, adulthood, and culture rather than to narrower psychological and emotional relations between particular adults and children. This narrower understanding reflects a growing ambivalence about the need for generalised norms and places an emphasis on the recognition of difference and diversity in more individuated and experiential terms. This is why the discussion of 'moral authority' in the twenty-first century tends to derive from inherently individualised accounts of 'lived experience' rather than from accounts that express or embody abstract or generalised precepts. While an investigation of, and sensitivity to, experiential differences and their relation to wider structures are important, we lose something when the idea that morality is important for social development is weakened. In social scientific discussions of the family, what stands out is the turn against the moral dimensions of socialisation and what it suggests about adulthood and the special authority of parents. As Guhin et al. (2021: 117) note, without an understanding of socialisation 'it is easy to lose sight of how people came to know the culture they know'.

In the period after the Second World War, Talcott Parsons grasped this problem most fully. In sociology textbooks and teaching, Parsons is often assigned the role of strawman functionalist, his insights on social integration being reduced to an apologism for fixed gender roles. His contemporary C. Wright Mills accused him of being 'a conservative "grand theorist" out of touch with the real world and its real problems' (Staubmann 2021: 178). Yet despite the limitations of Parsons' approach when it comes to understanding the dynamics of everyday life, his focus on ideas and institutions yielded some powerful insights on the difficulties of integrating younger generations into modern societies; and he grasped what was at stake with the moral aspect of socialisation. Parsons (2012 [1951]) linked social morality to thinking about the moral development of individuals: socialisation 'is necessary for both moral and logical capacity' and 'critical for the maintenance of both social continuity and social order' (Guhin et al. 2021: 111).

The social demographer Kingsley Davis, writing in 1940, also paid serious attention to the meaning of socialisation, its connections to morality, and the consequent need for society to validate parental authority. His discussion of 'parent–youth conflict' echoed Mannheim's sensitivity to the friction between adults and children that arises from having grown up in different times:

> Not only are parent and child, at any given moment, in different stages of development, but the content from which the parent acquired at the stage where the child is now, was a different content from that which the child is acquiring. Since the parent is supposed to socialise the child, he tends to apply the erstwhile but now inappropriate content. (Davis 1940: 524)

Kingsley regarded the 'readjustment of authority' between parent and child as a 'ticklish' process, but one that could be managed, provided that society shored up the authority of parents. Parents were charged with 'the responsibility of controlling and training the child in conformity with the mores, and thereby ensuring the maintenance of the cultural structure'; and, given this, 'the parent, to fulfil his duties, must have the privileges as well as the obligations of authority, and the surrounding community ordinarily guarantees both' (Davis 1940: 530). Parental authority, Davis argued, is unlike other forms of authority: it is not specific or instrumental; it is expansive and potentially unbearable, and can be made bearable only when the community has a shared understanding of moral norms.

In the early 1960s, a few scholars paid serious attention to the difficulties of integrating young people into a rapidly changing modern society. One notable collection brought together sociologists and psychologists from radical and conservative perspectives – including Talcott Parsons, S.N. Eisenstadt, Erik Erikson, Bruno Bettelheim, and Kenneth Keniston – to explore the problem that would inspire Erikson's (1963) title: *Youth: Change and Challenge.* In marked contrast to the narrow, evasive, and experiential focus of much academic discussion about the problem of youth today, this book tackled head-on the difficulties western societies were having with socialising and integrating their children.

A further important contribution came from the psychologist Diana Baumrind and her work on 'authoritative parental control' (Baumrind 1966) developed and elaborated through a long career that started in the 1950s. Until the twentieth century, observed Baumrind (1996: 406), 'few questioned the justification for parental authority'. But the context thrown up by profound changes in society and in children's place in it made both the justification and the meaning of authority demanding. The available thinking, which Baumrind characterised schematically as 'authoritarian' and 'permissive' parenting styles, was not sufficient to meet these challenges; and her efforts and energy went into explaining and practically investigating the 'authority problem'.

Baumrind (1996: 405) made the case for a middle way between 'authoritarian' and 'permissive' parenting styles, which she termed 'authoritative parenting'. As she summarised, '[e]ach polarised model contains its germ of truth, but each demonises the other'. Authoritativeness, she said, is a way of seeing upbringing as best based on control and warmth, alongside necessary efforts to discipline. 'Within the authoritative model', she explained:

> behavioral compliance and psychological autonomy are viewed not as mutually exclusive but rather as interdependent objectives; children are encouraged to respond habitually in prosocial ways *and* to reason autonomously about moral problems, and to respect adult authorities *and* learn how to think independently.

Baumrind's intention was to take seriously the matter of parental authority and develop a support for parents appropriate to a time in which children were seen, far more than previously, as 'developing individuals'. Crucial to this was explaining and upholding the necessity of adult authority, and especially that of the parent, which rested on making distinctions between child and adult.

Baumrind (1996: 406) argued for the need to think as deeply as possible about both what adulthood is constituted by in modern society and what this means for how we think of childhood and its demands. For example, she noted that John Stuart Mill 'restricted the ideal of self-determination to individuals capable of assuming adult responsibilities', recognising that, 'although the adult generation is not perfectly wise and good with regard to the interests of the next generation, it is wiser and better in its judgements of what would benefit them than that generation is itself'. The emphasis on the (imperfect) wisdom of the 'adult generation' as the starting point for how to think about socialisation also led her to clarity on what the point of being parent to a child is. Thus she wrote on the question of punishment, quoting Hegel (1952 [1821]: 61):

> The right of parents over the wishes of their children is determined by the object in view – discipline and education. The punishment of children does not aim at justice as such: the aim is more subjective and moral in character, that is to deter them from exercising a freedom still in the toils of nature and to lift the universal into their consciousness and will.

What matters here is the clarity on the difference between a child and an adult. No child should be placed on trial in order for the adult to pursue 'justice'. The authority of the parent is entirely unlike that of a court, as its focus is on what is specific to children; their domination by 'the toils of nature' cannot be left to run free, as it is not yet in their control. The purpose of what came to be called 'boundaries' is predicated on this recognition, and only by enforcing them can a child grow to a point where the exercise of will becomes possible.

Along similar lines, Baumrind (1996: 406) made the development of 'character' the focus of the purpose of childrearing (in marked contrast with 'being happy' and 'self-esteem', which characterise the goals of 'parenting'). She argued:

> Character consists of positive and cultivated habits of social responsibility, moral commitment, and self-discipline that provide the internal structure of conscience, regulating inner thoughts and volitions. . . Neither wicked nor good, children are born both with moral sentiments and destructive impulses.

For Baumrind, the socialisation process rests on the exercise of authority, for the goal of developing moral sense and competence. It can only happen where society sees what children can become, not what they are, and views adults as agents who can spur development. 'Socialisation', she said, 'is an adult-initiated process by which young persons, through education, training, and imitation, acquire their culture and the habits and values congruent with adaptation to that culture' (Baumrind 1996: 408). Her account of the specialness of parental authority as a part of a more general adult authority is compelling, and it is striking just how strong the reaction against her recognition of the necessity of discipline – and, with it, the wider understanding of the value of adulthood – has grown.

These problems, especially the problem of the foundation for authority that adult society needs to come to grips with, were captured by the sociologist Norbert Elias in the 1980s, as part of his discussion of what he termed 'the civilising process'. In his brilliant essay 'The Civilising of Parents', Elias (1997: 191) argues that society had found itself in 'a transition period' in which 'older, strictly authoritarian, and newer, more egalitarian parent–child relations exist alongside each other'. This transition 'produces, for both groups, a series of specific problems and, all in all, a rather high degree of uncertainty', in which

> [W]e are thoroughly sceptical about the notion that the unconditional authority of parents and the unconditional obedience of children is also the best, healthiest and most productive social arrangement from the standpoint of children themselves.

These contributions provide us with ways of thinking that genuinely recognise the difficulties of socialisation, but also the absolute necessity of shoring up parental authority and giving cultural support to the family. But, as we discuss below, parenting culture has taken things in the opposite direction. Furedi (2021: 70) notes that, '[i]n contrast to Davis' sympathetic depiction of an adulthood steeped in the experiences of the past, politically motivated commentators accused the older generations of wilfully misleading the young by subjecting them to their archaic prejudices'. Meanwhile, Baumrind's warnings about the dangers of professional interference in parent–child relationships have gone unheeded; her concept of authoritative parenting has been reduced to a set of instructions that parents should apply in order to turn out the best 'output'; and her balanced account of the necessity of aversive discipline has been condemned as justification for child abuse.

In media and popular discourses, Baumrind's understanding of 'parenting styles' is routinely mistranslated into a set of parenting identities, which represent the kind of parent you think you are – or the kind of parent you see others as being. There is the 'slummy mummy' proudly practising 'benign neglect'; the 'gentle parent', who believes that discipline is akin to child abuse; the 'Tiger Mom' pushing her child towards the best outcomes; the 'helicopter' or 'snowplough' parent focused on protecting their child from every physical or emotional hazard on the road to growing up. In reaction, we see the 'free range parent', who self-consciously sets out to encourage their child's developing independence in the face of cultural and legal prescriptions that push parents to focus on safety above all else; and there is even some discussion of a turn towards

'Boomer parenting' by mothers who grew up in the 1970s and think that what their own parents did provides a better model than the current rules.

The performative character of these parenting identities reflects how destabilising contemporary parenting culture has become for childrearing. As one thinks of oneself (or others) as practising a particular 'parenting style', attention is drawn away from the parent's relationship with the child and onto the parent's individual sense of herself or himself, as constructed in line with particular ways of thinking and performed under the spotlight of the outside world. As we discuss below, this represents what sociologists describe as the rationalisation of childrearing, where an intimate and sacred relationship is transformed into a set of skills and practices designed to meet a series of instrumental outcomes. Parents look outside the family to check that they are doing 'the right thing', while policymakers look inside the family to check that parents are feeling 'the right way'.

The rise of the parenting regime

Elias recognised, back in the 1980s, that rather than finding a way to address the uncertainty characterising authority relations, society seemed to be avoiding the problem. One form this took was to overturn the adult–child relationship altogether, ascribing a new status identity to children and endowing them with 'rights'. Unlike groups of adults who are oppressed by the denial of equal rights, children are 'a group of a completely different sort, an age group'.

> The behaviour of parents and children in their relations with each other is a form of group behaviour which is always co-determined by a specific socially determined code, and cannot be understood in terms of individual roles. In the

> case of children, it concerns a group of human beings whose behaviour, rights and obligations are always brought under normative social control. (Elias 1997: 190)

Subsequent decades have brought an inexorable movement away from confronting the task of giving adult authority a normative moral content. The rise of children's rights has symbolically reversed the authority relation, giving those adults appointed to determine what children's rights mean extensive power over parents within families. This is what happens, for example, with the criminalisation of particular forms of punishment, such as smacking: state authorities gain ground, and the issues raised by Baumrind about the place of discipline within authoritative parenting become completely lost. When policymakers and parenting experts then complain about the lack of discipline among 'kids today', one wonders whether they ever reflect on their own role in denuding parents of the ability to administer the kind of discipline they may feel is necessary.

The failure to bolster parental authority also means that we lose the sense that society *itself* socialises its new members through family-based morality. The individualised focus on 'parenting', with its specific techniques, styles, and identities, has resulted in a disappearance of 'the social' as something that can have a life and impact of its own, and of which 'the family' forms an institutionalised part. One outcome is a system populated by professionals designated as responsible for socialisation, presented as having the requisite training and insight to perform this task on behalf of society, and working with – or sometimes in place of – parents and families. Teachers, counsellors, doctors, mental health specialists, lawyers, and other appointed or self-appointed 'experts' try to counter the weakness of the socialisation process.

This point is elaborated in Emily Ball's (2021: 2) discussion of the tension between 'informalised parenting' – 'where authoritarian, violent and harsh parenting is discouraged and the autonomy of the child is encouraged' – and its 'reformalisation' through parenting interventions via state agencies. The uncertainty described by Elias, she writes, led to 'a proliferation of ideologies, theories and arguments in an attempt to reduce this unknown and guarantee the correct socialisation process'. This has included 'a saturation of parenting pedagogy guides' and 'the development of a cultural focus on the moral socialisation of children that includes tips for improving child social learning and increasing child social and emotional development'. Ultimately, Ball observes, a form of interaction driven by process has developed. This has 'problematised child outcomes and the relation between children and parents' (Ball 2021: 3).

The family has been flooded with external 'professional' advice on individual parenting methods, so that '[p]arents now need to consider how their interaction, disciplining and parenting style will successfully shape their children into upstanding adults' (Ball 2021: 3). At the same time, public policy seeks to detach children from the authority of their parents, bringing with it 'a shift from an understanding of care as something which takes place inside the private space of the family to a "public health issue" dealt with by the state'. This is what Ball (2021: 5) describes as the 'reformalisation' of parenting, as '[r]hetoric would suggest that the family cannot be trusted to care for children properly, and corporate state parenting via education, social care and child protection is more efficient at ensuring the socialisation process'.

The reformalisation of parenting is also tackled by Macvarish and Martin (2021: 436), in their discussion of a 'parenting regime', which reframes family relationships through the prism of 'parenting' – a term that 'reconceptualises the role and status of parents'. 'The emergence of new words to describe family relations and the raising of children, and the adoption of these words by policy makers, suggest the development of a new nexus through which families are understood,' they argue (p. 435). The parenting regime emphasises the inadequacy of parents and the need for them to be 'scaffolded' by professionals and others who understand the correct ways to raise a child fit for the twenty-first century. The purpose of scaffolding 'is not the self-development of a morally autonomous individual but a process involving external assistance, assessment and validation' (p. 442).

The parenting regime is explicitly therapeutic, aiming to scaffold parents' 'competencies' less by instructions about what to do than by training in how to feel. Macvarish and Martin observe that, over time, the more punitive approach to parents appears to have given way to an ostensibly more sympathetic account of 'the problem'. 'Rather than the weak transmission of parental authority, the diagnostic stick is increasingly bent towards the weak transmission of parental love, not because parents are cruel or distracted, but because they face psychological or emotional barriers to loving their children', they write (Macvarish & Martin 2021: 438). This perspective, as Gillies (2011) argues, has encouraged 'regular intervention at the level of the personal in the form of advice, training, expert consultation and sanctions for making the wrong choice'. In the twenty-first century, it is expected that parents need and want to be educated and trained in how to be a parent, through interventions ranging from daily advice on BBC Bitesize Parents' Toolkit (the equivalent of children's GCSE cribsheets) to compulsory parent training (Hennum 2014, Cucchiara & Steinbugler 2021).

The intrusion of modern parenting culture into the emotional domain, by seeking to reconfigure how individual parents feel about themselves and their children, has impacted the cultural meaning ascribed to the family both as a relationship and an institution. Discussion of the family, in policy and in academia, has become increasingly dominated by a focus on the 'lived experience' of people within families, with a heavy focus on 'feelings and introspective analysis' (Gillies 2011). In this perspective, diversity in 'families' is accomplished as a result of changes to the role of women and to all norms around both gender and sexuality, and any normative assumptions about relations between marriage and childbearing as the core of family are presented as radically transformed.

The family, write Gouveia and Castrén (2021: 259–60), is thus conceptualised 'less as a pre-given entity and more as comprising multiple kinds of relationships', with the sociological imaginary said to be moving 'away from preconceived notions of family based on normative expectations of relatedness' that include 'heteronormativity', and also 'co-residence' and 'genealogical proximity'. Viewed in this way, family comes to be understood in terms of 'feelings and practices of closeness that may or may not overlap with cultural understandings of kinship'. As Brigitte Berger (2002: 57) puts it more bluntly, '[t]his anti-conventional family agenda has entered the public arena with considerable fanfare. In some school districts in the United States this agenda has been adopted lock, stock and barrel.'

Attempts to manage the crisis of socialisation by seeking to rationalise parents' emotions and by reimagining the family as a set of diverse and conflictual individual relationships and practices have made the problem many times worse. Ashley Frawley's (2024: 12) review of the European Union's policies on the family finds the institutionalisation of fragmentation: while policy documents talk about '"parents", "women" and "men", and... "people with caring responsibilities", there are no "families"'. As Gillies (2011) argues, indifference towards the family as the locus for a meaning system beyond 'how it feels for me' becomes the wellspring for a mass of unstable but powerful projects and initiatives. These projects continually validate some forms of feeling and behaviour over others, and some 'lived experiences' are held up as being in need of extensive recognition while others are presented as 'problematic'.

Under the parenting regime, relationships are shorn of 'old' ideas about institutions and norms and reformalised in relation to therapeutic discourses that start from the individual's need to let go of their attachment to the old ways and to embrace change, fluidity, and diversity. The purpose of becoming and being a parent, once detached from 'family' understood as social institution, is altered beyond recognition by comparison with what it was in times past. The clearest example of this is the cultural onslaught on the biological core of the parent–child relationship.

Unlike 'social generations', which develop from social, cultural, and political dynamics, 'vertical' generations, running down from parent to child, are rooted first and foremost in the biological relationship of reproduction. Of course, 'parent' is not *merely* a biological relationship, and adopted or surrogate children have non-biological parents, but these exceptional relationships derive their meaning from the natural reproductive norm. Yet, as Macvarish and Martin (2021: 439–44) note, the 'naturalness' of the parent–child relationship, which has historically formed the basis of assumptions of family care, commitment, and responsibility, is confronted by the idea of 'parenting', which 'tends to separate the status of biological parenthood from acts which constitute "parenting" and raising children is reimagined as a collection of separate acts of "parenting" . . . with behavioural options'. In this respect, '"parenting" can be performed by people who need not be parents, and parents may not necessarily be "parenting" at all times or any time at all' (p. 440).

As Macvarish and Martin (2021: 439–41) argue, the detachment of 'parenting' from the specific figure of the parent has two linked consequences. The first is that familial childrearing becomes rationalised as a form of work, which undermines the distinction between public and private life and exposes intimate aspects of family life to the language and criteria of the public domain. This 'leads to parents becoming appreciated less in their specificity as individuals who love their own child more than anyone else could, but rather flattens them out into the rest of the childcare workforce'. The second is that it degenders and denaturalises parenthood. 'Parenting' as a word 'floats free from gendered meanings, moving us away from the cultural weight of the complex meanings carried by the words "mother" and "father"', they write; and this 'detaches them from some of the past foundations of their authority'.

The denaturalising and degendering of parenting, and its rationalisation as a form of work that can be done by anybody considered 'competent' in the ideas and skills deemed necessary for socialising children in the demands of the present moment, have powerful consequences both for the families living today and for those to be born tomorrow. Fundamentally, the effect of the parenting regime is to disenchant the family, stripping it of the mystique and meaning that for generations has spurred individuals to reproduce themselves, and in so doing to reproduce their societies.

In Chapter 7 we consider some of the bleak and lonely effects of this on today's young people, for whom the joy and purpose of sexual reproduction has become recast as a terrifying experience, best deferred or avoided in favour of an abstracted, individualised sexual or gender identity that lives in one's head and is given expression by the symbolic universe of social media and official validation. Below we consider how the disenchantment of the family is both a consequence of the crisis of socialisation and a cause of its further fragmentation.

Rationalisation, disenchantment, and meaning

In his powerful study of 'myth and ritual in family life', the historian John Gillis describes the tension between the families we live with and the families we live by. 'We not only live with families but depend on them to do the symbolic work that was once assigned to religious and communal institutions: representing ourselves to ourselves as we would like to think we are', explains Gillis (1997: xv). While the families we live with can be imperfect and impermanent, the families we live by – 'constituted through myth, ritual, and image' – are 'never allowed to let us down'.

In trying to capture the significance of 'the families we live by', Gillis was not only talking about the idealised versions of the family that have been periodically constructed by conservative moralisers: the Victorian paterfamilias, or the fifties' 'golden age' of stable, suburban nuclear families. By the mid-1990s, when he was writing, the world was well aware that these were ideal-type constructions, and the 'dark side' of the families we live with – domestic violence, child abuse, loveless marriages, careless divorces – had already suffered decades of exposure. Rather, Gillis was exploring the ways in which people derive a sense of meaning from family that they are increasingly unable to get in 'the cosmos or in the community'. Our attachment to family myths, rituals, and images comes about, he argues, because 'we no longer have access to other locations onto which we might map our deepest moral values' (Gillis 1997: xvi–xvii).

In Chapter 3 we discussed how the roots of our current culture wars lie in the normative upheavals of the 1960s, as the traditions and conventions of the old order were thrown into question and replaced by a focus on individual self-expression. But the twentieth-century culture wars were at least limited, for the most part, to battles over reproductive choice and family form. While supporters of the 'permissive society' wanted people to have more freedom over their sexual relationships and the circumstances in which they had children, there remained a sense that families mattered. Indeed, as Gillis explains, as Anglo-American societies became more confused and conflicted about what they stood for, the specialness of the family came to matter even more, creating additional tensions for the families we live with:

> Finding no other location for such values as cooperation, enduring loyalty, and moral consideration, modern Western culture has mapped these exclusively onto the families we live with, a cultural burden that members of these domestic groups find difficult, if not impossible, to sustain on an everyday basis. (Gillis 1997: xvi–xvii)

This wider crisis of meaning-making results in families being, simultaneously, the thing we most cherish and the thing we most rail against. It is true that this creates a burden for families, which constantly have to navigate the tensions, disappointments, flaws, and injustices of their everyday being, while at the same time representing a sense of how things should be. But this symbolic work also provides individuals with a sense of who they are, in a world where other attachments and principles seem to be constantly shifting. Young people can absorb the values of the families they live by, or reject them, or a bit of both; but they can do this only because their families have tried to create the meaning in the first place.

But, as we have discussed in this chapter, the twenty-first century parenting regime has brought a concerted attack on the families we live with, by rationalising the complex, tacit, and intimate work of childrearing into a series of instrumental tasks and 'appropriate' emotions. The idea that anybody outside the family can 'do' parenting aims to displace the generations-old sense of what it means to *be* a parent. At the same time, cultural and political institutions aim to recast the 'families we live by' as a dangerously outdated fiction that needs to be rewritten, discarding historical meanings related to tradition and continuity in favour of an open and fluid story of change.

In their quest for ever more 'inclusive' terminology, institutions such as schools now refer to parents as 'carers' – an instrumental term that barely captures the intimate relationship and the depth of responsibility that parents (and, indeed, grandparents, aunties, and adoptive families) have with their children. Sociologists talk about friends as alternatives to families, or 'families of choice'. The validation of 'families' outside previous normative expectations, including those rooted in biology and heterosexuality, is a core aspect of progressivist ideology. At the extreme end, the case for the outright 'abolition' of family has been mounted, with its target the 'traditional' structure of the family, its out-of-date supporters, and the assumptions it carries with it about what makes a mother or father what they are. The movement of our time is said to be with formations of relationships that proactively break down conventions based on vertical relationships between generations, including expectations of authoritativeness based on biological parenthood.

Biological relatedness to children, it is implied, provides no necessary grounds at all for 'knowing best': indeed, quite the opposite. Sophie Lewis's (2022) book *Abolish the Family: A Manifesto for Care and Liberation* takes the depiction of the 'dark side' of the nuclear family to intense lows. The family, she argues, is 'where most of the rape happens on this earth, and most of the murder. No one is likelier to rob, bully, blackmail, manipulate, or hit you, or inflict unwanted touch, than the family.' It is 'a shitty contract pretending to be biological necessity' (Lewis 2022: 14–15).

By casually reducing the complex and powerful relations of love, care, authority, responsibility, intimacy, and socialisation that have constituted the family across time and across cultures to 'a shitty contract pretending to be biological necessity', Lewis demonstrates the influence of the rationalised, disenchanted concept of parenting. At the same time, she also reveals the destructive logical consequence of progressive attempts to redefine the family out of its meaningful existence as a social institution. If the family is really nothing more than a set of lived relationships or parenting practices and parental authority the oppressive exercise of power, what does this say about our society's will and capacity to socialise our children?

As we noted at the start of this chapter, the family is diverse in form across societies and it changes over time. Indeed, some of the most illuminating sociological work and political analysis – and what inspired our own interest in the sociology of family, parenting culture, and generations – is based on exactly this observation. It understands the family in relation to wider aspects of economic, social, and cultural life and at its best articulates the complexities of the relation between the family and other dimensions of society.

Yet accounts of family change now routinely present us with a picture and suggest a process in which recent decades are said to have been more transformative of these relations than any other period in history. The downgrading of the significance of 'the family' as an 'institution' that has boundaries and purpose reduces the power of what Elias understood as the civilising process and Baumrind saw as authoritativeness on the part of parents, resulting in a tense and disorienting 'shared authority' between parents and the state (Furedi 2001). The shift from understanding the family from an institutional perspective to influential theories of 'individualisation', discussed in the next chapter, provides important observations about the fragmentary dynamics of post-modern western societies, but can end in a tacit celebration of individual self-realisation – the 'strengthening of reflexivity in individuals as actors and agents in their own biographies and relational worlds' (Gouveia & Castrén 2021: 261) – while downplaying the consequences for the social project of raising children.

Some have drawn attention to the importance of thinking through what is lost if the family ceases to be thought of as an institution. For example, Knapp and Wurm (2019: 216) discuss this with reference to the idea of deinstitutionalisation, where 'family relationships are increasingly theorised as being formed almost exclusively from within'. Noting that '[m]ost family scholars would likely interpret deinstitutionalisation in terms of some kind of emancipatory lens (i.e. individuals are now free to choose their own lifestyles instead of having social institutional roles and statuses imposed on them)', they warn that 'the focus on the emancipatory possibilities of new family forms, common to virtually all diversification scholarship, could easily slip into theorising family in noninstitutional terms, which ends up privileging individualisation' (p. 218). However, they argue:

> There is something about family life that is not reducible to individualisation. . . in the ways that diversification scholars have framed it. This something has its own inner logic or coherence . . . The familial is not merely something that we live by but an institutional substance that we live through and live for, even if we may do so in pluralistic ways. (Knapp & Wurm 2019: 223)

To us, the most important question raised by the shift from 'the family' to 'families' is whether the validation of fluidity really is about freeing up. Does the push against boundaries that may exist between what is and what is not 'family' make us better equipped to experiment creatively with the demands of raising children? Is it true that a borderless idea of family and how we imagine ourselves within it give us a way of thinking where we are more in control and better equipped to live our lives?

Our study of parenting culture over the years suggests that the demands of the parenting regime have neither freed up parents to enjoy their children nor bolstered their confidence in raising them. Indeed, media discussions and academic literature are replete with stories about parents feeling insecure and defensive about everything they do and exhausted, isolated, and 'burnt out'. As Jennifer Senior (2014) observes, the 'paradox of modern parenthood' is that so much is invested in what individual parents do and how they should feel that it has become 'all joy and no fun'.

And what about the children? As we discussed in Chapter 2, the problems afflicting today's kids, predominantly expressed in rocketing rates of mental ill health, have a complex set of causes. But, without confusing correlation and causation, it is fair to observe that the 'emancipatory' shift from 'family' to 'families' has not made children happier, stronger, or more secure. By opening up the privacy of family life to the meddling of external experts and by undermining parents' authority, the parenting regime has breached the family's defences as a 'haven in a heartless world' (Lasch 1995 [1977]), exposing children to the confusions and contradictions of our postmodern culture in a heartbreakingly unmediated way.

The parenting regime casts itself as child-centred. Incursions on parental authority and demands to validate children's 'rights' and 'identities' as though they were little adults are justified on this ground. But ironically, as Nancy McDermott (2020: loc. 1217–27) argues in *The Problem with Parenting*, what has happened is the opposite. America in the 1950s, she writes, is remembered as a time of political and social conformity, where racial and sexual discrimination were an accepted fact of life; 'few people would want to return to that era, even if such a thing were possible'. And yet, for all its faults, it was 'the last time in living memory that the family was child-centred'. Children in the 1950s 'were more numerous and more visible than they are today'. This made culture 'more child-friendly but also, paradoxically, more grown-up', as 'the very presence of children reminded adults of their own status'. Most adults were 'relaxed in their dealings with children' and were 'comfortable about exercising their authority over them'. Children were free to roam, but 'subject to the collective discipline of the adults they encountered on their travels', earning a rebuke for bad behaviour or help when they needed it. In consequence, she argues: 'What we describe as "free-range" kids was simply a normal childhood in a much more child-centred society.'

We suggest that the postmodern family has not been deinstitutionalised so much as reinstitutionalised in a therapeutic mode. At the centre of this process is the sublimation and disorganisation of an already fragile idea of socialisation as the core task of adult society. The almost tantrum-like rejection of the idea that 'the old' has any place in the raising of children means that the new cannot be grasped either. The result is an endless loop of reinventing new 'news' – for children and for relationships.

There is nothing creative in this. To the contrary, what emerges from the disintegration of the effort to develop meaningful social norms is an overbearing, bossy, intrusive regulation of family life, which is as bad for children as it is for parents. The consequences of this disorientation stretch forward, undermining young adults' capacity to see themselves as part of a social future in which they have both the desire and the ability to live beyond themselves. As Kearney et al. conclude on the basis of their detailed statistical examination of possible influences on fertility rates,

> One specific aspect of modern life that may contribute to young adults' views about having children is how the act of 'parenting' has evolved over recent decades . . . Changing norms regarding the intensity of parenting might change people's views toward how many children to have or whether to have them at all. (Kearney et al. 2022: 169)

Simonardottir's (2024: 1) research on the 'voluntarily childfree' in Iceland notes that, despite the policy emphasis on 'gender equality, diverse family structures, and policies that support both parents' participation in work and childcare', women perceive motherhood as 'mentally and emotionally draining, complex, and requiring significant personal sacrifices'. In this context, becoming a parent is seen as a choice 'which can even stand in the way of personal fulfilment and autonomy'. As we discuss in the next chapter, the perceived opposition between motherhood and 'personal fulfilment' is driven, at least in part, by the way in which 'parenting' is now constituted as an 'ordeal' (Furedi 2001). More importantly, what it means to develop *oneself* has become organised along lines that distance the self from intimacy and from the opportunities of taking immediate responsibility for others. A more disconnected, inward-looking self has come to the fore, trapped by the culture of identity.

Conclusion

As Oakeshott (2001 [1989]: 10) explained, '[t]he human family (whatever form it may take) is a practice devised, not for the procreation of children, nor merely for their protection, but for the early education of newcomers to the human scene'. When we have children, we don't just 'want a baby', and as our teenagers grow up, we don't merely want – let alone expect – them to 'be happy'. We understand that having children means raising them to be someone in the world, to contribute to our society through the work they do, the communities they build, and the children they will go on to have themselves. We know it doesn't always work out like that, and that's OK – any society has its share of individuals who cannot or will not work, and criminals who offend against the collective moral code. So long as most people are having children, it doesn't really matter if others can't, or don't. When, collectively, we socialise children into a landscape of norms, we can happily absorb the exceptions.

But the 'human scene' into which current parenting culture instructs mothers and fathers to introduce their children has become instrumentalised and hyperindividualised, to the point where social dysfunction is actively celebrated with such rhetorical frames as diversity, kindness, and self-realisation. Just as our collective need for cultural reproduction through education has been subsumed to the crisis management demands of presentism, our collective need for social reproduction is continually challenged by the idea that the thick ties generated by the family are an oppressive force standing in the way of young people's ability to 'be who they want to be'. This sort of commentary turns on a call to start again, to proactively reject perceived assumptions and tacit understandings of what makes parents best placed to know what is best, and to deliberately fashion relationships in families in a 'today' way. The progressive call is for newness – new families, new ideas about what a child, a parent, an adult means – and for these to be constructed on the basis of a rejection of tradition.

The idea that the children of the progressive future should be liberated from the archaic demands and ties of family is not itself entirely new. It has its roots in the individualised, therapeutic trend towards self-emancipation that developed in the sixties: the 'culture of narcissism' critically debunked by Christopher Lasch (2018 [1979]). It was subjected to a blistering attack by Tom Wolfe (of *Bonfire of the Vanities* fame) in 1976, in a lengthy essay for *New York* magazine in which he poured scorn on the voguish phrase '"If I've only one life, let me live it as a ——!" Fill in the blank, if you dare'. This notion, he argued, 'challenges one of those assumptions of society that are so deep-rooted and ancient, they have no name – they are simply lived by' – which in this case was 'man's age-old belief in serial immortality':

> Most people, historically, have *not* lived their lives as if thinking, "I have only one life to live". Instead they have lived as if they are living their ancestors' lives and their offspring's lives and perhaps their neighbors' lives as well. They have seen themselves as inseparable from the great tide of chromosomes of which they are created and which they pass on. The mere

> fact that you were only going to be here a short time and would be dead soon enough did not give you the license to try to climb out of the stream and change the natural order of things. (Wolfe 2023 [1976])

But whereas 50 years ago Wolfe's target was the individual who tried to 'climb out of the stream and change the natural order of things', today we have a much bigger problem. Parents are trying to raise their kids in a context where the 'natural order of things' has been recast as the barrier to the *desired* order of things, in which all individual children have both a right and a responsibility to live their lives 'as a ——!' – and it is the children alone who should 'fill in the blank'. That is the crisis of socialisation.

7

Identity blockers: How label fetishes stop the young from growing up

The story told by this book is one in which the institutions charged with the socialisation of young people in the UK and the US have, gradually but inexorably, turned their focus away from bringing up children into a common culture and towards the promotion of individual 'identities'. This identitarian turn is couched in the language of emancipation, choice, and future orientation; our young people are to be freed from the stultifying conventions of the past, whereby they would have been forced to be the kind of people society wanted them to be. Today our young can be free to be anything they think they can be, 'unburdened by what has been' (in Kamala Harris' much bandied about formula).

It's a lie, of course. We do not grow up in a symbolic, boundless universe in which we construct ourselves like an online avatar – the kind of 'hyperreality' theorised by Baudrillard (1983), where the distinction between reality and simulation is blurred to the point that we come to experience simulation as 'real life'. Despite the ubiquity of social media and the ways this has changed how we interact with one another, we grow up in physical spaces and within concrete relationships: families, communities, friends, and colleagues (Turkle 2015,

Livingstone & Blum-Ross 2020). We might imagine a future for ourselves, but our capacity to live that future is both aided and constrained by our personal limitations and our social location. Even if we did start out as blank slates, our biographies begin to be written early on, and not all by ourselves.

What a good thing that is. Imagine how brittle and lonely life would be if we could indeed dictate and curate everything about our lives as if they existed on Instagram, and how boring it would be to ensure that everybody talked to us in a way that echoed our opinions and our sense of ourselves at any particular moment. And think about how much worse that would be if we were teenagers – already shuttling through the lonely transition from childhood to adulthood and now tasked with bearing responsibility to tell the adults around us how we want to be affirmed.

But the cult of identity that has come to dominate our socialising institutions encourages children and young people into precisely this warped fantasy. Rather than seeking to provide them with the basis to become part of a common society, it flatters and fuels the classic youthful sentiments of being misunderstood, being on the outside, feeling at odds with yourself and with the world around you. In their celebration of shallow consumer identities based on difference and division, socialising institutions undermine young people's capacity to develop the identity that really matters: that of becoming an adult.

As we have discussed throughout, the project of raising children to become adults has always had its difficulties. We cannot look back to any moment in history and say, 'they got it right'. Nor can we point to one distinct cause of the growing up problem today. One challenge in writing this book is that the culture wars stretch back over generations, and the problems they cause cannot be breezily fixed by a change in outlook or policy. The past 30 years of education and family policy show that attempts to resolve the socialisation problem in such ways invariably end up making it worse.

Since we began working on this book, conservative objections to the influence of progressive ideology have become increasingly widely and loudly articulated. To the extent that these voices challenge the disintegrating effects of the 'war on the past' and defend the importance of the aspiration to integrate people into the norms and values associated with western civilisation, they are as welcome as they are necessary. But the conservative reaction has many of its own problems and contradictions, especially when it comes to grappling with what's distinctive about the present moment.

It is with all this in mind that we approach the question of what it means to become a grown-up in today's culture wars. We suggest that the development of an adult identity is bound up with three profound dimensions of social life: work, sex, and politics. The cult of identity interferes with all these dimensions, as it recasts relationships between people as abstracted, individualised character traits. This, in turn, thwarts young people's ability to develop their identity as adult social beings, keeping them trapped in a childlike state of dependence on others for affirmation.

Identity and infantilisation

In *Stop Mugging Grandma*, Jennie explored the curious ambivalence expressed by the Millennial generation – today's 30–40-year-olds, yesterday's benighted youth – about the prospect of growing up (Bristow 2019). The excitement and trepidation traditionally experienced by young people as they reached adulthood was never simply about gaining the legal rights that come with coming of age – to vote, to drink alcohol, to marry. It was about all the things you could finally do with your life: leave the parental home, earn a proper wage, start a life with an intimate partner, have children. You may not do all these things straightaway or at the same time, but they were all within your grasp – wherever you lived, and however rich or clever you were. It was the classic Game of Life that almost everybody wanted to play, and if you didn't like the rules, you could organise to change them. That's what politics was for.

But, for the children of the Baby Boomers, the milestones on the 'winding road' to emerging adulthood (Arnett 2015) had come to be perceived as both unfairly unobtainable and faintly undesirable. The Millennial angst that dominated the cultural narrative of the early noughties complained that the combination of insecure employment, flat wages, and spiralling cost of housing was preventing young people from leaving home and embarking upon coupledom, while the high costs of childcare and the even higher expectations of childrearing were holding them back from starting families of their own.

The Millennials had grounds for these complaints, and such problems continue to afflict youngsters growing into their twenties today. But while economic factors certainly add hurdles on the path to adulthood, the more significant barriers are cultural. Far from being associated positively with the time at which your life should begin, adulthood has become tainted by its association with closed opportunities, burdensome responsibilities, and the mundane tasks of that newly minted verb 'adulting' (Steinmetz 2016). In a society rhetorically in thrall to the cult of youth, adulthood is culturally situated as something to be avoided and apologised for.

Young people have always struggled with the problem of growing up. But since the late 1990s researchers and commentators have raised concerns about the ways in which contemporary culture promotes a curious reluctance even to *want* to become an adult. Andrew Calcutt's (1998) book *Arrested Development* explored the ways in which contemporary pop culture imported the cult of youth that dominated the 1960s counterculture and updated it to a *fin de siècle* yearning for safety over independence and a celebration of alienation over social connection and responsibility.

Jeffrey Arnett's (2000, 2015) influential thesis of 'emerging adulthood' put a positive spin on the phenomenon that others described as 'extended adolescence', positing that a combination of economic and cultural factors had created a 'new and historically unprecedented period of the life course', in which young people were 'neither adolescents nor young adults but something in-between'. Emerging adults were 'taking longer to grow up than young people had in the past, as measured by their entry to stable adult roles as well as their own self-perceptions of not-fully-adult status' (Arnett 2015: viii).

Many recognise that this dynamic does not come from young people themselves; nor does it benefit them. Critical attention has been paid to the process of 'infantilisation' (Furedi 2001, 2017, Hayes & Ecclestone 2008, Neiman 2015, Hayward 2024), whereby young adults are kept childlike through the concern to protect them from the slings and arrows of grown-up life. From the intervention of 'helicopter parents' into their children's lives at work and in college to the proliferation of 'safe spaces' on campuses and the normalisation of therapeutic mechanisms to reduce the anxiety and stresses of young adult life, there is growing recognition that young people's independence and resilience is being compromised by the imperative of overprotection (Bristow, Cant & Chatterjee 2020; Lee et al. 2023; Shrier 2024). The impulse behind this, on the part of individual adults, is often well meaning: nobody likes to see their children struggle and cry. But, in cultural and institutional terms, it comes from a darker place with more serious consequences.

The problem is not so much that young people are taking 'longer' to grow up than they used to, but that western societies have become confused and conflicted about what it means to grow up at all. 'Instability, uncertainty, and a desire to grow, but not grow up and settle down, persist into adults' thirties, forties, fifties, and sixties', explains Steven Mintz (2015: 68–9) in his history of modern adulthood. 'A script that shaped expectations of adulthood through much of the twentieth century has unravelled.'

Keith Hayward's (2024) *Infantilised* draws out some of the negative consequences of this state of things, illustrating the plethora of ways in which contemporary culture signals that we are all to be appealed to as if we were children. This goes beyond the inane emojification of advertisements; increasingly, it is how officials speak to citizens and how organisations message their employees. Hayward describes this trend as a 'cutesy' form of authoritarianism (p. 245), where those in power hide behind the voices and images of children to disarm their audience while simultaneously treating them as recalcitrant five-year-olds. One result is a kind of 'pantomime politics' in which politicians find it difficult to take themselves or their electors seriously.

The focus on identity is intimately bound up with this infantilising culture. Identity work demands protection from challenge and the amplification of grievance. Rather than encouraging individuals to get over themselves and become part of something bigger, it incites them to put their feelings front and centre and appeal to others to organise around them.

Alienated working identities

One area where we can see this situation having a profound impact on today's young is in the workplace, where it undermines the stabilising impact that work has historically had for young people: work develops both the material and the emotional foundation for the transition to adulthood. Here as in so many areas of public life, the idea that we should come together to work around a common interest and a shared sense of purpose is undermined by the fragmentary energy of the culture wars. Rather than focusing on the need to socialise young people into a world outside their own heads, much of contemporary workplace culture actively celebrates alienation.

Schools, universities, and workplaces are all spaces in which young people come to find their place in the world. In education, this has meant integration into their society's common culture through the curriculum, and socialisation into the rules and restrictions of social life via what sociologists like to term the 'hidden curriculum'. While the curriculum taught you what to know, the hidden curriculum taught you the implicit rules about how to behave and be. Obedience to authority, conformity to gender roles, and saying and doing the kind of things that made you popular – or cynically cool – were the kinds of expectations that you absorbed in school and would carry forward into your working life.

You might chafe against the demands of the hidden curriculum, or openly defy them, but you knew these rules were there to be navigated. You did this as an individual, as part of a collective body. The 'correspondence principle' developed by Bowles and Gintis (1977) captured the idea that these implicit social norms and behaviours learnt in school reflected those of the world of work – something that will be familiar to anybody who has dressed conservatively for the office or sucked up to the boss's bad jokes.

The hidden curriculum remains a powerful force in school, university, and work. But its prescriptions have changed in one important respect. Whereas the twentieth-century workers were encouraged to subsume their individual differences under the role of employee, the twenty-first-century workers are cajoled into accentuating their bespoke diversities. We are supposed to bring our 'whole selves' to work, curating the image that others might have of us by demanding that they address us by our chosen pronouns, respect our hidden disabilities, and pay heed to any potential offence caused by a racial microaggression.

This is sold as an entitlement, a basic right to receive 'respect' and 'support' – and when it fails, we are encouraged to snitch on our colleagues to HR, in the same way children are encouraged to tell tales on their classmates to the teacher. It is also sold as a freedom – a way to be who we want to be, rather than kowtowing to the hierarchical structures associated with the bad old days. But there is no freedom here, no actual individuality. Just as radical scholars exposed the hidden curriculum in the 1960s for the way it implicitly reproduced inequalities of class, race, and sex, critics of institutional DEI today point to its reproduction of divisive identitarian agendas and promotion of an unforgiving conformity of speech and etiquette.

For example, the injunction to declare one's pronouns and respect those of others is promoted as an inclusive measure designed to prevent trans people from becoming 'misgendered'. But it necessarily assumes that everybody has a chosen 'gender identity'; and this bemuses and even offends many of us, for whom being a man or a woman is simply something that one is born and raised as. As gender-critical feminists have clarified magnificently, the experience of living one's whole life as a woman or as a man *precisely because you had no choice* has a huge impact on your experience of the world and on who you become (Joyce 2021, Stock 2021, Sullivan & Todd 2024): but this powerfully rooted social identity is pushed aside by the individualising assumption that we should all declare what kind of entity we are at any given moment. This has the effect of unsettling our sense of self, while the fear of unintentionally misgendering our boss, colleague, pupil, or classmate makes us wary of those around us.

The pronouns problem is repeated in all the other ways in which students and workers have to navigate the identity minefield. Is the failure to acknowledge a colleague's ethnicity the hallmark of an egalitarian anti-racist, or is it an insensitive denial of their struggles with difference? If we fail to spot a hidden disability in our dealings with an anxious or unfriendly co-worker and focus on getting the job done, will we be praised for the results or condemned for the process? Motivational bosses remain fond of the catchphrase 'there's no I in team', while workplace policies remind us that every team is made up of diverse individuals whose feelings need to be appropriately managed.

The reorientation of education around the project of the self has played an important role in the fragmentation of the workplace. The explosion in mental health diagnoses in schools has unsettled attempts to impose normal standards of behaviour and achievement and sets in motion a process of identity labelling that accompanies a young person into the world of work. Employers increasingly present themselves as bewildered by the sense of entitlement that graduates seem to exhibit when they demand the right to work at home, during hours of their own choosing; expect that allowance will be made for myriad health conditions and personal circumstances; and insist that their voices and values are affirmed.

For all this, we shouldn't let businesses off the hook. Employers themselves encourage these expectations – both explicitly, via the rhetorical orientation of businesses towards 'values' rather than products or services, and implicitly, via the denigration of age and experience. They have waged their own version of the war against the past by casting the attitudes and working practices of older (more expensive) workers as outdated and inflexible – a barrier to the 'smart' working practices of the younger digital natives, who may not know much but are at least unafraid and unashamed to prompt ChatGPT for the answers. The politics of identity is an easy weapon in the corporate war on older workers, both because it flatters young people's sentiments of generational grievance, laid down in the script of Boomer blaming discussed in Chapter 4, and because it privileges newfangled consumer identities such as neurodiversity and LGBTQIA+ over traditional workplace identities and solidarities related to status or seniority.

Generational tensions and divisions at work became particularly pronounced during and after the pandemic, with the rapid adoption of hybrid working and working from home (WFH). Initially keen to cash in on potential savings on office costs and the opportunities for hi-tech restructuring, companies quickly realised that not only was less work getting done, but it was becoming far more difficult to train younger workers and socialise them into the workplace culture when they were left isolated and dangling on the end of disembodied video calls. But as with all social norms, once a work ethic and routine has been abandoned, bringing it back is easier said than done. Not only did older workers prove reluctant to come back to the office full-time, but the youngsters started demanding the flexibility of WFH as well, convinced that a once normal work routine would damage their physical and mental wellbeing. Disaffected and alienated, young workers boast about wanting 'lazy girl' jobs and practising 'quiet quitting', while looking enviously at friends who make their own bespoke careers through social media influencing.

The most damaging blow yet struck at the socialising potential of work has been directed at the idea that it is a good thing to have a job *at all*. In the UK, there has been much discussion about the extraordinary numbers of young people who are 'economically inactive' – that is, not in work or seeking work. A significant proportion of these youngsters are claiming sickness benefits related to loosely defined mental health conditions (Centre for Social Justice 2025, Latimer, Ray-Chaudhuri, & Waters 2025). One of the culprits here is the operation of the benefits system itself, which – especially since the pandemic – is easy to manipulate and contains perverse disincentives, which deter people from getting back into work even if they want to (Nelson 2024). But a large proportion of the youngsters caught up in this phenomenon are not deliberate skivers or spongers; they have internalised the idea that they are not up to the demands of work and therefore shouldn't have to do it.

Work, in short, has been culturally transformed from an important source of social identity into a threat to one's mental health and personal identity. Those who acknowledge that this is a problem tend to blame it on the attitudes or attributes of the young, and dream up technical solutions: spending more time in the office or less, making more use of technology or less. Rarely are these questions asked: what is it about today's culture that encourages young people to think that they can't work, or don't need to? When young people do roll up their sleeves and get stuck into paid work, why are they encouraged to feel that they really should be doing something else? And if work isn't providing them with the meaning they crave, where else are they looking for it?

'Perpetual postponement' and the problem of procreation

Over the latter part of the twentieth century, much of the debate about work as a source of social identity focused on women. Betty Friedan's (1963) landmark book *The Feminine Mystique*, one of the catalysts for second-wave feminism in the US, diagnosed the problem of middle-class women's dissatisfaction as their exclusion from 'meaningful work' in favour of an idealised role as housewife and mother. She wrote:

> There are aspects of the housewife's role that make it almost impossible for a woman of adult intelligence to retain a sense of human identity, the firm core of self or 'I' without which a human being, man or woman, is not truly alive. (Friedan 1963: 293)

Friedan's concern was that women were infantilised by being sequestered within the domestic sphere of home and childrearing and made dependent on their husbands. Friedan launched the National Organization of Women in order to campaign for equal rights in work. British feminist scholars such as Ann Oakley (1974) similarly focused on the housewife role as both cause and consequence of women's oppression. In both the US and the UK, legislation designed to equalise pay and conditions for working women became the basis of women's further integration into work and the institutions of public life.

It has become fashionable for today's progressives to sneer at second-wave feminism on account of its 'privileging' the experience of white middle-class women and to claim that the experience of women who were also poor, Black, or disabled is neither visible nor improved by a focus on opening up opportunities at work. There is some truth to this, of course, as there is to the argument that a focus on work as the source of personal fulfilment was always a rather one-sided perspective, which downplayed other sources of identity development in public life (Lasch 1997).

Friedan's framing of 'the problem that has no name' in psychological terms ushered in a way of understanding women's oppression as a problem of personal identity that spoke to the crumbling of the distinction between the private and the public, the personal and political – with the implications that we outlined in Chapter 3. Her hyperbolic negativity about the 'comfortable concentration camp' of the home underestimated the importance of marriage and motherhood both to society and to women's development of a sense of themselves as adults. This sparked a conservative backlash brilliantly dramatised in the mini-series *Mrs America*, which deals with the feminists' fight to ratify the Equal Rights Amendment in the 1970s (FX 2020).

But Friedan was writing in a very different time, when many women lacked the opportunity to gain independence and status at work and in public life even if they wanted to. Second-wave feminism did not dictate that women should not become housewives; it sought to open up the option for them to become something else. It was an optimistic approach, which saw women as capable of playing more than one role and regarded fulfilment through work not as an alternative to motherhood but as something that could be achieved as well as raising children and that generally contributed to the sum of human happiness. Sixty years on, this optimistic vision has been displaced by the grim suspicion that it was all a con. While Friedan saw work as a solution to women's anxiety and isolation, work is now frequently depicted as a burdensome source of stress. And, as we discussed in the previous chapter, contemporary parenting culture presents family life in a very similar way.

All this leaves young adults in something of a bind. Most young people are not self-consciously 'anti-family', and they crave the depth and stability that familial relations bring. But they struggle to situate this aspiration in the context of their lives right now, given all the things they feel they should do and achieve before getting there. Whereas in the twentieth century the teenage years were a time of getting ready for adulthood, now it is the twenties – the 'emerging adulthood' years – that are framed in this way. This results in a temporal paradox, where young people – particularly those who are middle class and university-educated – have far longer to play around in the present and establish the foundations for the rest of their lives, yet find themselves panicked by the possibility of fitting it all into a squeezed timeframe.

For young middle-class women, the immediate priority is establishing their career – this has been drummed into them during their time at university and, despite the ambivalence about work mentioned above, starting on a career remains an exciting, if daunting, opportunity. Alongside this are economic factors: once the job is found, the widening gulf between wage levels and the cost of renting or buying a home of one's own fosters an ongoing insecurity about the price of independence and an incentive to stay in the parental home. This anxiety about the cost of maintaining a middle-class standard of living stretches forward into thoughts about having kids 'one day', while the reality of needing to maintain a dual income and the high costs of childcare loom large.

All these are genuine problems, which illustrate how much has changed since Friedan's time. Working motherhood is no longer framed as a choice, but as a mundane reality of juggling time, money, and emotional commitment between two competing domains of life (Hochschild & Machung 2012, Hays 1996). While policy could go much further in helping with the costs of housing and childcare, at least by allowing a slightly better financial footing for the young to embark on starting families of their own, it can't resolve the underlying economic sluggishness that has resulted in this situation (Mullan 2000, 2017). More significantly, policy cannot resolve the cultural tensions that push young people to put off having children – or not have them at all.

There has recently been a remarkable expansion of the discussion on falling birth rates, with 'persistent sub-replacement fertility' recorded not only in the UK and Europe but all over the world (Kotowska et al. 2021: 159). It is beyond the scope of this book to delve into the complex reasons behind this phenomenon: as the political commentator Ros Douthat joked when asked for 'the' explanation, 'there are about 17!' (Oster 2024). It should also be noted that it is inaccurate to paint a picture of a stable past characterised by a prolonged period of birthrate stability, defined by 'replacement birth rates' of around 2.4 children; in reality, low fertility has been a feature of industrialised countries for many decades (McRae 1999, Lesthaeghe 2010).

However, it is worth drawing out some aspects of this phenomenon that reflect and interact with the struggles that young people in the UK and US experience in developing an adult identity. These are, first, the role played by postponement and delay in embarking on having children – the temporal paradox, which 'inevitably means that couples will have fewer children than they would like, and some will not have any' (Proudfoot, Welling, & Glasier 2009: 98). The second is the way in which the imperatives of personal identity construction have contributed to the 'transformation of intimacy' (Giddens 1992), producing a conflict between the social adult identity arising from having committed intimate relationships and children and the cultural self-identity arising from being 'yourself'.

It was observed in 2005 that, for the first time, British women in their early thirties had higher fertility rates than women in their late twenties; a similar trend was observed elsewhere (Kotowska et al. 2021). The UK's Office for National Statistics used the term 'perpetual postponers' as title of a 2004 commentary that emphasised how '[m]ore women in England and Wales are reaching the end of their reproductive careers without having had a live birth', and how 'the increase in childlessness has been the driving force behind the decline in average completed family size in England and Wales' (Berrington 2004: 9). While this trajectory to 'delayed fertility' after the post-war 'baby boom' has persisted ever since the mid-1970s, birth rates have now reached historic lows (Kearney et al. 2022, Simonardottir 2024).

One significant outcome of delayed fertility is that the first two decades of life as an adult have become increasingly 'childfree'. Becoming a parent, for those who do it, has come to be an experience associated with the beginning of what used to be called middle age. Another outcome of this trend towards delayed childbearing is the development of a social norm: that of the 'childfree twenties' and, increasingly, of the 'childfree thirties'. In historical terms, this situation is distinct.

Much media commentary on this trend focuses on women and runs along the lines of 'women are choosing to have children later in life'. This, in turn, leads many conservative commentators to blame reproductive technologies for allowing and encouraging this choice: abortion and contraception for delaying fertility in the first place, and assisted reproductive technologies – in vitro fertilisation (IVF), donor insemination, and egg freezing – for providing women with the opportunity to have children without a partner and beyond their natural fertile years (Perry 2022, Harrington 2024a). But while women's choices clearly have an impact on fertility trends, what commentary often misses is that it still takes two to make a baby – and the problem facing women today is often finding a partner to make one with.

For example, Proudfoot and colleagues' (2009: 98) exploration of why childless women over the age of 33 wish to use contraception noted that most were aware of the risks of delayed childbirth, but 'the most common reason for delay concerned lack of the "right" partner, something that does not lend itself to interventions'. Kearney and colleagues (2022: 169) conclude that their empirical analyses of the sustained post-2007 decline in US birth rates do not uncover a 'readily identifiable, contemporaneous cause'; and this leads them to speculate that the key explanation may lie in 'shifting priorities across cohorts of young adults' related to 'the way these cohorts were raised and how they experienced their childhoods' – rather than in a particular policy or cost factor.

It is tempting to extrapolate from these explanations a direct relationship with the culture wars issues hotly debated today: in particular, the growing polarisation of attitudes between young men and women, and trends in young people's self-identification as gay, bisexual, transgender, or non-binary. From the perspective of social reproduction, these trends are certainly troublesome – and they contribute to the difficulties experienced by Gen Z in finding its place in the world. But we should be careful not to read current debates into historical trends and leap at one-sided explanations. One obvious consequence of delayed fertility is that the data on birth rates (as opposed to fertility intentions) described here pertain to the Millennial generation, with trends stretching back to Gen X; and they are already anticipated by developments in the 1960s.

The contradictions of childfree adulthood

The interplay of the factors involved in the low fertility characteristic of western societies since the 1970s was carefully and brilliantly theorised by Ron Lesthaeghe in 2010, in his discussion of 'the second demographic transition'. 'Demographic transition' is a term used to describe change in population size and shape. It is a process that began back in the late eighteenth century, first in western countries and then, from the 1950s, in 'much of the rest of the world' (Lesthaeghe 2010: 211). Classically, demographic transition is associated with economic and social development: fewer children die in infancy and people live longer and healthier lives, meaning that there is less urgency for families and societies to 'replace' themselves. An important feature of this transition is that it occurred *prior to* the development of hormonal contraception, at a time when the means to prevent pregnancy were much less readily available than now.

According to Lesthaeghe (2010, 2014), the second demographic transition began in the 1970s and was the outcome of social, economic, technological, and cultural developments that had begun in the 1960s. These included the transformative influence of the pill, the legalisation of abortion, changes to education and to employment, especially for women, and increased migration. The balance between economic pressures and socio-cultural changes is also emphasised by Hobcraft (1996: 518). Writing about England and Wales and the 'baby bust' that followed the 'baby boom' of the 1960s, he explained that economic downturn served 'to reinforce an already low level of fertility, rather than inducing the change'. Alongside structural and material changes, Hobcraft noted the importance of 'ideas, cultures, attitudes and beliefs', which are 'more intangible, but there is strong circumstantial evidence that they exert important influences on fertility behaviour'.

The cultural significance of the 1960s, as discussed in Chapter 2, was the focus on individual and choice in personal life. According to Lesthaeghe (2010: 216), the 'sexual', 'gender', and 'contraceptive' revolutions took place within 'the framework of a rejection of authority and an overhaul of the normative structure' and, as such, impacted the subjective outlooks that influence childbearing. The motivation for choosing to have children became *'adult self-realisation'* (Lesthaeghe 2010: 213, our emphasis). This speaks to the formation of a kind of adulthood and sense of how it might be realised that were very different from their counterparts at previous points in history. Underpinned by a far greater expansion of choice, at the level of individual, regarding what to do in life and how to live it, the generational relationship and its purpose became differently calibrated.

From the 1970s onwards, bearing children and taking responsibility for them as the embodiment of the future became much more associated with how adults saw their future lives unfolding. As Ann Furedi (2021) explains in *The Moral Case for Abortion*, personal autonomy became more centrally situated and, with it, the individual responsibility for decision-making. If you could proactively plan your family – at least in terms of the number of children to have and when to have them – this logically required you to plan that other aspects of your life – partner, career, income – would provide you and your family with the best shot at happiness. And, up until the 1990s, there remained some optimism that happiness was in your grasp. For all the bitching and moaning about the latchkey kids of working mums and the problem of rising divorce rates and broken homes, people procreated on the assumption that it would all work out somehow.

But the sharp decline in fertility observed from the late 1990s was not merely a continuation of the shifts that marked the second demographic transition. 'On the eve of the new millennium', observed Scott (1999: 68–9), it seemed that 'old certainties are fast disappearing'; indeed, 'in just one generation, there have been dramatic changes in family life'. This period, as we discussed in the previous chapter, was characterised by a shift in the way in which policy and discourse framed the family, as the rise of the 'parenting regime' put a harsh spotlight on the responsibilities and difficulties faced by individual parents. Rather than family formation and childbirth being framed as a good thing for young adults to do and as something it was assumed that young adults *would* do, this whole endeavour was presented as a risky decision, which individuals took at their peril. The prospect of becoming a parent became disenchanted through associated warnings about losing out, feeling depressed, and not being up to the job.

The perception has been powerfully inculcated that 'parenting' is sufficiently high stakes and risky to be incompatible with most of what life in one's twenties or even early thirties is like. To be a parent, it is assumed that a person must be a sort of super adult, and then undergo training on top of that. What it means to be a responsible parent has changed from something you do when you feel ready and you learn to do with your peers to something you become when the time is perfect and you are prepared to be trained into (Gatrell 2005, Lee et al. 2023). This, in turn, has changed perceptions of contraception: while it gave previous generations of young women the freedom to avoid pregnancy at the wrong time or with the wrong person, now 'the decision to have children has been perceived increasingly as an individual's willing acceptance of these parental responsibilities' (Ruckdeschel 2024).

In policy terms, the nervousness and negativity surrounding parenthood was most explicit in the war on teenage pregnancy in the UK and US during the 1990s and early 2000s. As the literature observes, this trend was unrelated to changes to the objective incidence of conceptions: in the UK for example, at the point at which teenage pregnancy became an explicit policy concern, its rate was static and lower than it had been previously (Arai 2009). Rather, age had become identified by a range of claims-makers as a marker of 'unfitness' for motherhood and as a focal point for the case about the dangerousness of pregnancy and childbirth. Indeed, as Macvarish and Billings (2010: 50) observe, '[s]uch [was] the strength of the idea that young parenthood is inherently disastrous for mothers, babies and society, that at times policy . . . seemed to verge on a "zero tolerance" position on teenage pregnancy'.

Although the policy language around teenage pregnancy was coy, the problem was clearly conceptualised as one of class. The small proportions of women who, back in the 1990s, were having babies under the age of 20 tended to be working class. 'Throughout the developed world, teenage pregnancy is more common amongst young people who have been disadvantaged in childhood and have poor expectations of education or the job market', noted a report by the UK government's Social Exclusion Unit in 1999. One rationale for its launching the Teenage Pregnancy Strategy was that it would counter 'low expectations':

> One reason why the UK has such high teenage pregnancy rates is that there are more young people who see no prospect of a job and fear they will end up on benefits one way or the other. Put simply, they see no reason not to get pregnant. (Social Exclusion Unit 1999: 7)

The idea that preventing young working-class women from becoming pregnant would foster middle-class aspirations to engage in higher education and work was always rather fanciful. A quarter of a century on, we can see that the outcome of the Teenage Pregnancy Strategy – described by the commentator Polly Toynbee (2013) as 'the success story of our time' – was a plummeting number of births to women under 20, and also between the ages of 20 and 30. At the same time, as discussed above, anxieties about the growing proportion of 'economically inactive' under-thirties languishing on benefits have grown.

But the problem of teenage pregnancy was not only about class: it was also framed explicitly as a problem of age. The term 'teenage pregnancy' brought with it the assumption that children were having babies, although most of these births happened to women aged 17 and 18, and the discussion often slipped into a worry about young motherhood in general. The anxiety was that these young adults were unprepared to accept the responsibilities of adulthood – which by this point meant waiting until one was in an optimal personal situation to accept the rigour of the 'parenting regime'. Not surprisingly, the upshot of all this was to fuel the idea that, overall, one could never feel ready to have a child – and that growing up somehow happened prior to, and separately from, becoming an adult.

The dynamic underlying all this was a reframing of the notion of adult self-realisation. Up until the 1990s, the realisation of adulthood was bound up with the assumption of motherhood and fatherhood. Tacitly, and often explicitly, taking responsibility for children was inherent in the idea of becoming an adult. This didn't mean just assuming that most people would have families of their own, but believing that all adults would play a role in the education and socialisation of children in their communities. But with the development of the idea of emerging adulthood and the 'childfree twenties', a situation arose in which young adults were no longer expected to take responsibility for children – and, in many ways, were cautioned against doing so. Adult self-realisation became reframed as, and reduced to, the protection of one's personal identity against the relationships and responsibilities that might constrain one's freedom to become whatever one wanted to be. This included not only children but sex and intimate relationships.

Sex, fear, and gender identity

At the same time as the monstering of teenage mothers, a significant shift happened in the discussion of sexual relationships. By the 1970s, abortion and contraception had technically allowed the separation of sexual intercourse from reproduction, at least to the extent that sex didn't have to lead to bearing an unwanted child. The 'transformation of intimacy' (Giddens 1992) that took place from the 1990s brought the possibility of the *cultural* separation of sex from reproduction, in the sense that sex became portrayed as an act that was predominantly about self-identity and satisfaction, rather than something that implied an intimate relationship that might stretch forward into something more.

A number of influential social theorists have analysed the impact of social and cultural changes around the millennium on conceptions of love, intimacy, and family life. So-called individualisation theorists situated these changes in the context of an increasingly insecure and atomised 'risk society' (Beck 1992), where traditional values had eroded in favour of new lifestyles based on consumerism and choice and intimate relations became 'democratised'. Traditional authority relations between the generations, and boundaries between femininity and masculinity, motherhood and fatherhood, childhood and adulthood, became open to question and revision (Giddens 1992, Beck & Beck-Gernsheim 1995, Beck-Gernsheim 2002, Bauman 2013).

The most prominent theorist to analyse these as positive changes was Anthony Giddens (1992: 2), who developed the concept of 'plastic sexuality': a 'decentred sexuality, freed from the needs of reproduction', which 'can be moulded as a trait of personality and thus is intrinsically bound up with the self'. This gave rise to a 'transformation' of intimate relationships and the emergence of 'confluent love': an emotional connection that is risky and reflexive, active and contingent, and 'jars with the "for-ever", "one-and-only" qualities of the romantic love complex' (p. 61). Giddens also theorised the 'pure relationship', which was shaped by trust and emotional interaction within the couple rather than by external demands or standards. The pure relationship implied therapeutic relations of intimacy guided less by duty and more by negotiation between individuals.

Not all the 'individualisation theorists' were so upbeat about this shift. In *The Normal Chaos of Love,* Beck and Beck-Gernsheim (1995) warned that atomisation led to family fragmentation and to thinner, more temporary and insecure relationships. This increased the pressure on the family, as people focused on home as the only site of potential constancy and fulfilment, echoing Gillis' (1997) point about the difficulties caused by the conflation of 'the families we live with' with 'the families we live by'. They also observed the increased pressure this brought to parenting, as, when intimate partnerships become more fraught and temporary, 'the child becomes the last remaining, irrevocable, unique primary love object. Partners come or go, but the child stays' (Beck & Beck-Gernsheim 1995: 37). Charlotte Faircloth's (2021) study of Millennial couples who attempt to practise the newly democratised, equitable, and self-fulfilling strictures of the pure relationship reveals the contradictions and dissatisfactions that come to the fore when these notions are applied to the messy, practical, and unpredictable daily business of raising children.

Other critical scholars have argued that cultural shifts do not lead directly or always observably to changes in people's behaviour or experiences and that the 'pure relationship' expressed the construction of a new 'ideal type' family, which was not supported by empirical research (Jamieson 1998, Lewis 2001). In this ideal type, the degree of individual choice was exaggerated and the level of obligation to children and other families was downplayed, particularly in the experience of working-class women. Hochschild's (2003) discussion of the commercialisation of intimate life points to the rationalisation of love as an emotion out of sync with the individualising dynamics of late modern capitalism. She emphasises that the key shift is not that 'people enter relationships more lightly' than they used to or that they 'think shallow connections are better than deeper ones', but rather that 'one important strategy of emotional management *is to develop the ability to limit emotional connection since this strategy adapts us to survival in a destabilizing culture of capitalism*' (Hochschild 2003: 125).

These observations provide an important balance to considering how cultural individuation frames the predicament of Gen Z today. We should not leap on cultural trends as the single reason for why this cohort seems to be having less sex, identifying as non-heterosexual, and thinking that it is totally fine to identify as a gender different from their biological sex. Individuals are not pure expressions of cultural trends – and only when the young have grown up will we be able to see exactly how these trends have intersected with fertility rates, family formation, and expressions of intimacy. As we discuss towards the end of the chapter, the twists and turns in this latest phase of the culture wars are taking young people's orientation to both public and private life in all kinds of directions, and it would be premature to predict any one dominant outcome.

But we can certainly make some observations about how this cultural context has framed the ideas about intimacy and adulthood into which today's young have been socialised. In her review of sex education in British schools during the 1990s, Sarah Moore (2012) drew attention to the way sex was presented to teenagers as a danger to their personal health and emotional wellbeing. At the time, this took 'two distinctive forms': a focus on the risks of HIV/AIDS and teenage pregnancy; and 'a non-curricular sex education based on a discourse of emotional wellbeing and personal development'. 'Far from being mutually exclusive, these two forms of education have, in recent years, started to overlap', argued Moore, as '[m]astering a certain style of emotional expression is regularly framed as a means of avoiding "high risk" sexual encounters and teenage sex is often described as damaging one's emotional wellbeing'. In critiquing these developments, Moore (2012: 25) argued: 'Sex and relationship education prescribes a certain emotional disposition, mystifies sex for young people, and transforms teenage pregnancy and sexually transmitted infections into problems of emotional maturity.'

Self-consciously detached from the moralised discourses that traditionally framed underage or 'casual' sex, the adoption of a discourse of risk promoted a highly individualised wariness of both sex and intimate relationships. Over a decade later, this approach has become thoroughly institutionalised and has expanded in such forms as 'comprehensive sexuality education', defined by UNESCO (2023: 1) as 'a curriculum-based process of teaching and learning about the cognitive, emotional, physical and social aspects of sexuality' that

> aims to equip children and young people with knowledge, skills, attitudes and values that will empower them to: realize their health, well-being and dignity; develop respectful social and sexual relationships; consider how their choices affect their own well-being and that of others; and understand and ensure the protection of their rights throughout their lives.

As Joanna Williams (2024a: 8) writes, proponents of sexuality education view it as providing 'an effective means of reducing the risks associated with sexual activity' that 'helps cultivate positive attitudes towards sex, sexuality, relationships, gender equality and gender identity'. However, she argues, there are a number of reasons to be concerned about this approach – not least the extent to which it sexualises children, imbuing them with the kind of emotions and capacities around sex and sexuality that are developed through adulthood.

Contemporary culture's approach to young people, sex, and sexuality has thus become thoroughly confused. On one hand, children are taught from an early age to regard both sex and intimate emotional relationships as a danger, on the premise that growing up should not be about developing relationships beyond yourself, but about learning to safeguard against incursions on your personal identity and autonomy. On the other, they are encouraged to view all kinds of emotions and experiences through the prism of sexuality – as though how they feel about their playground friends, or their bodies, or the stuff they watch on social media constitutes an affirmation of, or an attack on, their sexual identity. Sex and sexuality are constituted simultaneously as the most fundamental feature of your identity and as something abstract and alien to what you do with other people. It is sexualisation without sex.

The separation of sex and sexuality from relationships via the cultivation of sexual identity in children may be one reason why today's teenagers find it plausible to identify as gay or bisexual even if they have never had a relationship with, or romantic feelings for, somebody of the same sex. If sexual identity is mainly in the mind – and if openness to all things queer is the approved attitude – why would you select anything else from the drop-down menu? This may also suggest that one of the drivers behind the cult of transgender identification is that it allows for the cultivation of a sexualised identity that protects you from the complications bound up with intimate relationships, as your identity becomes fully expressed by how you feel about yourself, rather than how you may feel about others.

Of course, a complex set of additional factors is involved in the transgender trend, just as in the adoption of a range of sexual and gender identities (asexual, pansexual, nonbinary, furry, etc.) that were unknown in the twentieth century. As emphasised above, individuals are not only the expression of cultural trends, and a sensitive exploration of the gender identity crisis among today's young people should avoid jumping to single, pat explanations (Shrier 2020, Barnes 2023, Cass 2024). But, as part of our discussion about growing up in the culture wars, we should acknowledge the powerful hold that these ideas have over the ways in which young people have been socialised to think and talk about sex, relationships, and identity – and that these ideas have become disturbingly detached from the kind of adult identity that is grounded in the aspiration to reproduction.

In this context, it is intriguing to observe the forms taken by the conservative backlash against this sexless sexualisation. They range from an apparent resurgence of chastity (or 'voluntary celibacy'), through a hankering for strictly defined gender roles in the home (the 'tradwife' phenomenon), to the kind of positive pronatalism articulated by the late Charlie Kirk: more people should get married young and have more kids than they can afford. For those of us who grew up in the 1970s and 1980s, when 'sexual liberation' resonated with women's struggle to gain equality and independence, the attraction, to young women, of the idea of domestic subservience and fulfilment through breeding seems naïve at best and frightening at worst. Sexual equality and freedom took centuries to achieve – could it really be overturned in a couple of generations?

Cautionary tales abound, such as that of the radical Canadian right-winger Lauren Southern, who tried to live out the tradwife dream with terrible real-life consequences, including an abusive marriage from which she had to escape into a period of poverty and precarity (Harrington 2024b). The overturning of *Roe v Wade* in the US represents a major setback for the idea that women have a right to control their fertility: as Ann Furedi (2022) argues, while this won't stop women from having abortions, it has dragged women's bodies and choices back to the centre of the culture wars, politicising what should be private decisions.

But rather than falling down the rabbit hole of *Handmaid's Tale* fantasies, we should consider what lies behind the conservative reaction's appeal to sections of Gen Z. In pushing back against the alienating fantasies promoted by progressives and pushed by centrist policymakers, the conservative reaction expresses a demand for meaning, security, and adult leadership. While we can argue about the forms this should take, the tendency to represent this reaction as illegitimate and dangerous significantly underestimates the threat posed by the celebration of insecure personal identities to our young people's ability to thrive. If there is anything positive to say about growing up in the culture wars today, it is that these big questions of meaning are now, finally, coming back into the public arena for discussion. This presents Gen Z with both a massive problem and a huge opportunity.

Cultural insecurity and the quest for meaning

The development of an adult identity through sexual relationships and parenthood depends on decisions and dynamics in the private sphere of life. This is why it is always problematic – and counterproductive – for commentators and policymakers to start meddling with teenage pregnancy, sex and relationships education, or birth rates. As we have indicated, it exposes these intimate areas to a public and politicised gaze and makes it harder for people to work matters out for themselves (Jenkins 2025). At the same time, intervention in the pre-political domain is a distraction from the problem of public life: the sense of integration into a society with a common purpose. This, above all, is where Gen Z is struggling.

The Millennials' obsession with identity was driven by an insecure sentiment of entitlement. 'We were raised to dream big', writes Kamenetz (2006: 93) of US college graduates, in her extended whinge, *Generation Debt: Why Now Is a Terrible Time to Be Young.* When the dream crashed against a reality of 'job erosion, temp hell, the intern trap, low pay, no benefits, and the uncertain quest for a fulfilling career', the result was 'chronic dissatisfaction'. One reason why sensitivities around identity were so marked among the most privileged sections of youth, university educated and working in sectors such as journalism and publishing, was a desperate attempt to hold on to that sense that they were, indeed, unique and special – and that this was what society wanted from them.

The Millennials were the last generation to grow up in the post-war liberal order. Initially feted as its bright-eyed saviours, its oldest members approached adulthood during the nineties tech bubble, the end of the Cold War, and the ascendancy of the centrist Third Way politics of Clinton and Blair. This generation is lauded for its open minds and its attachment to open borders, qualities seen to relate to 'its racial and ethnic diversity'. This in turn would allegedly provide a 'demographic bridge to America's diverse future' that would 'pave the way for the generations behind them as workers, consumers, and leaders in business and government in their acceptance by and participation in tomorrow's more racially diverse America' (Frey 2018: 4).

Even when the sunny uplands of the 'end of history' darkened with the terrorist outrage of 9/11 in 2001 and the GFC of 2008, the Millennials clung stubbornly to the dream of technocratic consumerism. They voted overwhelmingly against Brexit, arguing bitterly that the result should be weighted more in their favour, as it was unfair to make them live with choices made 'by people who have already lived their lives' (Graham-Harrison 2016, Bristow 2019: 166–7). They didn't want change: they just wanted real life to match up to the consumer fantasy they had been sold. As Kamenetz (2006: xv) opined:

> I don't think it's America's self-image that's wrong. It's the gulf that has grown up between ideal and reality. Mom, Dad, listen up: Things have changed. We're not doing as well as you did. And if something doesn't change soon, it's unlikely that we ever will.

Gen Z has a somewhat different set of problems. The Millennials were famously encouraged to think of themselves as special, fragile 'snowflakes' who struggled to cope once real life didn't deliver everything they had been raised to think they were entitled to; but at least they weren't incited to believe that they were born in the wrong body and to cut off their breasts. The sentiment of grievance and victimhood had been firmly established for the Millennials via the idea that their parents, the Boomer generation, had experienced nothing but good things while growing up and had left their kids to deal with the problems; but at least they weren't schooled in the idea that western history was nothing but an exercise in colonialist exploitation requiring a constant performance of atonement and 'grievance archaeology' in the present day (Furedi 2024).

But while it would be easy to slip into a litany of the ways in which Gen Z has it worse than the Millennials, that would be a mistake. Not only would it lead to the dead end of generationalism, which made Millennial commentators into whiny victims and has scripted a bleak, fatalistic situation for the 'Covid generation'; it would miss what is genuinely distinct about the historical moment that Gen Z finds itself in.

Even before the Covid-19 pandemic, Gen Z was culturally framed with reference to the *Hunger Games* – a dystopian young adult book and movie series in which children from impoverished districts of a fictional country are selected to compete in a televised death match (Collins 2009). Noting that the internet styled the Millennials 'a bunch of entitled, attention-hungry, selfie-taking adults who believe they deserve – and can achieve – whatever they want', an article in *Teen Vogue* (Webster 2016) contrasted that portrait with Noreena Hertz's investigation into the plight of Gen Z – which Hertz (2016) preferred to call 'Generation K', after the *Hunger Games* heroine Katniss Everdeen: 'Like Katniss, they feel the world they inhabit is one of perpetual struggle – dystopian, unequal and harsh.' Hertz went on to offer the bleak examples that have now become familiar: not only economic insecurity and rising debt, but rising levels of anxiety and loneliness, the ubiquity of phones and social media, declining levels of social trust, and lack of faith in the meritocratic promises of the social contract.

As we noted in Chapter 4, much of the discussion about generations is symbolic – so it is not surprising that dystopian young adult fiction becomes a reference point for generalisations about a whole cohort. Yet by 2020 the world was in the grip of its real-life dystopia, as the response to the Covid-19 pandemic brought the tensions of the dying days of the post-war liberal order rushing out into the open. The institutions of centrist technocracy became openly authoritarian – not only by locking down their populations but by doubling down on their desperate attempts to construct a future in line with their post-material values: they shut down the discussion of all manner of issues via policies that demanded 'respect' and 'kindness'. The institutions of education, which were already doing a terrible job of socialising the Millennials, literally collapsed during the pandemic and, during recovery, have gone further than ever in encouraging the state of cultural fragmentation.

We are living through an historical hiatus, in which, as Gramsci put it in the 1930s, 'the old world is dying, and the new world struggles to be born' (quoted in Žižek 2010). 'Now is the time of monsters', warned Gramsci back then, referring to the morbid symptoms of societal collapse. A century on, a number of different monsters are bearing down on us, and we have named some of them in this book. The most terrifying is the cultural nihilism that has turned our education systems into engines of disintegration, attempting to socialise young people into the conviction that western culture is not a heritage to be absorbed and renewed, but an evil force to be resisted and destroyed. When elite kids on college campuses call to 'globalise the intifada', they are not really talking about Palestine – they are expressing alienation from their own culture and offering themselves up as a sacrifice.

The other monsters lie closer to home – in the parenting regime that seeks to detach children from their parents, in the identitarian re-presentation of intimacy that seeks to detach young people from one another, in the discouragement of having children of one's own, in the various ways in which young people are encouraged to internalise the difficulties and contradictions of our times as problems generated by their own mental health and failure to cope. This does not only lead to a lonely, alienating existence; it blocks young people from developing a stable adult identity, where they feel secure in the world and prepared to take responsibility for it. The tragedy of the Millennials was not only that they were infantilised in these ways but that infantilisation was celebrated and sought after. The opportunity for Gen Z lies in the fact that this stifling comfort blanket has been ripped away, and nobody is even pretending to look after them.

Conclusion

Infantilisation does not simply mean that young people are treated like children for longer than they should be. It effectively means that adults are collectively reduced to a childlike status; they are dependent on the affirmation, permission, and 'support' they receive from official agencies and assorted experts. One effect of this is to weaken the cultural distinction between adults and children. Hayward (2024) observes that, paradoxically, for all the exaggeration of generational differences and conflict, the actual situation is better described as a 'generational mulch' in which it is increasingly difficult to see where the differences in behaviour and expectations lie between adults and children.

Generational mulch is often indulged as a cute recognition of how much more tolerant and relaxed we are than in the days when *Harry Potter* would have been regarded merely as a series of children's books and parents would never have thought of considering their kids as friends. In reality, it leads to a warped kind of 'adultification', whereby children are simultaneously discouraged from growing up and regarded as though they were adults already. The dilemma confronting Gen Z is that the 'adults in the room' have essentially checked out, leaving it to the kids to find their own ways of making sense of the world – and to find a meaning to their lives.

In speculating on how they are going to do that, we have to take care not to rush to premature conclusions. As observed throughout this book, the culture wars are moving very fast, and whole cohorts never respond to events in the same way (Mannheim 1952). When we see sections of Gen Z glorying in the death of Charlie Kirk, calling for the globalisation of the intifada, and claiming that it is acceptable to use violence to prevent a public speaker from speaking at a university campus, we can worry that young people's response to the nihilism of the moment will be to push it further towards destruction. When we see reports of record numbers of young people flocking to Christianity, voting for right-wing populist parties, and reasserting 'traditional' ideas of masculinity and femininity, we can worry that they are looking back into a mystified past to find a solution to the problems of the present.

We can interpret indicators of increasing political polarisation between young men and women and worry about whether these kids will ever find a way of being together. We can obsess on the madnesses of social media and torment ourselves with the fear that young people have lost touch with reality altogether. Then we can look around us at the kids hanging out together at school, festivals, gyms, and clubs and comfort ourselves that it's all fine really and that the culture wars are merely a weird, confected online panic.

But in the end we need to face up to the fact that this combination of self-indulgent catastrophising and wishful thinking is what has brought us to this place; and its time is over. The fragmentary trends behind the culture wars have been developing for decades, and there is little point in hoping that they can be turned around tomorrow. But their effects are now out in the open, providing a space in which all ideas about change can be developed in all kinds of directions. We should be trying neither to predict nor to control how Gen Z will work up its experience of these febrile times: rather we should turn the focus back on ourselves and consider what we can do to support our young people in their battles against the monsters of postmodernity.

8

Starting a conversation

We began our discussion of growing up in the culture wars by diagnosing the two big problems of our time as cultural pessimism and panic-stricken presentism. Western societies have allowed themselves to slide into an unapologetic state of gloom about our capacity to do anything bold and creative to tackle the big problems that have been ratcheting up for a long time, from moribund economies and spiralling national debt to political fragmentation and rising tensions both within and between nations.

At the same time, western elites and social institutions have failed to confront the questions at the heart of the culture wars: what our societies stand for and what it means to be a part of them. They have evaded these questions by embracing fragmentation in the name of 'diversity' and by fuelling trends towards individuation and division through the promotion of 'identity'. In their quest to paper over the cracks and maintain their position as the leaders and managers of today, they have disowned their societies' cultural heritage and, with it, the knowledge, values, and social bonds that could give young people the security to discover who they are and what they want to become. The critical, shock-absorbing institutions of socialisation – education and the family – have been weakened and weaponised by the conceit that children need to break free of the past if they are to adapt to the demands of the modern world. Our irresponsible elites have used the language of 'the future' to sell out our tomorrow.

So what can we do? We imagine that the starting point for anybody who reads this book has been a concern about the predicament of our young: if you thought that everything was just fine, you wouldn't bother reading about it. Likewise, our motivation for writing was not to offer some lofty sociological insights on why things are so messy and confusing for the teenagers and young adults known as Gen Z. As parents and teachers, we wanted to understand the problem so we can help to address it. This puts us in something of a bind.

We can't shy away from the understanding that the difficulties facing kids today have their roots in a long-running, slow-motion moral collapse, which began before they were born and shows no signs of being resolved anytime soon. Nor, as we noted in the Introduction, can our concluding chapter offer a fashionable 'how to' list of expert tips. As we have shown, this kind of initiative has done a lot to make the problems worse, presenting societies' struggles with socialisation as individuals' failures to adopt a particular kind of teaching method or parenting style.

But we can offer some suggestions as to how to think constructively about the issues that have become so fraught and febrile, and how to develop those conversations across the generations.

Helping our young to weather the storm of the culture wars requires us to do two things simultaneously: to step back and to lean in. Whatever it is that worries us most – be it social media or transgender identification, climate change or the impact of the Covid lockdowns, the rise in mental health problems or the increase in political polarisation, or anything else – we should avoid the compulsion simply to react to the slogans and memes coming from the progressive left or the identitarian right and spend more time thinking about them and discussing the ideas behind them.

The young are not the only ones to demonstrate the simplistic, 'dichotomous' thinking (Twenge 2023) characteristic of current debates, and this is not only a feature of social media. When politicians take the knee to show 'solidarity' with BLM, universities fly Pride flags, police officers display pronouns to perform their commitment to 'inclusion', and British pensioners offer themselves up for arrest by protesting in support of Just Stop Oil or Palestine Action, it's clear that the kids are not the generals of the culture wars, but their conscripts. In our experience, young people tend to be more open to thinking through the tensions and contradictions of the fashionable 'omnicauses' than are many older people. This is partly because they are young and open to exploring what they don't yet know. It's also because of the temper of the times: as we have shown throughout this book, the unstable character of cultural conflicts means that positions, motivations, and ideas can change overnight.

As discussed in Chapter 4, the condition of being young means that the teenagers and emerging adults confront experiences, issues, and ideas for the first time. During periods of rapid social change, this can result in a schism between the generations, as young people, being closer to the problems of their time, 'are dramatically aware of a process of destabilization and take sides in it', while 'the older generation cling to the re-orientation that had been the drama of *their* youth' (Mannheim 1952: 301). This febrile situation is made worse by the ways in which members of older generations tend to panic in the face of a confrontation with new developments and interpret arguments and events as though they were the same as they were in the 1970s or 1980s.

Viewed through the lens of the progressive movements associated with the 1960s, flying the English or British flag can seem like a straightforward statement of racism, flying the Pride flag can seem like a statement of tolerance, and the machinery of DEI can appear as a way of safeguarding equality at work. This blinds us to what has changed; and when we load these assumptions onto the young, we, rather than engaging with what actually is going on, are essentially asking them to believe a fictionalised account of what we think should be happening.

So, instead of leaping to conclusions about current events and loudly demanding that the young should accept them, we should first take a moment to step back and listen to what they are saying. Young people – like older people – are a heterogeneous group with very different ideas and experiences; second-guessing what a young person is bound to think about any particular issue betrays the same kind of ignorant arrogance as 'OK Boomer'. We can learn a lot from the ways in which they are working up their experience of the present hiatus, and the aim of the generational transaction should not be to score points. In our increasingly fractious society pluralism, tolerance, and good faith matter more than ever.

At the same time we should be less hesitant about leaning into the culture wars, engaging in these messy and difficult discussions, and trying to provide some perspective and clarity where we can. For too long, there has been a tendency to avoid engaging in the debates that exercise the young, either because we're nervous about offending them or because we have bought into the progressivist conceit that any idea that originated before the late 1990s stands in the way of the more enlightened perspective of today's youth. By removing ourselves from the battlefields, we flatter the young that they have all the answers when, in reality, all we're doing is desertion.

Young people are as entitled to hear the views of their elders as we are to air them. That's how conversation works. So, whatever happens next in the culture wars, let's keep talking.

Notes

Notes to Chapter 3

1 Legislation included the Civil Rights Act (1964) in the US and the 1965 Race Relations Act in the UK; *Roe v Wade* (1973) in the US and the 1967 Abortion Act in the UK; and the 1970 Equal Pay Act and 1975 Sex Discrimination Act in the UK.

Notes to Chapter 4

1 Because generation labels are cultural constructions, analysts differ in the birth dates they assign to each cohort. This box draws on the dates and definitions offered by the Resolution Foundation (UK), the Pew Research Center (US), and Twenge (2023), among others.

2 The traits that Twenge ascribes to Gen Z are: 'gender fluidity'; 'more lesbian, gay, and bisexual people'; 'less sexually active'; 'growing up slowly'; 'delayed adulthood'; 'restricting speech'; 'interest in physical and emotional safety'; 'racial consciousness'; 'dissatisfied and depressed'; 'more online communication'; 'less likely to be physically healthy'; 'pessimism'; 'perceiving discrimination and having an external locus of control'; 'political polarization'; 'political activism and increased voter turnout'; 'liberal unhappiness and depression'; 'shaped by the pandemic'.

3 Twenge (2023: 7, Fig. 1.1) presents an historical periodisation that shows how ‘certain technological developments have ultimately led to behavioral and attitude changes far beyond the device itself’. The items involved are: television (1947–1990), home appliances (microwaves, washing machines, refrigerators) (1947–1985), air conditioning (1950s–1980s), birth control (1960–1969), computer technology (1964–2005), internet news (2000–2010), and social media (2006–2015).

Bibliography

Anonymous (2025a) 'A racist mob menacing refugee children and our town: Read this and see what lies ahead, unless we act now'. *Guardian*, 9 September. https://www.theguardian.com/commentisfree/2025/sep/09/racist-mob-menacing-refugee-children-far-right.

Anonymous (2025b) 'Faversham Community clean up'. Leaflet distributed to Faversham households, September.

Arai, L. (2009) *Teenage Pregnancy: The Making and Unmaking of a Problem.* Policy Press.

Arendt, H. (2006 [1961]) *Between Past and Future: Eight Exercises in Political Thought.* Penguin.

Arnett, J.J. (2000) 'Emerging adulthood: A theory of development from the late teens through the twenties'. *American Psychologist* 55(5): 469–80.

Arnett, J.J. (2015) *Emerging Adulthood: The Winding Road from the Late Teens through the Twenties.* Oxford University Press.

Asher, J. (2007) *Thirteen Reasons Why.* Penguin.

Badshah, N. (2025) 'Oxford Union condemns president-elect's reported comments on Charlie Kirk shooting'. *Guardian*, 11 September. https://www.theguardian.com/education/2025

/sep/11/oxford-union-condemns-president-elects-reported-comments-on-charlie-kirk-shooting.

Ball, E. (2021) 'The tension between Elias' informalisation of parenting and the reformalisation of parenting interventions'. *People, Place and Policy* 15(1): 1–18.

Barnes, H. (2023) *Time to Think: The Inside Story of the Collapse of the World's Largest Gender Service for Children*. Pitchstone Publishing.

Baudrillard, J. (1983) *Simulacra and Simulation*, trans. by Paul Foss, Paul Patton, and Philip Beitchman. Semiotext(e).

Bauman, Z. (2013) *Liquid Love: On the Frailty of Human Bonds*. John Wiley & Sons, Inc.

Baumrind, D. (1966) 'Effects of authoritative parental control on child behavior'. *Child Development* 37: 887–907.

Baumrind, D. (1996) 'The discipline controversy revisited'. *Family Relations* 45(4): 405–14.

Beaumont-Thomas, B. (2025) 'Bruce Springsteen says Trump is running "rogue government" and "siding with dictators"'. *Guardian*, 15 May. https://www.theguardian.com/music/2025/may/15/bruce-springsteen-trump-manchester-rogue-government-siding-with-dictators.

Beck, U. (1992) *Risk Society: Towards a New Modernity*. SAGE.

Beck, U. & Beck-Gernsheim, E. (1995) *The Normal Chaos of Love*. Polity.

Beck-Gernsheim, E. (2002) *Reinventing the Family: In Search of New Lifestyles*, trans. by P. Camiller. Polity.

Becker, H. (1997 [1963]) *Outsiders: Studies in the Sociology of Deviance*. Free Press.

Bell, D. (1979) *The Cultural Contradictions of Capitalism* (2nd edn). Heinemann.

Berger, B. (2002) *The Family in the Modern Age: More than a Lifestyle Choice*. Transaction.

Berrington, A. (2004) 'Perpetual postponers? Women's, men's and couple's fertility intentions and subsequent fertility behaviour'. *Population Trends* 117: 9–19.

Bloom, A. (2012 [1987]) *The Closing of the American Mind: How Higher Education Has Failed Democracy and Impoverished the Souls of Today's Students.* Simon & Schuster.

Bogost, I. (2025) 'A new kind of crisis for American Universities'. *Atlantic,* 10 February. https://www.theatlantic.com/health/archive/2025/02/nih-trump-university-crisis/681634.

Bolton, P. (2025) *Higher Education Student Numbers.* House of Commons Library. (Research Briefing, 25 March.) https://researchbriefings.files.parliament.uk/documents/CBP-7857/CBP-7857.pdf.

Booker, C. (1980) *The Seventies: Portrait of a Decade.* Penguin.

Booker, C. (1992 [1969]) *The Neophiliacs.* Collins.

Bowles, N. (2024) *Morning after the Revolution: Dispatches from the Wrong Side of History.* Penguin.

Bowles, S. & Gintis, H. (1977) *Schooling in Capitalist America: Educational Reform and the Contradictions of Economic Life.* Basic Books.

Brant, P. (2018) 'What is a graduate job? The Open University's Peter Brant explains the curious official distinctions between graduate and non-graduate jobs'. Wonkhe, 27 November. https://wonkhe.com/blogs/what-is-a-graduate-job.

Bristow, J. (2015) *Baby Boomers and Generational Conflict.* Palgrave Macmillan.

Bristow, J. (2016a) 'The making of "Boomergeddon": The construction of the Baby Boomer generation as a social problem in Britain'. *British Journal of Sociology* 67(4): 575–91.

Bristow, J. (2016b) *The Sociology of Generations: New Directions and Challenges.* Palgrave Macmillan.

Bristow, J. (2019) *Stop Mugging Grandma: The 'Generation Wars' and Why Boomer Blaming Won't Solve Anything.* Yale University Press.

Bristow, J. (2021a) 'Post-Brexit Boomer blaming: The contradictions of generational grievance'. *Sociological Review* 69(4): 759–74.

Bristow, J. (2021b) *Growing Up in Lockdown.* Academy of Ideas Ltd.

Bristow, J. (2023) 'The real chaos of the "new normal"'. *UnHerd*, 1 November. https://unherd.com/2023/11/the-real-chaos-of-the-new-normal.

Bristow, J. (2025a) 'The battle for the voice of Faversham'. Jennie Bristow website, 12 September. https://jbristow.co.uk/the-battle-for-the-voice-of-faversham.

Bristow, J. (2025b) 'Sociology and the problem of "social generations"'. In H. Kingstone & J. Bristow, eds, *Studying Generations: Multidisciplinary Perspectives*. Bristol University Press.

Bristow, J. (2025c) 'No, Gen Z is not "yearning for fascism"'. *spiked*, 3 February. https://www.spiked-online.com/2025/02/03/no-gen-z-is-not-yearning-for-fascism.

Bristow, J. & Gilland, E. (2020) *The Corona Generation: Coming of Age in a Crisis*. John Hunt Publishing.

Bristow, J., Cant, S., & Chatterjee, A. (2020) *Generational Encounters with Higher Education: The Academic–Student Relationship and the University Experience*. Bristol University Press.

Burnham, B. (2021) *Inside*. Netflix. https://www.netflix.com/gb/title/81289483.

Calcutt, A. (1998) *Arrested Development: Pop Culture and the Erosion of Adulthood*. Cassell.

Cass, H. (2024) *Independent Review of Gender Identity Services for Children and Young People: Final Report*. NHS England. https://cass.independent-review.uk/home/publications/final-report.

Castells, M. (2009 [1996]) *The Rise of the Network Society* (2nd edn). Wiley Blackwell.

Centre for Parenting Culture Studies (2025) CPCS blog. https://blogs.kent.ac.uk/parentingculturestudies.

Centre for Social Justice (2025) *Wasted Youth: Helping Britain's Young Adults into Work*. Centre for Social Justice, August. https://www.centreforsocialjustice.org.uk/wp-content/uploads/2025/08/CSJ-Wasted_Youth.pdf.

Clements, D. (2026) *The Crisis in the Classroom: How the Needs Explosion Is Destroying Education*. Luath Press.

Cohen, P.N. (2021) 'Open letter to the Pew Research Center on generation labels'. Family Inequality, 26 May. https://docs.google.com/forms/d/e/1FAIpQLSecsM1JavYMlNI-XlKDYngFKsEFBGFs_imv7R5KO8e15NYeCg/viewform.

Cohen, S. (2011 [1972]) *Folk Devils and Moral Panics*. Routledge.

Cole, L. & Kingsley, M. (2022) *The Children's Inquiry: How the State and Society Failed the Young during the Covid-19 Pandemic*. Pinter & Martin.

Collins, S. (2009) *The Hunger Games*. Scholastic.

Combi, C. (2015) *Generation Z: Their Voices, Their Lives* (Kindle edn). Hutchinson.

Cucchiara, M. & Steinbugler, A.C. (2021) '"The books make you feel bad": Expert advice and maternal anxiety in the early twenty-first century'. *Sociological Forum* 36: 939–961. https://doi.org/10.1111/socf.12748.

Cunningham, H. (2006) *The Invention of Childhood*. Random House.

Davis, K. (1940) 'The sociology of parent–youth conflict'. *American Sociological Review* 5(4): 523–535.

Deconinck, C. (2024) 'Greta Thunberg: "Fuck Germany! And fuck Israel!"' Brussels Signal, 9 December. https://brusselssignal.eu/2024/12/greta-thunberg-fuck-germany-and-fuck-israel.

DES (1991) *Higher Education: A New Framework*. White Paper (Cm 1541). HMSO.

Dingwall, R. (2021) 'Has UK sociology marginalized itself on some of the great issues of our time?' Social Science Space, 23 November. https://www.socialsciencespace.com/2021/11/has-uk-sociology-marginalised-itself-on-some-of-the-great-issues-of-our-time.

Doyle, A. (2022) *The New Puritans: How the Religion of Social Justice Captured the Western World*. Constable.

Duffy, B. (2021) *Generations: Does When You're Born Shape Who You Are?* Atlantic Books.

Duffy, B. and Hewlett, K. (2021) 'How culture wars start'. King's College London News Centre, 24 May. https://www.kcl.ac.uk/news/how-culture-wars-start.

Duffy, B. & Skinner, G. (2023) 'Woke vs anti-woke? Culture war divisions and politics'. KCL Policy Institute & Ipsos, October. https://www.kcl.ac.uk/policy-institute/assets/woke-vs-anti-woke-culture-war-divisions-and-politics.pdf.

Duffy, B. & Skinner, G. (2025) 'The UK's changing "culture wars": Division, tension and common ground'. KCL Policy Institute & Ipsos, November. https://www.kcl.ac.uk/policy-institute/assets/uks-changing-culture-wars-division-tension-and-common-ground.pdf.

Duffy, B., Stoneman, P., Hewlett, K., May, G., Skinner, G., & Gottfried, G. (2022) 'Freedom of speech in the UK's "culture war"'. KCL Policy Institute & Ipsos, May. https://www.kcl.ac.uk/policy-institute/assets/freedom-of-speech-in-the-uks-culture-war.pdf.

Durkheim, E. (2002 [1925]) *Moral Education.* Dover Publications.

Dylan, B. (1964) *The Times They Are a-Changin'.* Vinyl LP. Columbia Records.

Edmunds, J. & Turner, B.S. (2005) 'Global Generations: Social change in the twentieth century'. *British Journal of Sociology* 56(4): 559–77.

Elias, N. (1997) 'The civilizing of parents'. In J. Goudsblom & S. Mennell, eds, *The Norbert Elias Reader.* Wiley Blackwell.

Elliott, R. (2021) 'Generationalism: Understanding the difference between what generations are and what they do'. LSE blogs, 11 November. https://blogs.lse.ac.uk/covid19/2021/11/11/generationalism-understanding-the-difference-between-what-generations-are-and-what-they-do.

Elliott, R. (2022) 'The "Boomer remover": Intergenerational discounting, the coronavirus and climate change'. *Sociological Review* 70(1): 74–91.

Erikson, E.H., ed. (1963) *Youth: Change and Challenge.* Basic Books.

Erikson, E.H. (1995 [1950]) *Childhood and Society.* Vintage.

Faircloth, C. (2021) *Couples' Transitions to Parenthood: Gender, Intimacy and Equality.* Springer Nature.

FIRE (2025) 'The 2026 College Free Speech Rankings'. Foundation for Individual Rights and Expression. https://rankings.thefire.org.

France, A. & Roberts, S. (2015) 'The problem of social generations: A critique of the new emerging orthodoxy in youth studies'. *Journal of Youth Studies* 18(2): 215–30.

Frawley, A. (2024) *Families in Fragments: Why the EU Must Bring Back the Family*. MCC Brussels. https://brussels.mcc.hu/uploads/default/0001/01/d199e23aed7ff0436fbc88c46081ce716fd2687a.pdf.

Freeman, H. (2024) 'Welcome to The Omnicause, the fatberg of activism'. *Jewish Chronicle*, 17 June. https://www.thejc.com/opinion/welcome-to-the-omnicause-the-fatberg-of-activism-rw849dht.

Frey, W.H. (2018) *The Millennial Generation: A Demographic Bridge to America's Diverse Future*. Brookings Institution. https://www.brookings.edu/wp-content/uploads/2018/01/2018-jan_brookings-metro_millennials-a-demographic-bridge-to-americas-diverse-future.pdf.

Friedan, B. (1963) *The Feminine Mystique*. W.W. Norton.

Fukuyama, F. (1992) *The End of History and the Last Man*. Penguin.

Furedi, A. (2021) *The Moral Case for Abortion: A Defence of Reproductive Choice*. Palgrave Macmillan.

Furedi, A. (2022) 'You can ban abortion, but you cannot stop abortion'. *spiked*, 24 June. https://www.spiked-online.com/2022/06/24/you-can-ban-abortion-but-you-cannot-stop-abortion.

Furedi, F. (2001) *Paranoid Parenting: Abandon Your Anxieties and Be a Good Parent*. Allen Lane.

Furedi, F. (2005) *Politics of Fear: Beyond Left and Right*. Continuum.

Furedi, F. (2009) *Wasted: Why Education Isn't Educating*. Continuum.

Furedi, F. (2014) *First World War: Still No End in Sight*. Bloomsbury Continuum.

Furedi, F. (2017) *What's Happened to the University? A Sociological Exploration of Its Infantilisation*. Routledge.

Furedi, F. (2018) *How Fear Works: Culture of Fear in the Twenty-First Century*. Bloomsbury Publishing.

Furedi, F. (2020) *Why Borders Matter: Why Humanity Must Relearn the Art of Drawing Boundaries*. Routledge.

Furedi, F. (2021) *100 Years of Identity Crisis: Culture War over Socialisation*. De Gruyter.

Furedi, F. (2024) *The War Against the Past: Why the West Must Fight for Its History*. Polity.

Furedi, F. (2025) 'White nationalism: A willing servant of victim culture'. *Roots and Wings*, Substack, 11 November. https://open.substack.com/pub/frankfuredi/p/white-nationalism-a-willing-product?r=lud7o&utm_campaign=post&utm_medium=web&showWelcomeOnShare=false.

FX (2020) *Mrs America*, created by D. Waller. Television miniseries. https://www.fxnetworks.com/shows/mrs-america.

Gatrell, C. (2005) *Hard Labour: The Sociology of Parenthood*. Open University Press.

Gibney, B.C. (2017) *A Generation of Sociopaths: How the Baby Boomers Betrayed America*. Hachette.

Giddens, A. (1992) *The Transformation of Intimacy: Sexuality, Love and Eroticism in Modern Societies*. Polity.

Giddens, A. & Sutton, P.W., eds (2017) *Sociology* (8th edn). Polity.

Gillies, V. (2011) 'From Function to Competence: Engaging with the New Politics of the Family'. *Sociological Research Online* 16(4): 11.

Gillis, J.R. (1997) *A World of Their Own Making: A History of Myth and Ritual in Family Life*. Oxford University Press.

Glover, E. (2025) 'The last flags of Faversham: Why night-time vigilantes are stripping hundreds of St George's Crosses from Kent lamp-posts'. *New Statesman*, 1 November. https://www.newstatesman.com/politics/society/2025/11/the-last-flags-of-faversham

Goddard, R. (2025) 'Students at King's College London sign open letter against recent examination proposals'. *The Tab*, 10 December. https://thetab.com/2025/12/10/students-at-kings-college-london-sign-open-letter-against-recent-examination-proposals.

Goffman, E. (1990a [1959]) *The Presentation of Self in Everyday Life*. Penguin.

Goffman, E. (1990b [1963]) *Stigma: Notes on the Management of Spoiled Identity*. Penguin.

Gouveia, R., & Castrén, A. (2021) 'Redefining the boundaries of family and personal relationships'. In A.M. Castrén et al., eds, *The Palgrave Handbook of Family Sociology in Europe*. Palgrave Macmillan.

Grabien Staff (2023) 'Here are four straight minutes of Kamala Harris being unburdened', 18 December. https://news.grabien.com/story/here-are-four-straight-minutes-of-kamala-harris-being-unburdened.

Graham-Harrison, E. (2016) 'Young people on the EU referendum: "It is the end of one world, of the world as we know it"'. *Observer*, 26 June. https://www.theguardian.com/politics/2016/jun/26/young-people-vote-anger.

Grasso, M., & Smith, K. (2021) 'Gender inequalities in political participation and political engagement among young people in Europe: Are young women less politically engaged than young men?' *Politics* 42(1): 39–57. https://doi.org/10.1177/02633957211028813

Guhin, J., Calarco, J.M. & Miller-Idriss, C. (2021) 'Whatever happened to socialization?' *Annual Review of Sociology* 47(1): 109–29.

Guldberg, H. (2009) *Reclaiming Childhood: Freedom and Play in an Age of Fear*. Routledge.

Haidt, J. (2024) *The Anxious Generation: How the Great Rewiring of Childhood Is Causing an Epidemic of Mental Illness*. Allen Lane.

Hamburger, J. (2017) 'The Closing of the American Mind'. *The Point*, issue 15, 27 November. https://thepointmag.com/criticism/the-closing-of-the-american-mind-allan-bloom.

Hanisch, C. (1969) 'The personal is political'. https://www.carolhanisch.org/CHwritings/PIP.html.

Hareven, T. K. (1977) 'Family time and historical time'. *Daedalus* 106(2): 57–70.

Harkness, T. (2024) *Technology Is Not the Problem*. HQ.

Harrington, M. (2024a) *Feminism against Progress*. Forum.

Harrington, M. (2024b) 'Lauren Southern: How my tradlife turned toxic'. *UnHerd*. https://unherd.com/2024/05/lauren-southern-the-tradlife-influencer-filled-with-regret/

Hayes, D. & Ecclestone, K. (2008) *The Dangerous Rise of Therapeutic Education.* Routledge.

Hays, S. (1996) *The Cultural Contradictions of Motherhood.* Yale University Press.

Hayward, K.J. (2024) *Infantilised: How Our Culture Killed Adulthood.* Constable.

Hegel, G. (1952 [1821]) *The Philosophy of Right and the Philosophy of History.* University of Chicago (Great Books).

Hennum, N. (2014) 'Developing child-centred social policies: When professionalism takes over'. *Social Sciences* 3: 441–59.

Henry, J. and Harding, E. (2026) 'King's College accused of "dumbing down" after overlooking poor grammar to be more "inclusive"'. *Daily Mail,* 6 April. https://www.dailymail.co.uk/news/article-15707863/Kings-College-exams-inclusive.html.

Hertz, N. (2016) 'Think millennials have it tough? For "Generation K", life is even harsher'. *Guardian,* 19 March. https://www.theguardian.com/world/2016/mar/19/think-millennials-have-it-tough-for-generation-k-life-is-even-harsher.

Hillman, N. (2022) '"You can't say that!" What students really think of free speech on campus'. HEPI Policy Note 35, Higher Education Policy Institute. https://www.hepi.ac.uk/wp-content/uploads/2022/06/You-cant-say-that-What-students-really-think-of-free-speech-on-campus.pdf.

Hillman, N.W. (2024) 'An overview of US higher education'. HEPI Report 175, Higher Education Policy Institute, 4 July. https://www.hepi.ac.uk/wp-content/uploads/2024/07/An-overview-of-US-higher-education.pdf.

Hobcraft, J. (1996) 'Fertility in England and Wales: A fifty-year perspective'. *Population Studies* 50(3): 485–524.

Hochschild, A.R. (1979) 'Emotion work, feeling rules, and social structure'. *American Journal of Sociology* 85(3): 551–75.

Hochschild, A.R. (2003) *The Commercialization of Intimate Life: Notes from Home and Work.* University of California Press.

Hochschild, A.R. (2018 [2016]) *Strangers in Their Own Land: Anger and Mourning on the American Right.* New Press.

Hochschild, A. & Machung, A. (2012 [1989]) *The Second Shift: Working Families and the Revolution at Home*. Penguin.

Howker, E. & Malik, S. (2010) *Jilted Generation: How Britain Has Bankrupted Its Youth*. Icon.

HSS, Department of Education, & GSA (2025) 'Letter sent to Harvard'. Harvard University, 11 April. https://www.harvard.edu/research-funding/wp-content/uploads/sites/16/2025/04/Letter-Sent-to-Harvard-2025-04-11.pdf.

Hunter, J.D. (1991) *Culture Wars: The Struggle to Define America*. Basic Books.

Hunter, J.D. & Wolfe, A. (2007) *Is There a Culture War? A Dialogue on Values and American Public Life*. Bloomsbury Publishing.

Ibbetson, C. (2021) 'How do people feel about national lockdown in the UK?' YouGov, 20 January. https://yougov.co.uk/politics/articles/33795-britons-attitudes-toward-national-lockdown.

ISE (2024) 'Is career readiness in decline?'. Institute of Student Employers, 1 May. https://ise.org.uk/knowledge/insights/195/is_career_readiness_in_decline.

Jack, P. (2025) 'Almost half of employers think graduates "lack resilience": Survey highlights concerns that university leavers are less prepared for work than previous generations'. *Times Higher Education*, 7 May. https://www.timeshighereducation.com/news/almost-half-employers-think-graduates-lack-resilience.

Jamieson, L. (1999) 'Intimacy transformed? A critical look at the "pure relationship"'. *Sociology* 33(3): 477–94.

Jenkins, P. (2006) *Decade of Nightmares: The End of the Sixties and the Making of Eighties America*. Oxford University Press.

Jenkins, T. (2025) *Strangers and Intimates: The Rise and Fall of Private Life*. Pan Macmillan.

Joyce, H. (2021) *Trans: When Ideology Meets Reality*. Simon & Schuster.

Khalil, H. (2026) 'Molly Russell's dad says under-16 social media ban would be wrong'. BBC News, 18 January. https://www.bbc.com/news/articles/cpwn1vjy0y5o.

Kamenetz, A. (2006) *Generation Debt: Why Now Is a Terrible Time to Be Young*. Riverhead Books.

Kauffmann, E. (2025) 'The decline of trans and queer identity among young Americans'. Centre for Heterodox Social Science Report No. 5, 10 October. https://www.heterodoxcentre.com/research/chss-report-no-5.

KCL News Centre (2023) 'Public increasingly see politicians as stoking culture wars, study finds'. King's College London, 3 November. https://www.kcl.ac.uk/news/public-increasingly-see-politicians-as-stoking-culture-wars-study-finds.

KCL News Centre (2025) 'UK's sense of division reaches new high as culture war tensions grow, study finds'. King's College London, 7 November. https://www.kcl.ac.uk/news/uks-sense-of-division-reaches-new-high-as-culture-war-tensions-grow-study-finds.

Kearney, M.S., Levine, P.B., & Pardue, L. (2022) 'The puzzle of falling US birth rates since the Great Recession'. *Journal of Economic Perspectives* 36(1): 151–76.

Kennedy, A. & Panton, J., eds (2019) *From Self to Selfie: A Critique of Contemporary Forms of Alienation*. Palgrave Macmillan.

Kingstone, H. & Bristow, J., eds (2025) *Studying Generations: Multidisciplinary Perspectives*. Bristol University Press.

Knapp, S.J. & Wurm, G. (2019) 'Theorizing family change: A review and reconceptualization'. *Journal of Family Theory & Review* 11(2): 212–29.

Kotowska, I.E., Mynarska, M., & Gauthier, A.H. (2021) 'Family transformations and sub-replacement fertility in Europe'. In A.M. Castern et al., eds, *The Palgrave Handbook of Family Sociology in Europe*. Palgrave.

Latimer, E., Ray-Chaudhuri, S., & Waters, T. (2025) *The Role of Changing Health in Rising Health-Related Benefit Claims*. Institute for Fiscal Studies, 12 March 2025. https://ifs.org.uk/publications/role-changing-health-rising-health-related-benefit-claims.

Lasch, C. (1985) *The Minimal Self: Psychic Survival in Troubled Times*. W. W. Norton.

Lasch, C. (1995 [1977]) *Haven in a Heartless World: The Family Besieged*. W. W. Norton.

Lasch, C. (1997) *Women and the Common Life*, ed. by Elisabeth Lasch-Quinn. W.W. Norton.

Lasch, C. (2018 [1979]). *The Culture of Narcissism: American Life in an Age of Diminishing Expectations*. W. W. Norton.

Lawson, E. & Jefford, W. (2025) 'Why have thousands of St George's flags gone up in cities and towns?' BBC News, 21 August. https://www.bbc.co.uk/news/articles/c626vxyxgj6o.

Leatherdale, D. (2026) 'Hospital violated trans complaint nurses' dignity, tribunal rules'. BBC News, 16 January. https://www.bbc.com/news/articles/c0jv9l5n32zo.

Lebedíková, M., Tkaczyk, M., Mýlek, V., & Smahel, D. (2024) 'Do smartphones really cause mental illness among adolescents? Ten problems with Jonathan Haidt's book'. LSE Blogs, 15 May. https://blogs.lse.ac.uk/parenting4digitalfuture/2024/05/15/haidt.

Leccardi, C. (2016) 'Facing uncertainty: Temporality and biographies in the new century'. In C. Leccardi & Ruspini, E., eds, *A New Youth? Young People, Generations and Family Life*. Routledge.

Leccardi, C., Jedlowski, P., & Cavalli, A. (2023) *Exploring New Temporal Horizons: A Conversation between Memories and Futures*. Bristol University Press.

Lee, E., Bristow, J., Faircloth, C., & Macvarish, J. (2023) *Parenting Culture Studies* (2nd edn). Palgrave Macmillan.

Lesthaeghe, R. (2010) 'The unfolding story of the second demographic transition'. *Population and Development Review* 36(2): 211–51.

Lesthaeghe, R. (2014) 'The second demographic transition: A concise overview of its development'. *Proceedings of the National Academy of Sciences of the United States of America* 111(51): 18112–15.

Lewis, H. (2020) 'How J. K. Rowling became Voldemort'. *Atlantic*, 6 July. https://www.theatlantic.com/international/archive/2020/07/why-millennial-harry-potter-fans-reject-jk-rowling/613870.

Lewis, J. (2001) *The End of Marriage?* Edward Elgar Publishing.

Lewis, S. (2022) *Abolish the Family: A Manifesto for Care and Liberation*. Verso Books.

LGB Alliance (2024) 'Time to stop "transing the gay away"'. Blog on LGB Alliance, 27 February. https://lgballiance.org.uk/conversion-practices-bill-blog.

Lichtenstein, B. (2021) 'From "Coffin Dodger" to "Boomer Remover": Outbreaks of ageism in three countries with divergent approaches to coronavirus control'. *Journals of Gerontology: Series B* 76(4): e206–e212.

Livingstone, H. (2026) 'Australia has banned social media for kids under 16: How does it work?' BBC News, 23 January. https://www.bbc.com/news/articles/cwyp9d3ddqyo.

Livingstone, S.M. & Blum-Ross, A. (2020) *Parenting for a Digital Future: How Hopes and Fears about Technology Shape Children's Lives*. Oxford University Press.

Lovell, J. (2025) 'The majority of UK parents are AGAINST a smacking ban – with dads more opposed than mums'. Netmums, 16 September. https://www.netmums.com/child/43-of-uk-parents-want-smacking-to-remain-legal-with-dads-more-in-favour-than-mothers.

Lukianoff, G. & Goldstein, A. (2025) 'Trump's college funding threat puts free speech at risk'. *UnHerd*, 5 March. https://unherd.com/newsroom/trumps-college-funding-threat-puts-free-speech-at-risk.

Lukianoff, G. & Haidt, J. (2018) *The Coddling of the American Mind: How Good Intentions and Bad Ideas Are Setting Up a Generation for Failure*. Penguin.

Lukianoff, G. & Schlott, R. (2023) *The Canceling of the American Mind: How Cancel Culture Undermines Trust, Destroys Institutions, and Threatens Us All*. Allen Lane.

Macvarish, J. & Billings, J. (2010) 'Challenging the irrational, amoral and anti-social construction of the "teenage mother"'. In S. Duncan, R. Edwards, & C. Alexander, eds, *Teenage Pregnancy: What's the Problem?* Tuffnell Press.

Macvarish, J. & Martin, C. (2021) 'Towards a "parenting regime": Globalising tendencies and localised variation'. In A.M. Castrén et al., eds, *The Palgrave Handbook of Family Sociology in Europe*. Palgrave.

Mannheim, K. (1952 [1928]) 'The problem of generations'. In P. Kecskemeti, ed., *Essays on the Sociology of Knowledge*. Routledge.

Marwick, A. (1999) *The Sixties: Cultural Revolution in Britain, France, Italy and the United States, c.1958–c.1974*. Oxford University Press.

McCrindle (2025) 'Welcome Gen Beta'. McCrindle, 7 February. https://mccrindle.com.au/article/topic/generation-beta/welcome-gen-beta.

McDermott, N.A. (2020) *The Problem with Parenting: How Raising Children Is Changing across America* (Kindle edn). Praeger.

McRae, S. (1999) 'Preface'. In S. McRae, ed., *Changing Britain: Families and Households in the 1990s*. Oxford University Press.

Mehring, K., Off, G., & Wojnicka, K. (2025) 'The populist radical right, the gender gap and protective masculinity across European countries'. *European Journal of Politics and Gender*. Advance of publication. https://doi.org/10.1332/25151088Y2025D000000101.

Meisner, B.A. (2022) 'Are you OK, Boomer? Intensification of ageism and intergenerational tensions on social media amid COVID-19'. In B. Lashua, C.W. Johnson, & D.C. Parry, eds, *Leisure in the Time of Coronavirus: A Rapid Response*. Routledge.

Melley, J. (2024) 'Census may have overestimated number of trans people in England and Wales'. BBC News, 13 September. https://www.bbc.co.uk/news/articles/c3030519849o.

Mills, C.W. (1970 [1959]) *The Sociological Imagination*. Penguin.

Milosav, Đ., Dickson, Z., Hobolt, S. B., Klüver, H., Kuhn, T., & Rodon, T. (2025) 'The youth gender gap in support for the far right'. *Journal of European Public Policy* 33(2): 1–25 (= 444–68). doi: 10.1080/13501763.2025.2481181.

Milotay, N. (2020) 'Next generation or lost generation? Children, young people and the pandemic'. European Parliamentary Research Service, December. https://www.europarl.europa.eu/RegData/etudes/BRIE/2020/659404/EPRS_BRI(2020)659404_EN.pdf.

Mintz, S. (2015) *The Prime of Life: A History of Modern Adulthood*. Belknap Press of Harvard University Press.

Moore, S. E. H. (2012) 'Controlling passion? A review of recent developments in British sex education'. *Health, Risk & Society* 14(1): 25–40.

Mullan, P. (2000) *The Imaginary Time Bomb: Why an Ageing Population Is Not a Social Problem*. I.B. Tauris.

Mullan, P. (2017) *Creative Destruction: How to Start an Economic Renaissance*. Policy Press.

Navabi, A. (2023) '"Queers for Palestine" and the death of irony'. *Queer Majority*, 17 October. https://www.queermajority.com/essays-all/queers-for-palestine-and-the-death-of-irony.

Nebehay, S. (2020) 'WHO message to youth on coronavirus: "You are not invincible"'. Reuters, 20 March. https://www.reuters.com/article/us-health-coronavirus-who/whomessage-to-youth-on-coronavirus-you-are-not-invincibleidUSKBN21733O.

Neiman, S. (2015) *Why Grow Up? Subversive Thoughts for an Infantile Age*. Macmillan.

Nelson, F. (2024) 'Inside Britain's £48 billion benefits scandal'. Documentary in the *Dispatches* series on Channel 4, 2 December. https://www.benefitstrap.com.

Niederhelman, E.F. & Rai, A.B. (2025) 'A majority of frozen federal funding has been restored, Harvard says'. *Harvard Crimson*, 14 October. https://www.thecrimson.com/article/2025/10/14/majority-federal-funds.

Nisbet, R. (1994 [1980]) *History of the Idea of Progress*. Transaction.

Oakeshott, M. (2001 [1989]) *The Voice of Liberal Learning*. Liberty Fund.

Oakley, A. (1974) *Housewife*. Allen Lane.

O'Hear, A. (2001) 'Michael Oakeshott 1901–92'. In J. Palmer, ed., *Fifty Modern Thinkers on Education: From Piaget to the Present*. Routledge.

Oster, E. (2024) 'Should you have kids?' Episode 8 in the podcast *Raising Parents with Emily Oster*, 13 November. https://podcasts.apple.com/nz/podcast/ep-8-should-you-have-kids/id1766973918?i=1000676780684.

Parker, K. (2023) 'How Pew Research Center will report on generations moving forward'. Pew Research Center, 22 May. https://www.pewresearch.org/short-reads/2023/05/22/how-pew-research-center-will-report-on-generations-moving-forward.

Parsons, T. (2012 [1951]) *The Social System*. Quid Pro LLC.

Perna, M.C. (2025) 'New data reveals just how deep the college crisis goes'. *Forbes*, 28 January. https://www.forbes.com/sites/marckcperna/2025/01/28/new-data-reveals-the-depth-of-college-crisis.

Perry, L. (2022) *The Case against the Sexual Revolution: A New Guide to Sex in the Twenty-First Century*. Polity.

Peters, J.W. (2024) 'It's not just Gaza: Student protesters see links to a global struggle'. *The New York Times*, 1 May. https://www.nytimes.com/2024/05/01/us/pro-palestinian-college-protests.html.

Pew Research Center (2015) 'Most Millennials resist the "Millennial" label'. Report, 3 September. https://www.pewresearch.org/politics/2015/09/03/most-millennials-resist-the-millennial-label.

Pink Floyd (1979) *Another Brick in the Wall, Part 2*. On the album *The Wall*, Harvest Records/Columbia Records, 30 November.

Plastina, A.F. (2022) '# BoomerDoomer and# BoomerRemover: Discriminatory discursive strategies in the representation of the COVID-19 risk group on Twitter'. *Journal of Language & Discrimination* 6(1): 114–37.

Postman, N. (1971 [1969]) *Teaching as a Subversive Activity*. Penguin.

Postman, N. (1979) *Teaching as a Conserving Activity*. Delacorte Press.

Postman, N. (1994) *The Disappearance of Childhood*. Vintage Books.

Postman, N. (1996) *The End of Education: Redefining the Value of School*. Vintage.

Proudfoot, S., Wellings, K., & Glasier, A. (2009) 'Analysis why nulliparous women over age 33 wish to use contraception'. *Contraception* 79(2): 98–104.

Purhonen, S. (2016) 'Generations on paper: Bourdieu and the critique of "generationalism"'. *Social Science Information* 55(1): 94–114.

Reece, H. (2013) 'The pitfalls of positive parenting'. *Ethics and Education* 8(1): 42–54.

Reilly, K. (2016) 'Read Hillary Clinton's "basket of deplorables" remarks about Donald Trump supporters'. *Time*, 10 September. https://time.com/4486502/hillary-clinton-basket-of-deplorables-transcript.

Ritchie, H. (2024) 'Australia approves social media ban on under-16s'. BBC News, 29 November. https://www.bbc.co.uk/news/articles/c89vjj0lxx9o

Ritzer, G. (2002) 'Enchanting McUniversity: Toward a spectacularly irrational university quotidian'. In D. Hayes & R. Wynyard, eds, *The McDonaldization of Higher Education*. Bergin & Garvey.

Robbins, L. (1963) *Higher Education: Report of the Committee Appointed by the Prime Minister under the Chairmanship of Lord Robbins, 1961– 63*. Command Paper 2154. HMSO.

Ruckdeschel, K. (2024) Ready for parenthood? On intensive parenting ideals and fertility. *Journal of Family Issues* 45(12): 2985–30087. https://journals.sagepub.com/doi/full/10.1177/0192513X241227872.

Rudolph, C.W. & Zacher, H. (2020) '"The COVID-19 generation": A cautionary note'. *Work, Aging and Retirement* 6(3): 139–45.

Ruspini, E. (2013) *Diversity in Family Life: Gender, Relationships, and Social Change*. Policy Press.

Ryder, N.B. (1965) 'The cohort as a concept in the study of social change'. *American Sociological Review* 30(6): 843–61.

SAGE (2020) 'Options for increasing adherence to social distancing measures'. Scientific Advisory Group for Emergencies, 22 March. https://assets.publishing.service.gov.uk/government/uploads/system/uploads/attachment_data/file/882722/25-options-for-increasing-adherence-to-social-distancing-measures-22032020.pdf.

Savage, J. (2007) *Teenage: The Creation of a Youth Culture*. Viking.

Scott, J. (1999) 'Family change: Revolution or backlash in attitudes?'. In S. McRae, ed., *Changing Britain: Families and Households in the 1990s*. Oxford University Press.

Scott, P. (2012) 'It's 20 years since polytechnics became universities – and there's no going back'. *Guardian*, 3 September. https://www.theguardian.com/education/2012/sep/03/polytechnics-became-universities-1992-differentiation.

Sculthorp, F. (2025) 'Meet Faversham's answer to Akhmed Yakoob: A young activist is embracing working-class rage'. *UnHerd*, 21 November. https://unherd.com/2025/11/meet-favershams-answer-to-akhmed-yakoob.

Sehgal-Cuthbert, A. & Standish, A. (2021) *What Should Schools Teach? Disciplines, Subjects and the Pursuit of Truth* (2nd edn). UCL Press.

Senior, J. (2014) *All Joy and No Fun: The Paradox of Modern Parenthood.* Hachette.

Sex Matters (2025) 'What happened at Sussex University?' Briefing by Sex Matters, 1 April. https://sex-matters.org/wp-content/uploads/2025/04/What-happened-at-Sussex-University-Sex-Matters.pdf.

Shrier, A. (2020) *Irreversible Damage: The Transgender Craze Seducing Our Daughters.* Simon & Schuster.

Shrier, A. (2024) *Bad Therapy: Why the Kids Aren't Growing Up.* Penguin.

Sigsworth, T. (2025) 'Don't say "able-bodied" – use "non-disabled", Britain's tourist board tells guides'. *Daily Telegraph*, 8 February. https://www.telegraph.co.uk/news/2025/02/08/able-bodied-is-harmful-language-says-britains-tourist-board/#:~:text=The%20word%20%E2%80%9Cable%2Dbodied%E2%80%9D,who%20do%20not%20have%20disabilities.

Simonardottir, S. (2024) '"Unless I could be like the typical dad": Exploring parenthood through the perspective of the voluntarily childfree'. *Acta Sociologica* 67(4): 1–15 (= 463–77).

Skipper, A.D. & Rose, D.J. (2021) '# BoomerRemover: COVID-19, ageism, and the intergenerational twitter response'. *Journal of Aging Studies* 57: art. 100929.

Smith, V. (2023) *Hags: The Demonisation of Middle-Aged Women.* Little, Brown.

Smith, C., with Christoffersen, K., Davidson, H., & Snell Herzog, P. (2011) *Lost in Transition: The Dark Side of Emerging Adulthood.* Oxford University Press.

Social Exclusion Unit (1999) *Teenage Pregnancy: Presented to Parliament by the Prime Minister by Command of Her Majesty.* Command Paper 4342. Stationery Office. https://dera.ioe.ac.uk/15086/1/teenage-pregnancy.pdf.

Springsteen, B. (1984) *Born in the USA.* Columbia Records/CBS Inc.

Staubmann, H.C. (2021) 'Wright Mills' *The Sociological Imagination* and the construction of Talcott Parsons as a Conservative grand theorist'. *American Sociologist* 52: 178–93.

Steinmetz, K. (2016) 'This is what "adulting" means'. *Time,* 8 June. http://time.com/4361866/adulting-definition-meaning.

Stock, K. (2021) *Material Girls: Why Reality Matters for Feminism.* Hachette.

Stock, K. (2023) 'The Oxford kids are alright'. *UnHerd,* 1 June. https://unherd.com/2023/06/the-oxford-kids-are-alright.

Strömmer, S.T. et al. (2022) 'Young people's experiences of COVID-19 messaging at the start of the UK lockdown: Lessons for positive engagement and information sharing'. *BMC Public Health* 22(1): art. 352.

Sullivan, A., Murray, K., & Mackenzie, L. (2024) 'Why do we need data on sex?' In A. Sullivan & S. Todd, eds, *Sex and Gender: A Contemporary Reader.* Routledge.

Sullivan, A. & Todd, S., eds (2024) *Sex and Gender: A Contemporary Reader.* Routledge.

Taylor, J. (2024) 'Labor's plan to ban children from social media might actually create more harm, charity says'. *Guardian,* 11 September. https://www.theguardian.com/media/article/2024/sep/12/australia-plan-to-ban-children-from-social-media-might-actually-create-more-harm-charity-says.

Telegraph Reporters (2025) 'Gen Z says smacking children is unacceptable amid calls for ban'. *Daily Telegraph,* 21 August. https://www.telegraph.co.uk/news/2025/08/21/gen-z-smacking-children-unacceptable-calls-ban.

Tenbarge, K. (2020) 'Gen Z sparked backlash by calling coronavirus the "Boomer Remover", but actual teens say it's not a serious trend'. *Business Insider*, 26 March. https://www.businessinsider.com/gen-z-boomer-remover-coronavirus-teen-vanessa-hudgens-toilet-seat-2020-3.

Tondo, L. & Carrington, D. (2025) 'Israel accused of detaining Greta Thunberg in infested cell and making her hold flags'. *Guardian*, 4 October. https://www.theguardian.com/world/2025/oct/04/greta-thunberg-israel-gaza-sweden.

Toynbee, P. (2013) 'The drop in teenage pregnancies is the success story of our time'. *Guardian*, 13 December. https://www.theguardian.com/commentisfree/2013/dec/13/drop-teenage-pregnancies-success-story-children.

Trilling, L. (1965) *Beyond Culture*. Viking.

Trow, M. (2010) *Twentieth–Century Higher Education: Elite to Mass to Universal*, ed. by M. Burrage. Johns Hopkins University Press.

Turkle, S. (2015) *Reclaiming Conversation: The Power of Talk in a Digital Age*. Penguin.

Twenge, J.M. (2006) *Generation Me: Why Today's Young Americans Are More Confident, Assertive, Entitled – and More Miserable than Ever Before*. Atria Books.

Twenge, J.M. (2017) *Igen: Why Today's Super-Connected Kids Are Growing Up Less Rebellious, More Tolerant, Less Happy – and Completely Unprepared for Adulthood: And What That Means for the Rest of Us*. Simon & Schuster.

Twenge, J.M. (2023) *Generations: The Real Differences between Gen Z, Millennials, Gen X, Boomers, and Silents – and What They Mean for America's Future*. Atria Books.

UCAS (2021) 'LGBT+ freshers looking forward to being open and out at university, new UCAS research shows'. Press Release, 24 September. https://www.ucas.com/corporate/news-and-key-documents/news/lgbt-freshers-looking-forward-being-open-and-out-university-new-ucas-research-shows.

UCAS (2025) 'Gender options in the UCAS application'. Admissions

Guidance, 15 January. https://www.ucas.com/gender-options-ucas-application.

UNESCO (2023) *Global Education Monitoring Report: Comprehensive Sexuality Education (CSE) Country Profiles*. UNESCO. https://unesdoc.unesco.org/ark:/48223/pf0000384494.

UnHerd Staff (2025) 'Third of US students say violence is acceptable response to speech'. *UnHerd*, 9 September. https://unherd.com/newsroom/third-of-us-students-say-violence-is-acceptable-response-to-speech.

Warren, G. (2021) 'University of Kent in Canterbury and Medway defends diversity course all students are being asked to take'. Kent Online, 29 September. https://www.kentonline.co.uk/canterbury/news/compulsory-uni-white-privilege-course-branded-thought-pol-254801.

Webster, E.S. (2016) 'The sad reason Gen Z is being named after Katniss Everdeen'. *Teen Vogue*, 23 March. https://www.teenvogue.com/story/generation-z-katniss-everdeen-anxiety.

Whalen, A. (2020) 'What is "Boomer Remover" and why is it making people so angry?' *Newsweek*, 13 March. https://www.newsweek.com/boomer-remover-meme-trends-virus-coronavirus-social-media-covid-19-baby-boomers-1492190.

Whalen, J. & Flacks, R. (1989) *Beyond the Barricades: The Sixties Generation Grows Up*. Temple University Press.

White, J. (2013) 'Thinking generations'. *British Journal of Sociology* 64(2): 216–47.

Williams, J. (2013) *Consuming Higher Education: Why Learning Can't Be Bought*. Bloomsbury.

Williams, J. (2024a) *Sexualising Children? The Rise of Comprehensive Sexuality Education*. MCC Brussels, July. https://brussels.mcc.hu/uploads/default/0001/01/5af421de2164389456d75fa542b8b1baa859bc02.pdf.

Williams, J. (2024b) *Teachers or Parents: Who Is Responsible for Raising the Next Generation?* Civitas, September. https://www.civitas.org.uk/content/files/Teachers-or-Parents-pdf.pdf.

Williams, T. C. (2025a) *Summer of Our Discontent: The Age*

of Certainty and the Demise of Discourse. Knopf Publishing Group.

Williams, T. C. (2025b) '2020: The summer we lost our minds'. Interview on *The Brendan O'Neill Show. spiked,* 4 September. https://www.youtube.com/watch?v=gRc4wjTfCAM

Willetts, D. (2010) *The Pinch: How the Baby Boomers Took Their Children's Future: And Why They Should Give It Back.* Atlantic Books.

Winnicott, D. W. (2021 [1964]) *The Child, the Family, and the Outside World.* Penguin.

Witherington, E. (2026) 'Alton Towers U-turns on plan to restrict disability pass'. BBC News, 12 February. https://www.bbc.com/news/articles/cx2gyggxv4no.

Wohl, R. (1980) *The Generation of 2014.* Weidenfeld & Nicolson.

Wolf, A. (2002) *Does Education Matter? Myths about Education and Economic Growth.* Penguin.

Wolfe, T. (2023 [1976]) 'The "Me" decade'. *New York,* 15 September. https://nymag.com/article/tom-wolfe-me-decade-third-great-awakening.html.

Woodman, D. & Wyn, J. (2015) *Youth and Generation: Rethinking Change and Inequality in the Lives of Young People.* SAGE.

Woods, J. (2025) '"Patriots" vs "de-flaggers": How a war over the Union Flag is dividing Faversham'. *Daily Telegraph,* 9 October. https://www.telegraph.co.uk/news/2025/10/09/faversham-union-flag-division.

Young, M. (1971) *Knowledge and Control: New Directions in the Sociology of Education.* Macmillan.

Young, M. (2007) *Bringing Knowledge Back In: From Social Constructivism to Social Realism in the Sociology of Education.* Routledge.

Žižek, S. (2010) 'A Permanent Economic Emergency'. *New Left Review* 2(64): 85–106. https://newleftreview.org/issues/ii64/articles/slavoj-zizek-a-permanent-economic-emergency.